Written and Drawn by
BRIAN MICHAEL BENDIS

Collection Editor:
JENNIFER GRÜNWALD

Cover and Publication Design:
PATRICK McGRATH and CURTIS KING JR.

Publisher:
ALISA BENDIS

PEFC Certified

This product is from sustainably managed forests and controlled sources

www.pefc.org

FIRE

Published by DC Comics. Original compilation published as FIRE: THE DEFINITIVE COLLECTION. Copyright © 1994, 2001 Jinxworld, Inc. All Rights Reserved.

Originally published in single magazine form in FIRE 1-2. Copyright © 1993 Jinxworld, Inc. All Rights Reserved. FIRE, its logo design, the Jinxworld logo, all characters, their distinctive likenesses and related elements featured in this publication are trademarks of Jinxworld, Inc. The stories, characters and incidents featured in this publication are entirely fictional. DC Comics does not read or accept unsolicited submissions of ideas, stories or artwork.

DC Comics, 2900 West Alameda Ave., Burbank, CA 91505
Printed by LSC Communications, Owensville, MO, USA. 1/25/19.
First Printing. ISBN: 978-1-4012-9053-5

Library of Congress Cataloging-in-Publication Data is available.

"Don't trust the CIA."

—Ronald Reagan to George Bush,
from Bob Woodward's *Veil*

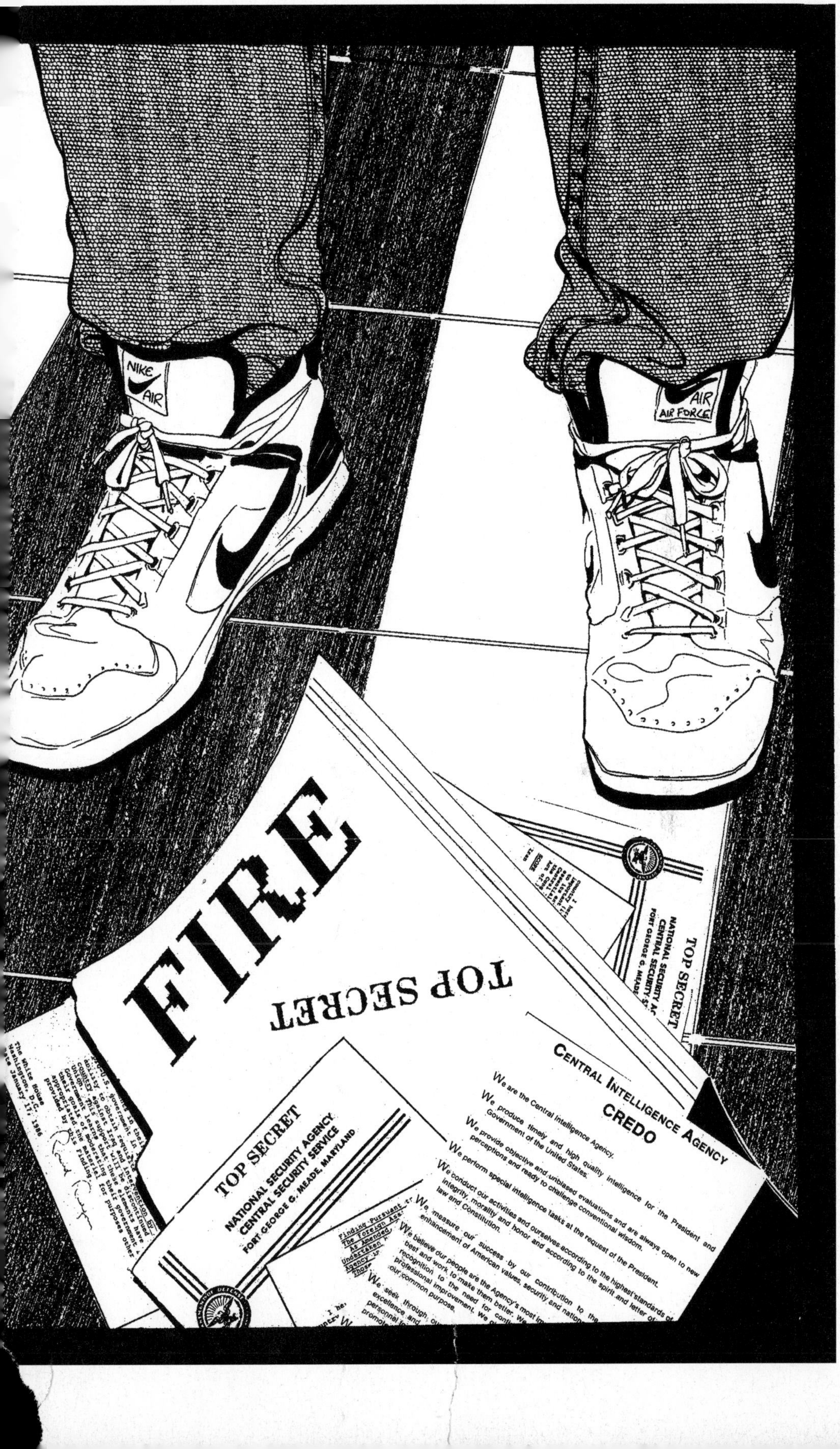
NIKE AIR
AIR
AIR FORCE
FIRE
TOP SECRET
CENTRAL INTELLIGENCE AGENCY
CREDO
We are the Central Intelligence Agency.
TOP SECRET
NATIONAL SECURITY AGENCY
CENTRAL SECURITY SERVICE
FORT GEORGE G. MEADE, MARYLAND

"What do you think spies are: priests, saints, martyrs? They're a squalid procession of vain fools, traitors, too, yes; pansies, sadists and drunkards, people who play cowboys and Indians to brighten their rotten lives."

—John le Carré, *The Spy Who Came in from the Cold*

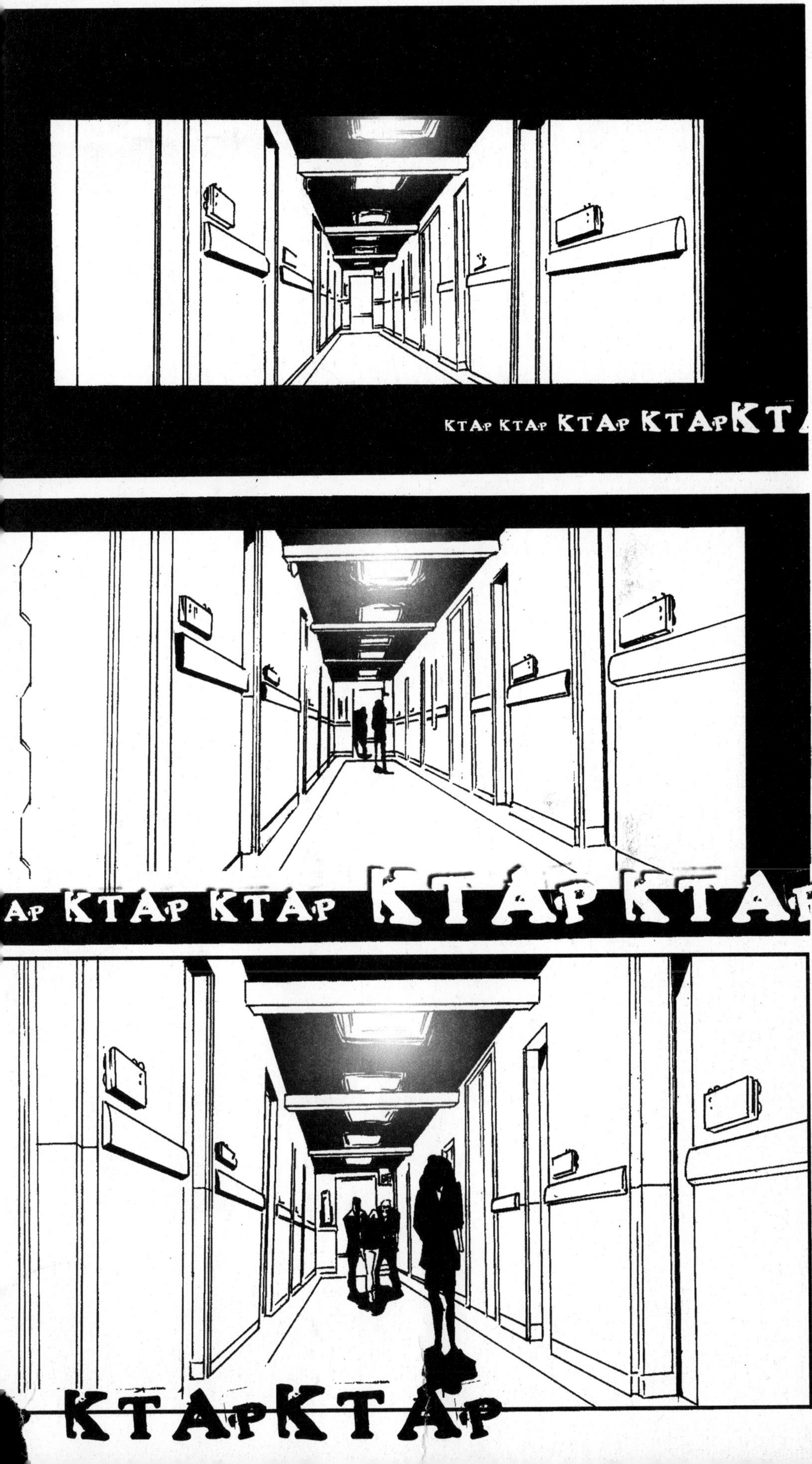
KTAp KTAp KTAp KTAp KTA
Ap KTAp KTAp KTAp KTAp
KTApKTAp

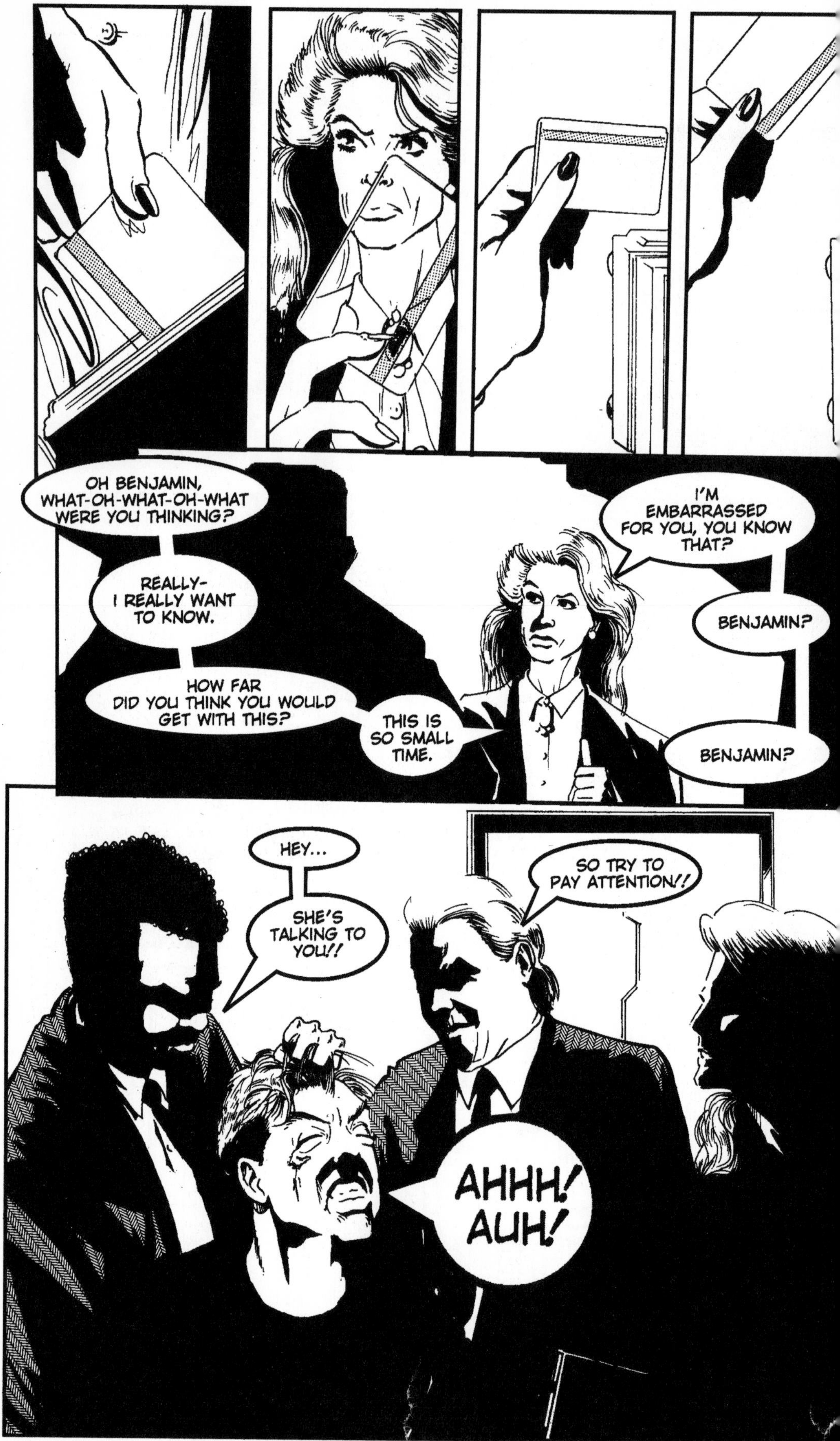
OH BENJAMIN, WHAT-OH-WHAT-OH-WHAT WERE YOU THINKING?
REALLY- I REALLY WANT TO KNOW.
HOW FAR DID YOU THINK YOU WOULD GET WITH THIS?
THIS IS SO SMALL TIME.
I'M EMBARRASSED FOR YOU, YOU KNOW THAT?
BENJAMIN?
BENJAMIN?
HEY...
SHE'S TALKING TO YOU!!
SO TRY TO PAY ATTENTION!!
AHHH! AUH!

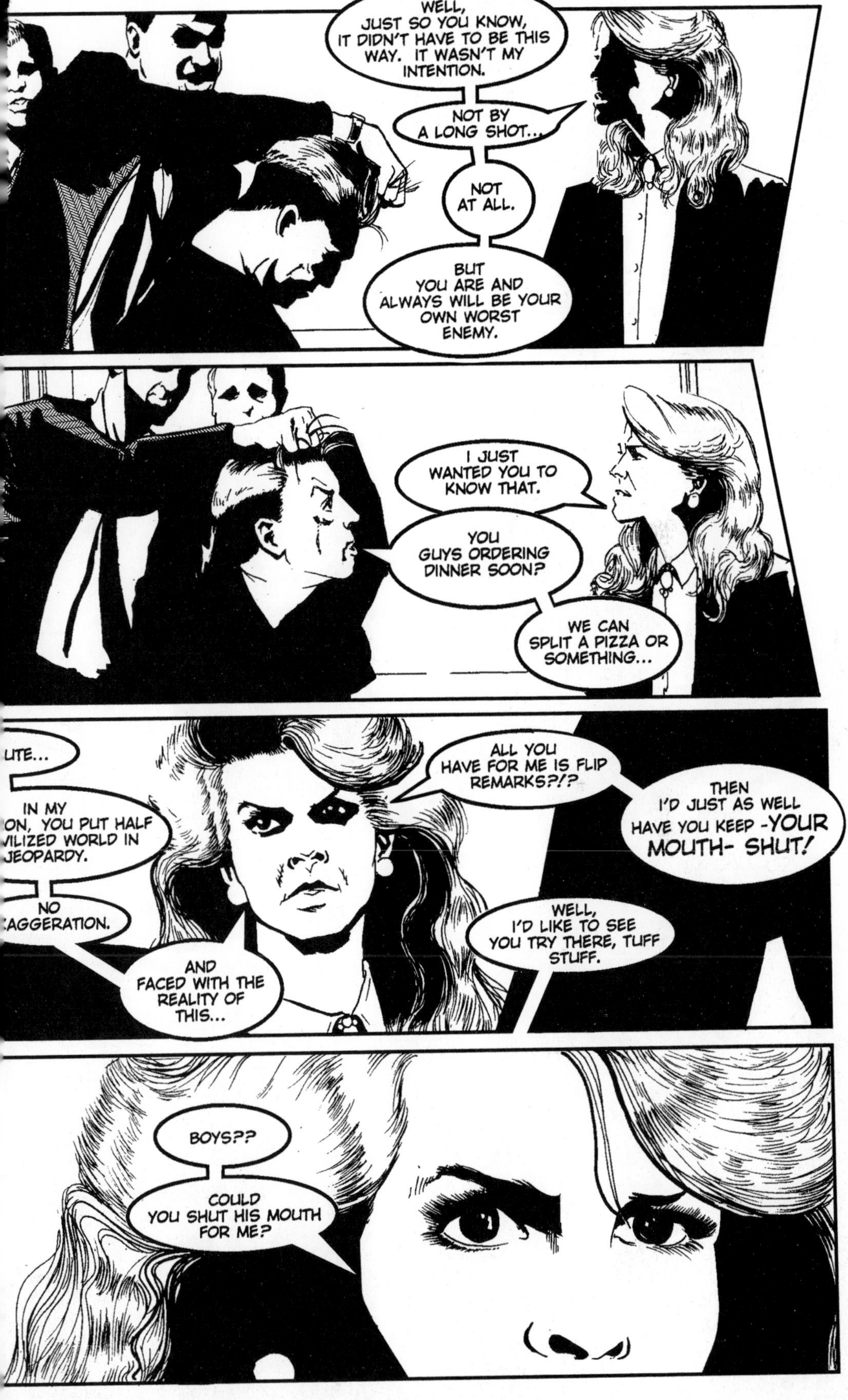
WELL, JUST SO YOU KNOW, IT DIDN'T HAVE TO BE THIS WAY. IT WASN'T MY INTENTION.
NOT BY A LONG SHOT...
NOT AT ALL.
BUT YOU ARE AND ALWAYS WILL BE YOUR OWN WORST ENEMY.
I JUST WANTED YOU TO KNOW THAT.
YOU GUYS ORDERING DINNER SOON?
WE CAN SPLIT A PIZZA OR SOMETHING...
UTE...
IN MY
ON, YOU PUT HALF
VILIZED WORLD IN
JEOPARDY.
NO
AGGERATION.
AND FACED WITH THE REALITY OF THIS...
ALL YOU HAVE FOR ME IS FLIP REMARKS?!?
THEN I'D JUST AS WELL HAVE YOU KEEP -YOUR MOUTH- SHUT!
WELL, I'D LIKE TO SEE YOU TRY THERE, TUFF STUFF.
BOYS??
COULD YOU SHUT HIS MOUTH FOR ME?

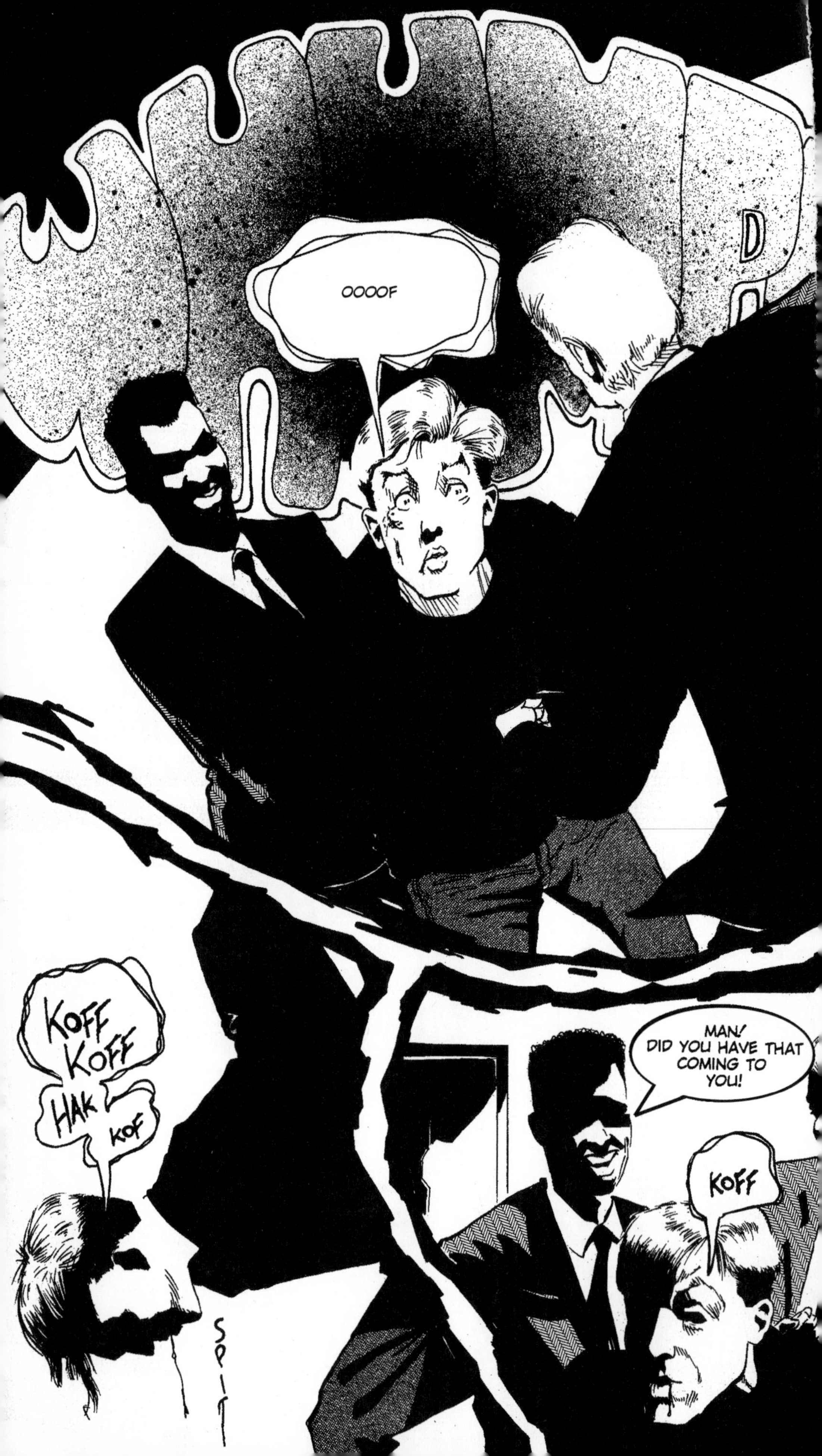
OOOOF
KOFF KOFF
HAK
KOF
SPIT
MAN! DID YOU HAVE THAT COMING TO YOU!
KOFF

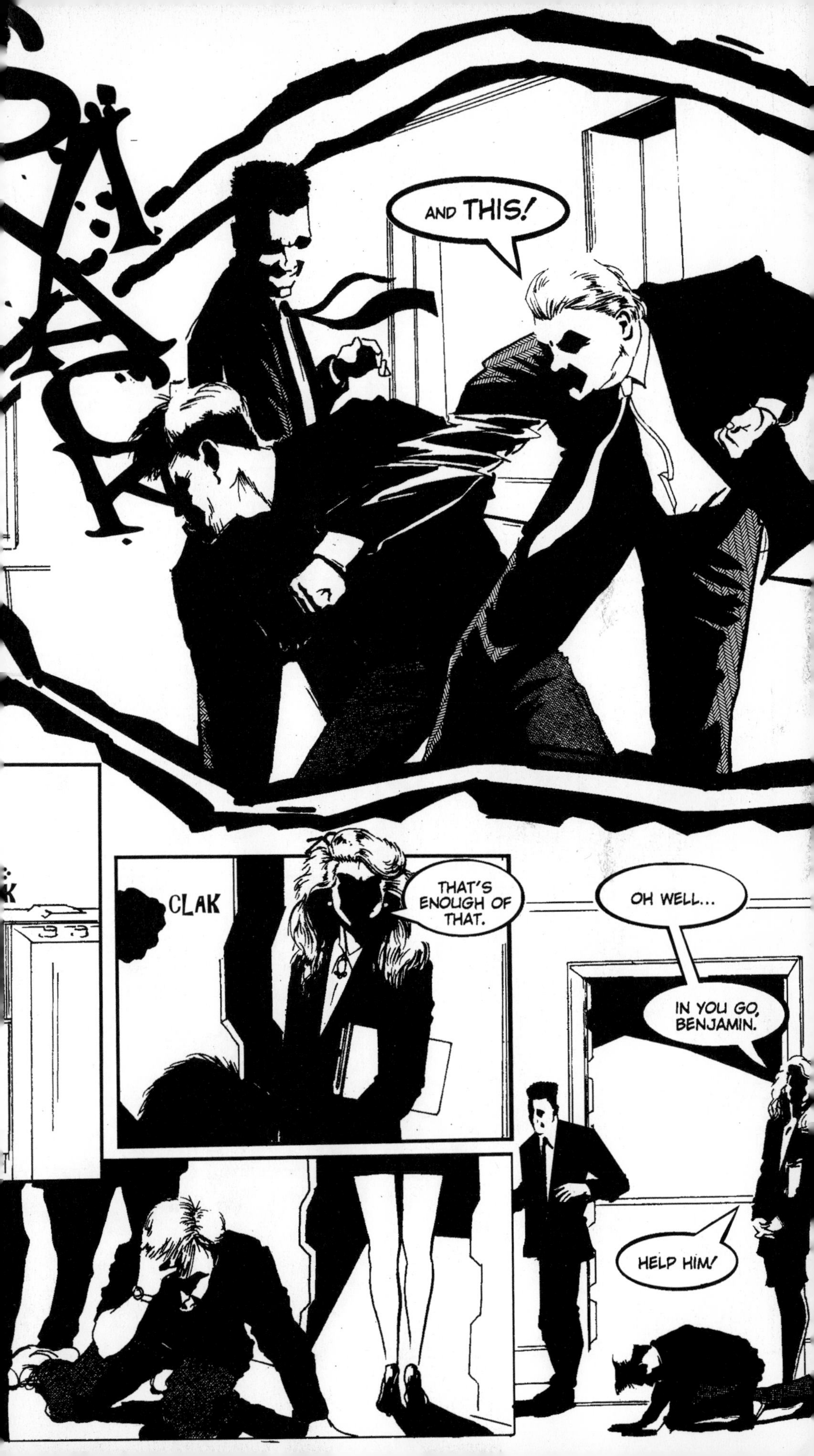
AND THIS!
CLAK
THAT'S ENOUGH OF THAT.
OH WELL...
IN YOU GO, BENJAMIN.
HELP HIM!

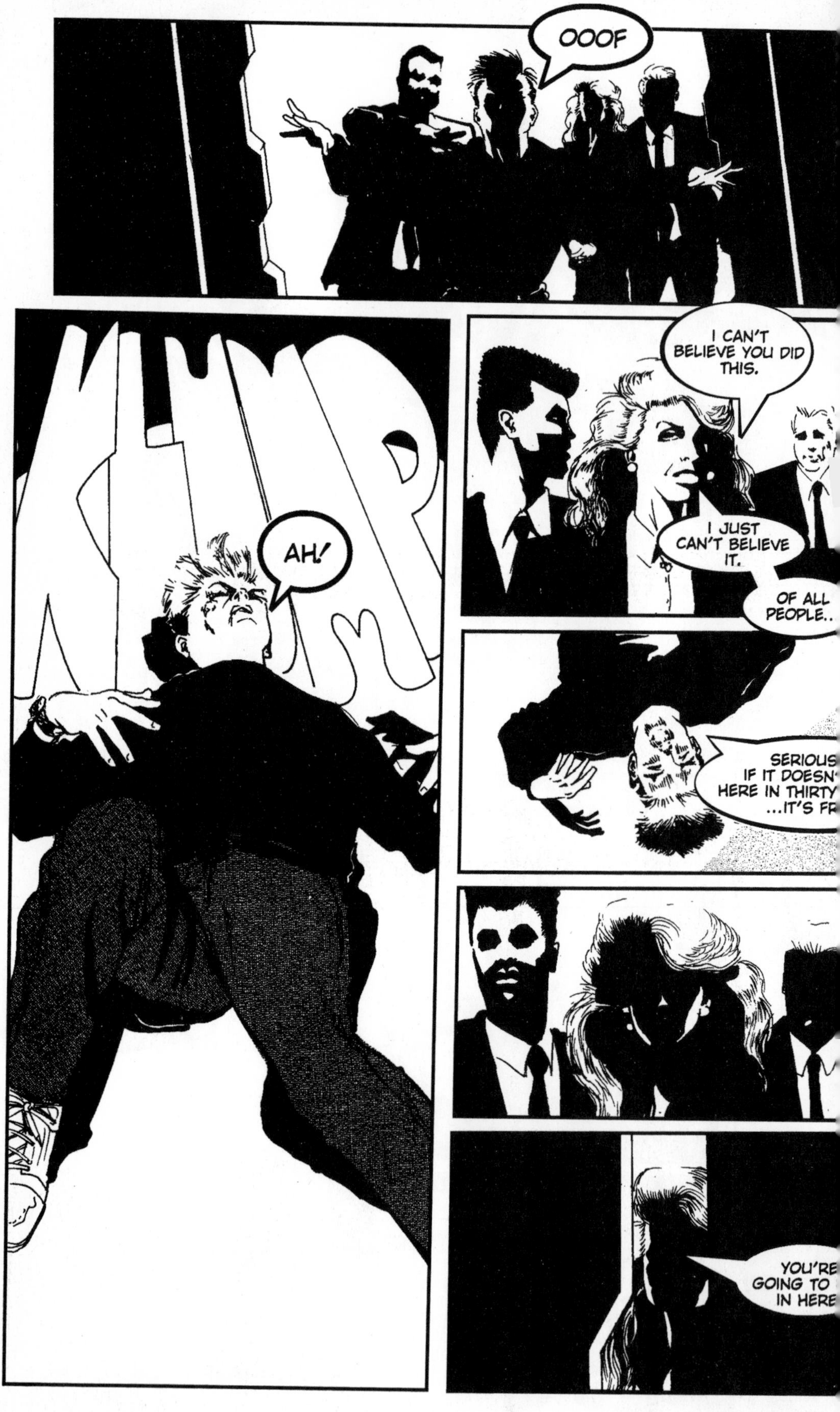

OOOF
AH!
I CAN'T BELIEVE YOU DID THIS.
I JUST CAN'T BELIEVE IT.
OF ALL PEOPLE..
SERIOUS IF IT DOESN' HERE IN THIRTY ...IT'S FR
YOU'RE GOING TO IN HERE

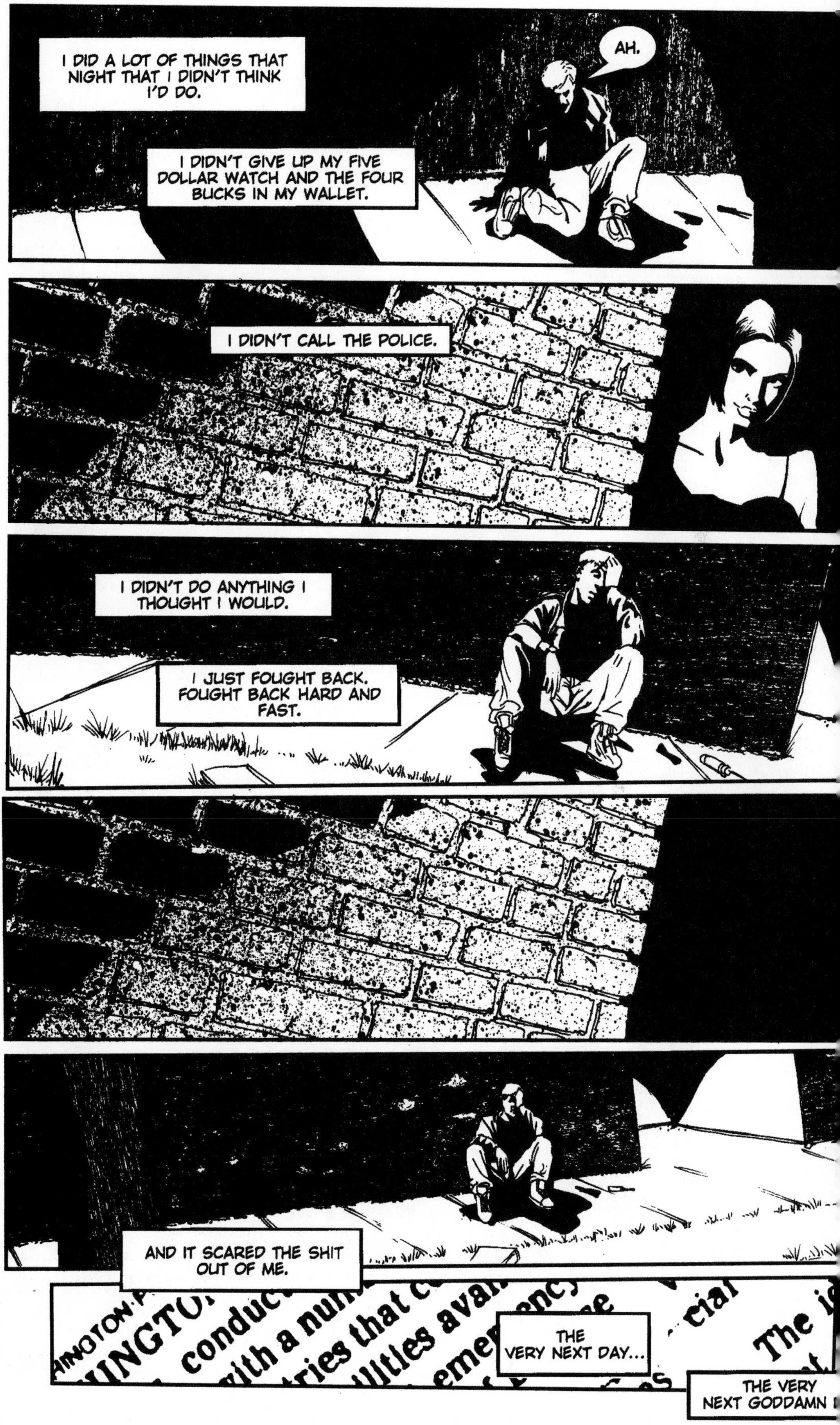
I DID A LOT OF THINGS THAT NIGHT THAT I DIDN'T THINK I'D DO.
AH.
I DIDN'T GIVE UP MY FIVE DOLLAR WATCH AND THE FOUR BUCKS IN MY WALLET.
I DIDN'T CALL THE POLICE.
I DIDN'T DO ANYTHING I THOUGHT I WOULD.
I JUST FOUGHT BACK. FOUGHT BACK HARD AND FAST.
AND IT SCARED THE SHIT OUT OF ME.
THE VERY NEXT DAY...
THE VERY NEXT GODDAMN

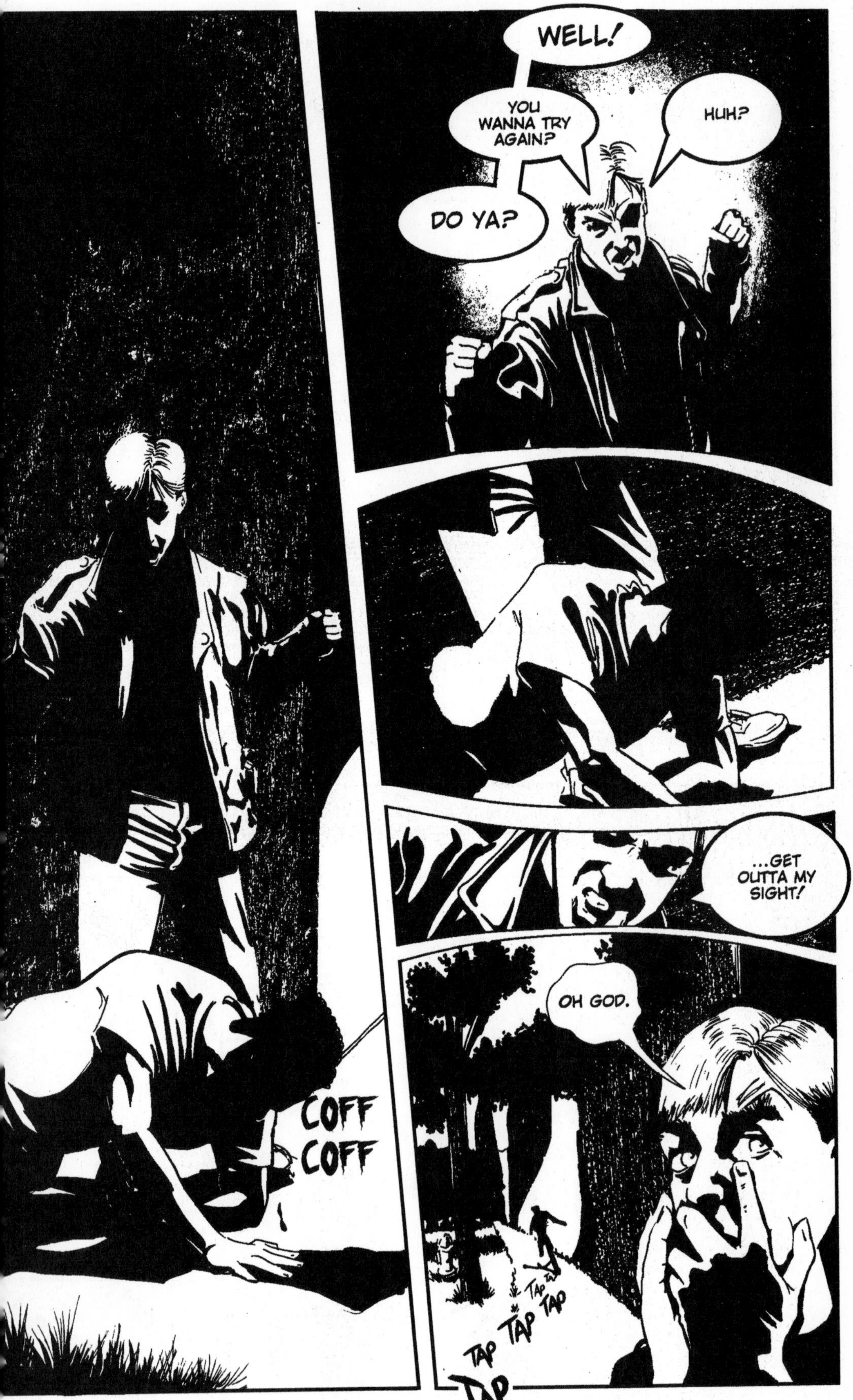
COFF
COFF
WELL!
YOU WANNA TRY AGAIN?
DO YA?
HUH?
...GET OUTTA MY SIGHT!
OH GOD.
TAP TAP TAP TAP
TAP
TAP

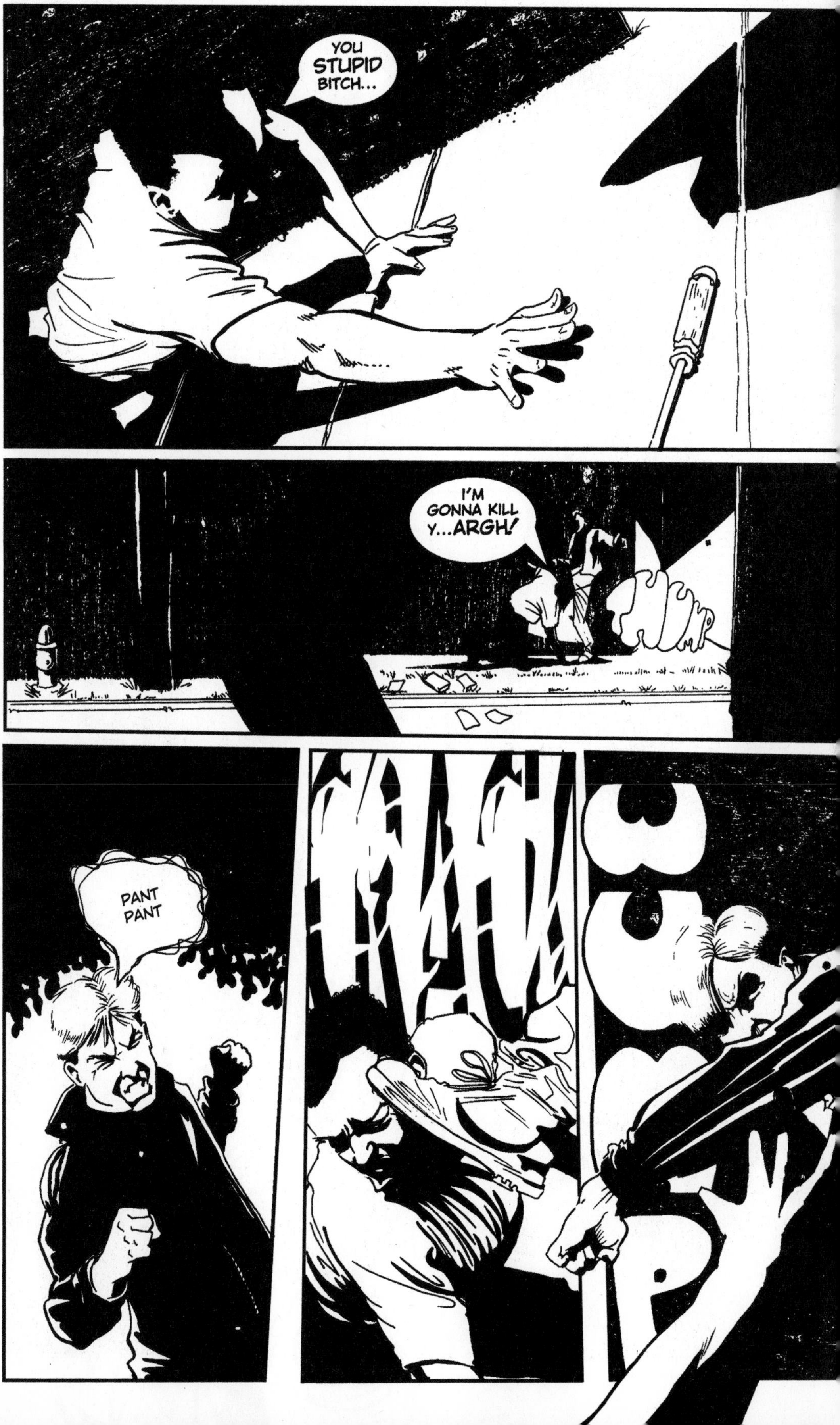
YOU STUPID BITCH...
I'M GONNA KILL Y...ARGH!
THUMP
PANT PANT

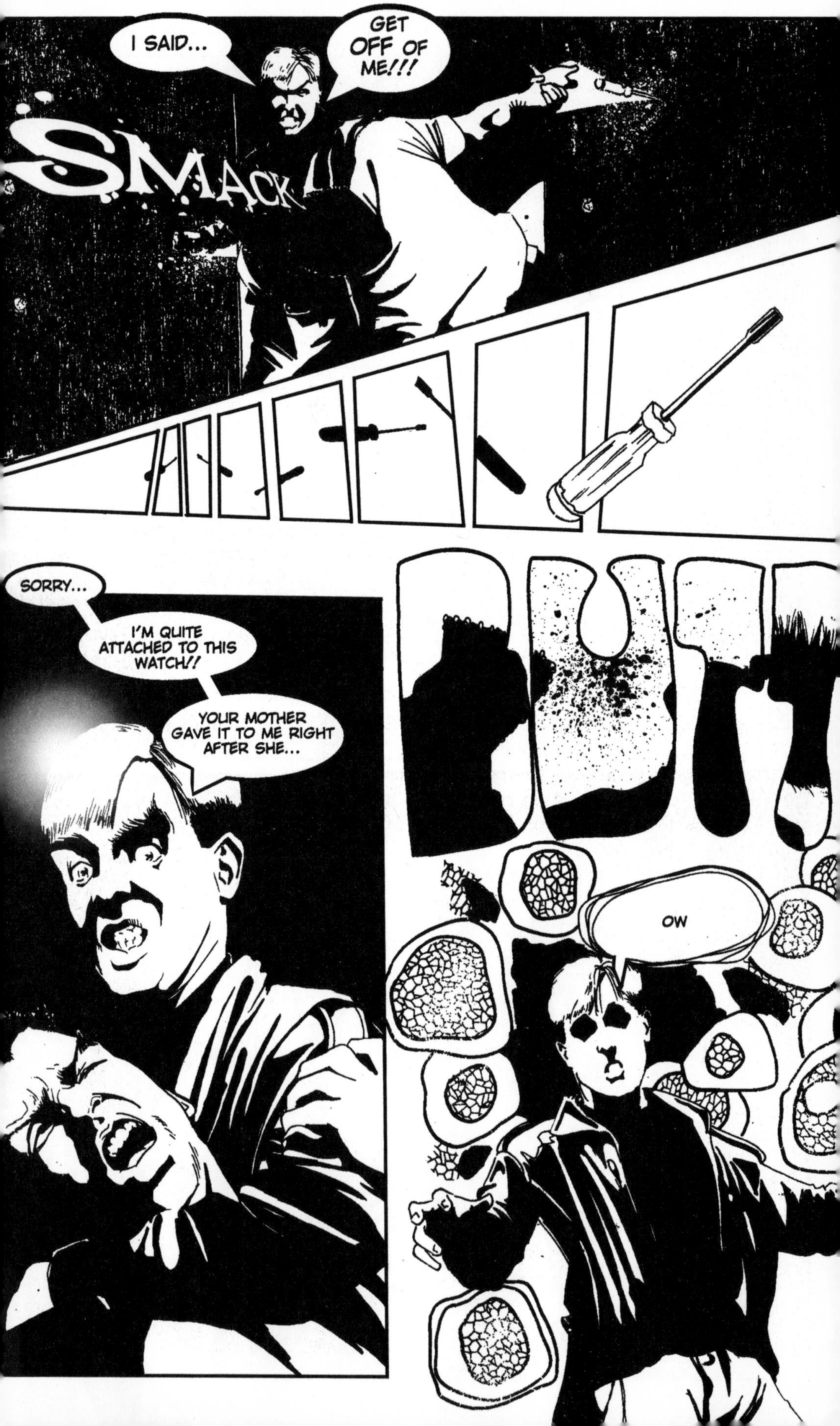
I SAID...
GET OFF OF ME!!!
SMACK
SORRY...
I'M QUITE ATTACHED TO THIS WATCH!!
YOUR MOTHER GAVE IT TO ME RIGHT AFTER SHE...
OW

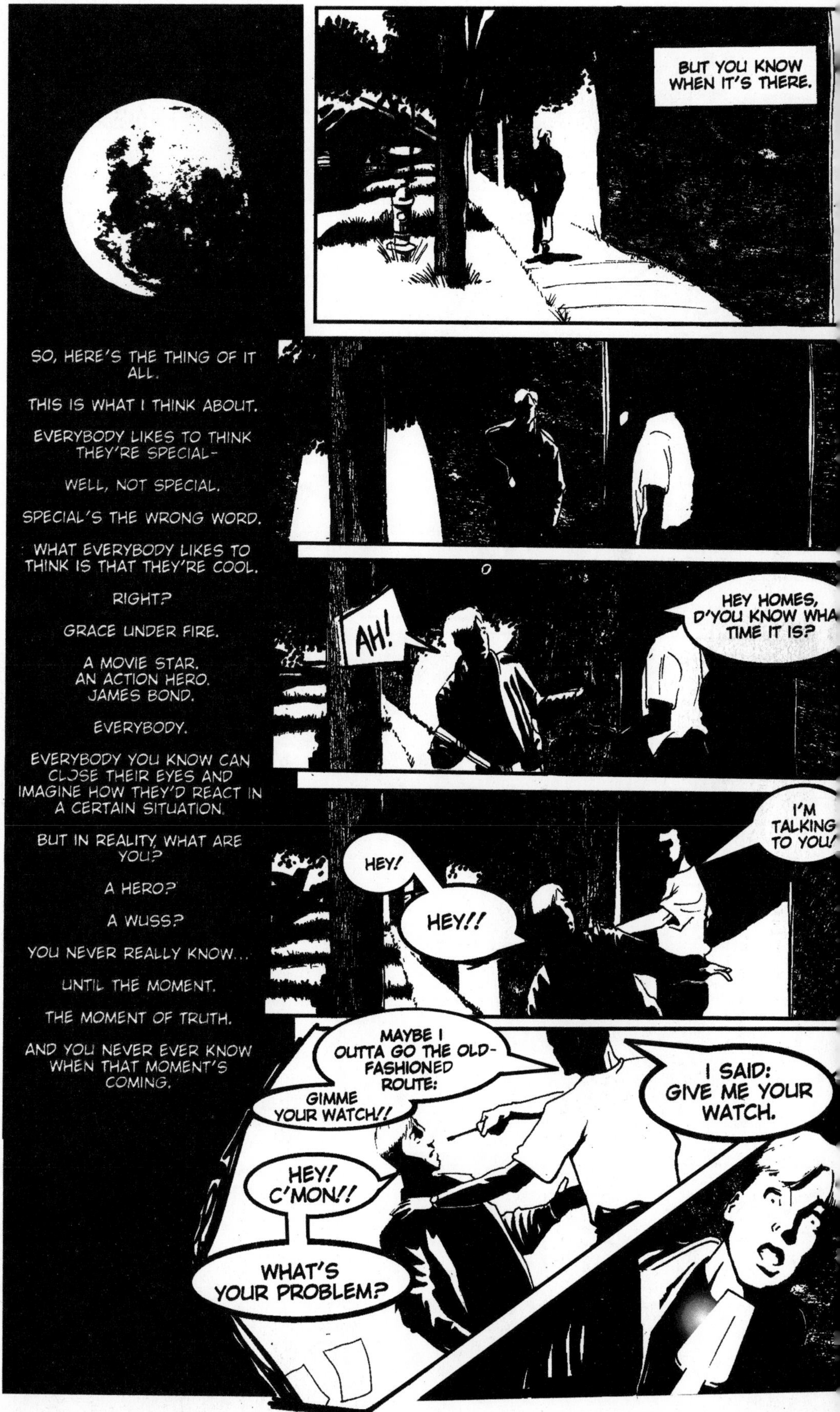
BUT YOU KNOW WHEN IT'S THERE.
SO, HERE'S THE THING OF IT ALL.
THIS IS WHAT I THINK ABOUT.
EVERYBODY LIKES TO THINK THEY'RE SPECIAL-
WELL, NOT SPECIAL.
SPECIAL'S THE WRONG WORD.
WHAT EVERYBODY LIKES TO THINK IS THAT THEY'RE COOL.
RIGHT?
GRACE UNDER FIRE.
A MOVIE STAR. AN ACTION HERO. JAMES BOND.
EVERYBODY.
EVERYBODY YOU KNOW CAN CLOSE THEIR EYES AND IMAGINE HOW THEY'D REACT IN A CERTAIN SITUATION.
BUT IN REALITY, WHAT ARE YOU?
A HERO?
A WUSS?
YOU NEVER REALLY KNOW...
UNTIL THE MOMENT.
THE MOMENT OF TRUTH.
AND YOU NEVER EVER KNOW WHEN THAT MOMENT'S COMING.
AH!
HEY HOMES, D'YOU KNOW WHA
TIME IT IS?
HEY!
HEY!!
I'M TALKING TO YOU!
MAYBE I OUTTA GO THE OLD-FASHIONED ROUTE:
GIMME YOUR WATCH!!
I SAID: GIVE ME YOUR WATCH.
HEY! C'MON!!
WHAT'S YOUR PROBLEM?

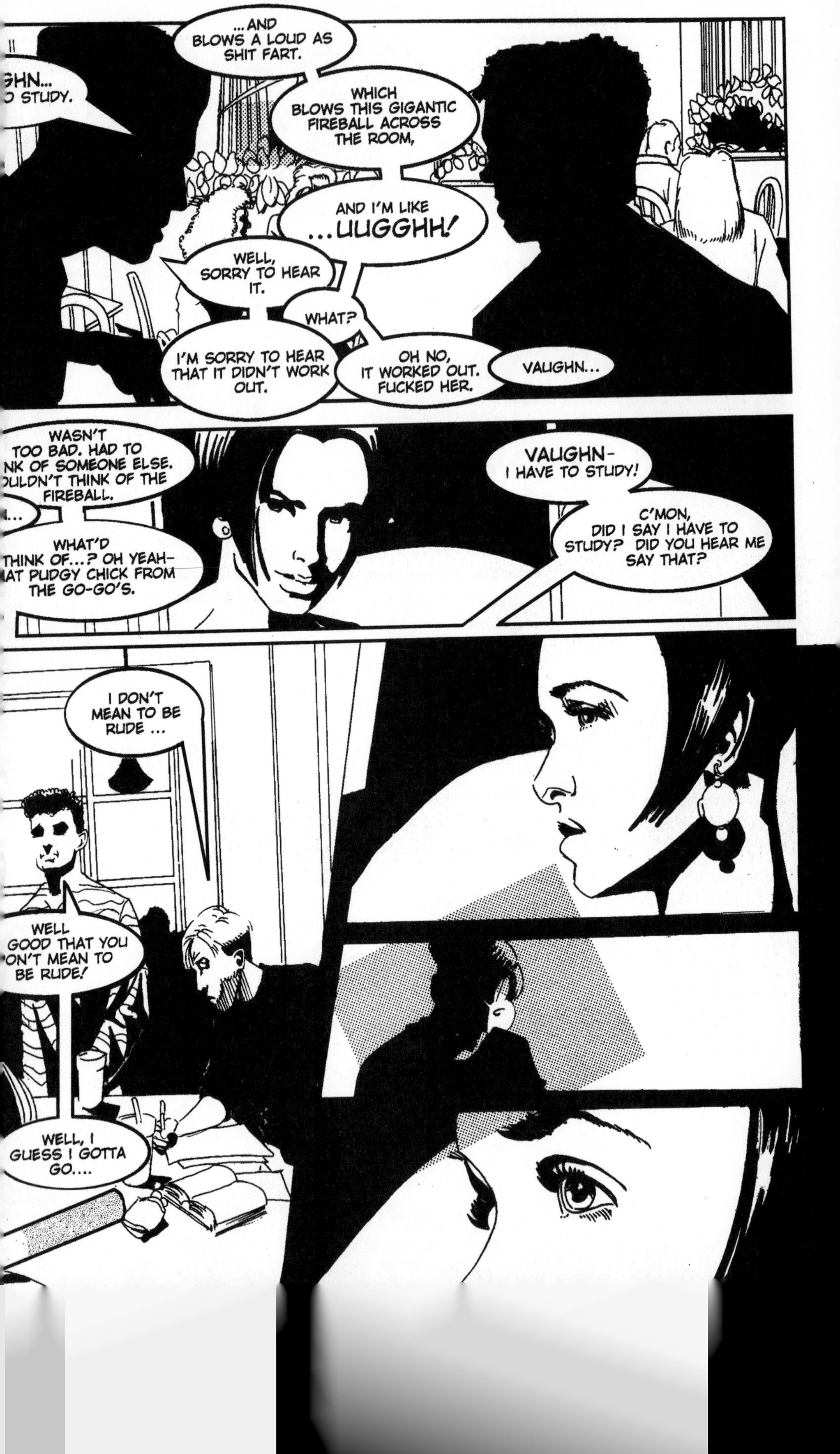

GHN...
O STUDY.
...AND BLOWS A LOUD AS SHIT FART.
WHICH BLOWS THIS GIGANTIC FIREBALL ACROSS THE ROOM,
AND I'M LIKE ...UUGGHH!
WELL, SORRY TO HEAR IT.
WHAT?
I'M SORRY TO HEAR THAT IT DIDN'T WORK OUT.
OH NO, IT WORKED OUT. FUCKED HER.
VAUGHN...
WASN'T TOO BAD. HAD TO NK OF SOMEONE ELSE. OULDN'T THINK OF THE FIREBALL.
WHAT'D THINK OF...? OH YEAH- AT PUDGY CHICK FROM THE GO-GO'S.
VAUGHN- I HAVE TO STUDY!
C'MON, DID I SAY I HAVE TO STUDY? DID YOU HEAR ME SAY THAT?
I DON'T MEAN TO BE RUDE ...
WELL GOOD THAT YOU ON'T MEAN TO BE RUDE!
WELL, I GUESS I GOTTA GO....

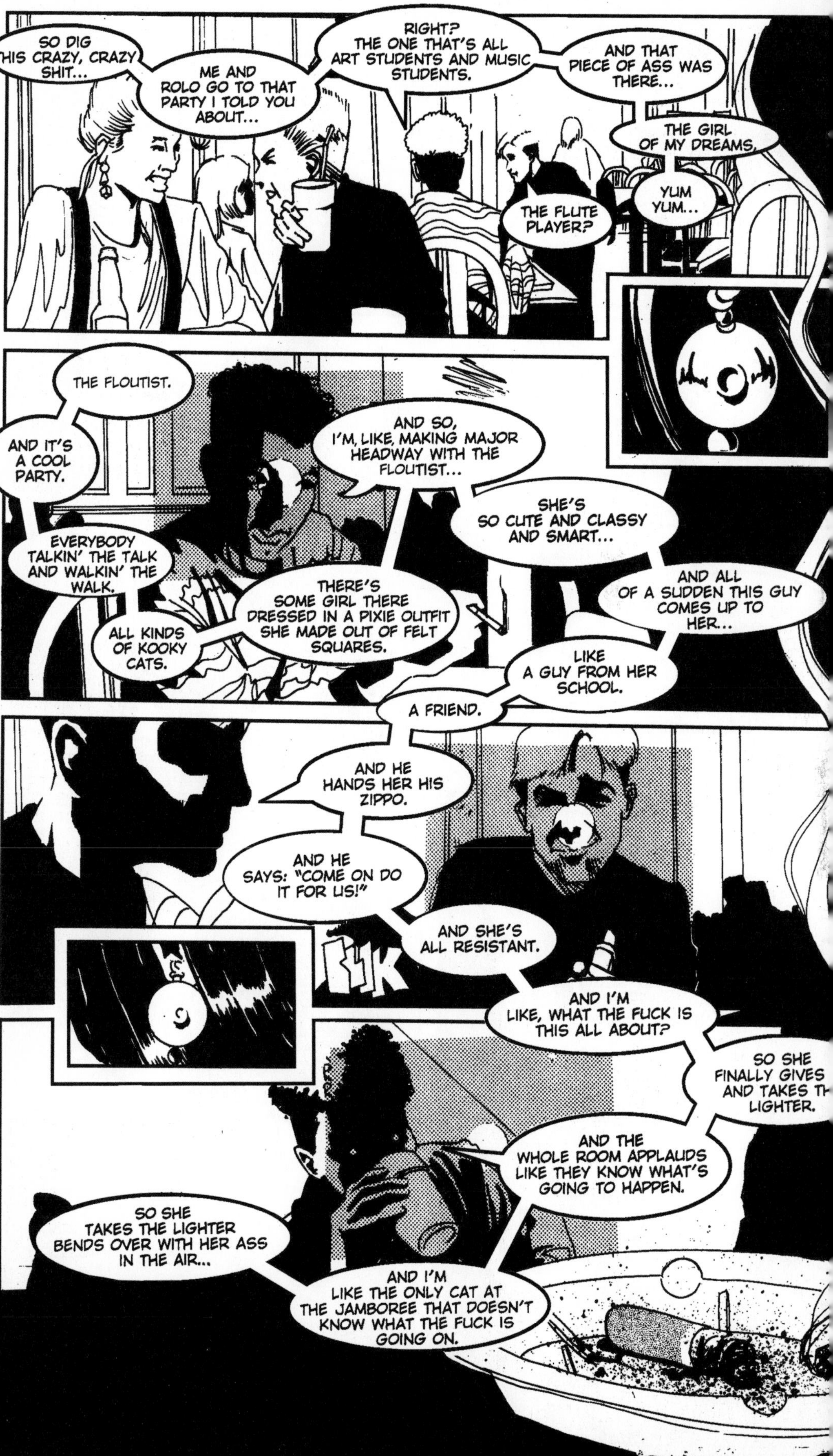
SO DIG THIS CRAZY, CRAZY SHIT...
ME AND ROLO GO TO THAT PARTY I TOLD YOU ABOUT...
RIGHT? THE ONE THAT'S ALL ART STUDENTS AND MUSIC STUDENTS.
AND THAT PIECE OF ASS WAS THERE...
THE GIRL OF MY DREAMS,
YUM YUM...
THE FLUTE PLAYER?
THE FLOUTIST.
AND IT'S A COOL PARTY.
EVERYBODY TALKIN' THE TALK AND WALKIN' THE WALK.
ALL KINDS OF KOOKY CATS.
THERE'S SOME GIRL THERE DRESSED IN A PIXIE OUTFIT SHE MADE OUT OF FELT SQUARES.
AND SO, I'M, LIKE, MAKING MAJOR HEADWAY WITH THE FLOUTIST...
SHE'S SO CUTE AND CLASSY AND SMART...
AND ALL OF A SUDDEN THIS GUY COMES UP TO HER...
LIKE A GUY FROM HER SCHOOL.
A FRIEND.
AND HE HANDS HER HIS ZIPPO.
AND HE SAYS: "COME ON DO IT FOR US!"
AND SHE'S ALL RESISTANT.
AND I'M LIKE, WHAT THE FUCK IS THIS ALL ABOUT?
SO SHE FINALLY GIVES AND TAKES TH LIGHTER.
AND THE WHOLE ROOM APPLAUDS LIKE THEY KNOW WHAT'S GOING TO HAPPEN.
SO SHE TAKES THE LIGHTER BENDS OVER WITH HER ASS IN THE AIR...
AND I'M LIKE THE ONLY CAT AT THE JAMBOREE THAT DOESN'T KNOW WHAT THE FUCK IS GOING ON.

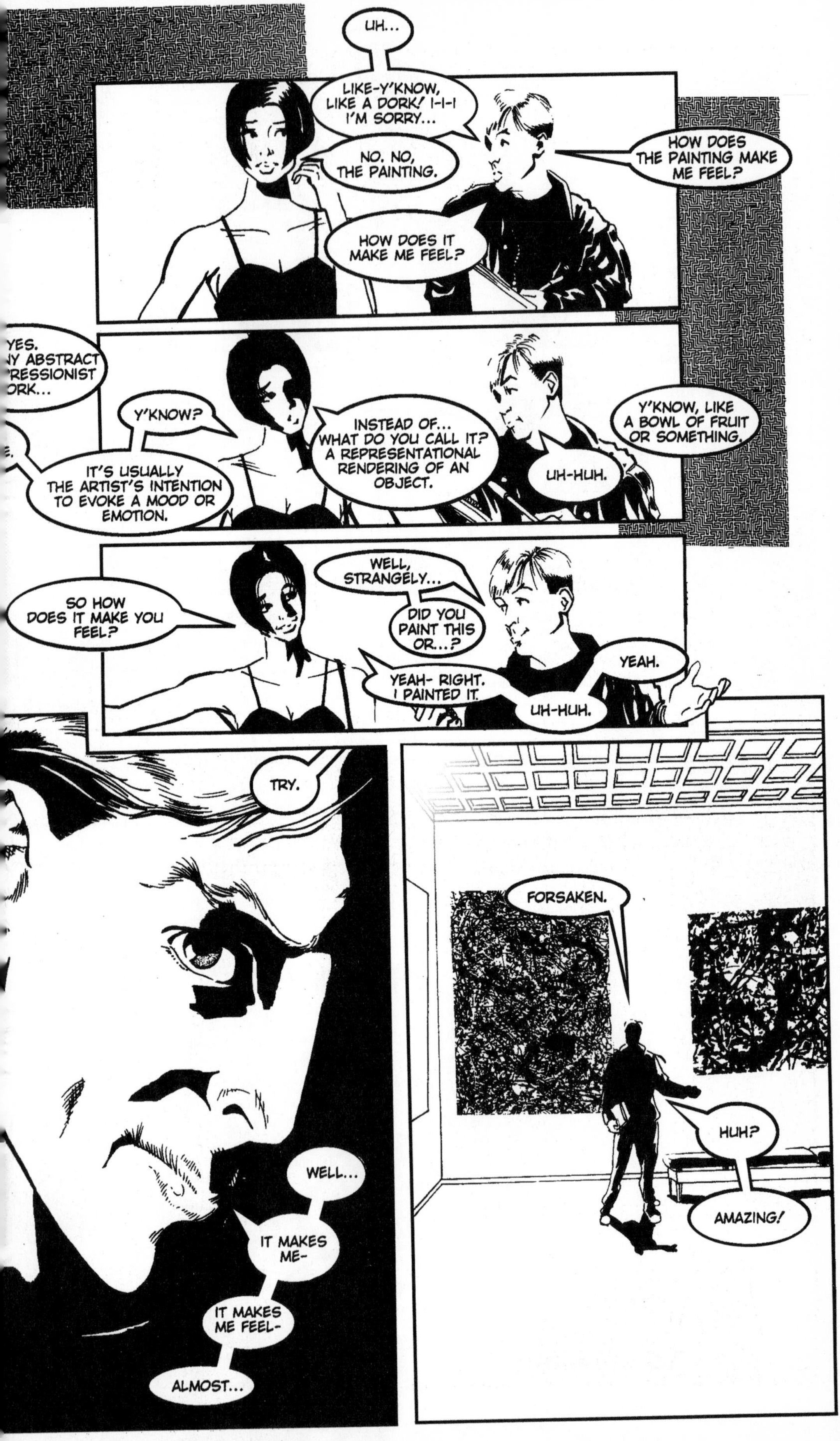
UH...
LIKE-Y'KNOW, LIKE A DORK! I-I-I I'M SORRY...
HOW DOES THE PAINTING MAKE ME FEEL?
NO. NO, THE PAINTING.
HOW DOES IT MAKE ME FEEL?
YES. NY ABSTRACT RESSIONIST ORK...
IT'S USUALLY THE ARTIST'S INTENTION TO EVOKE A MOOD OR EMOTION.
Y'KNOW?
INSTEAD OF... WHAT DO YOU CALL IT? A REPRESENTATIONAL RENDERING OF AN OBJECT.
UH-HUH.
Y'KNOW, LIKE A BOWL OF FRUIT OR SOMETHING.
SO HOW DOES IT MAKE YOU FEEL?
WELL, STRANGELY...
DID YOU PAINT THIS OR...?
YEAH- RIGHT. I PAINTED IT.
UH-HUH.
YEAH.
TRY.
WELL...
IT MAKES ME-
IT MAKES ME FEEL-
ALMOST...
FORSAKEN.
HUH?
AMAZING!

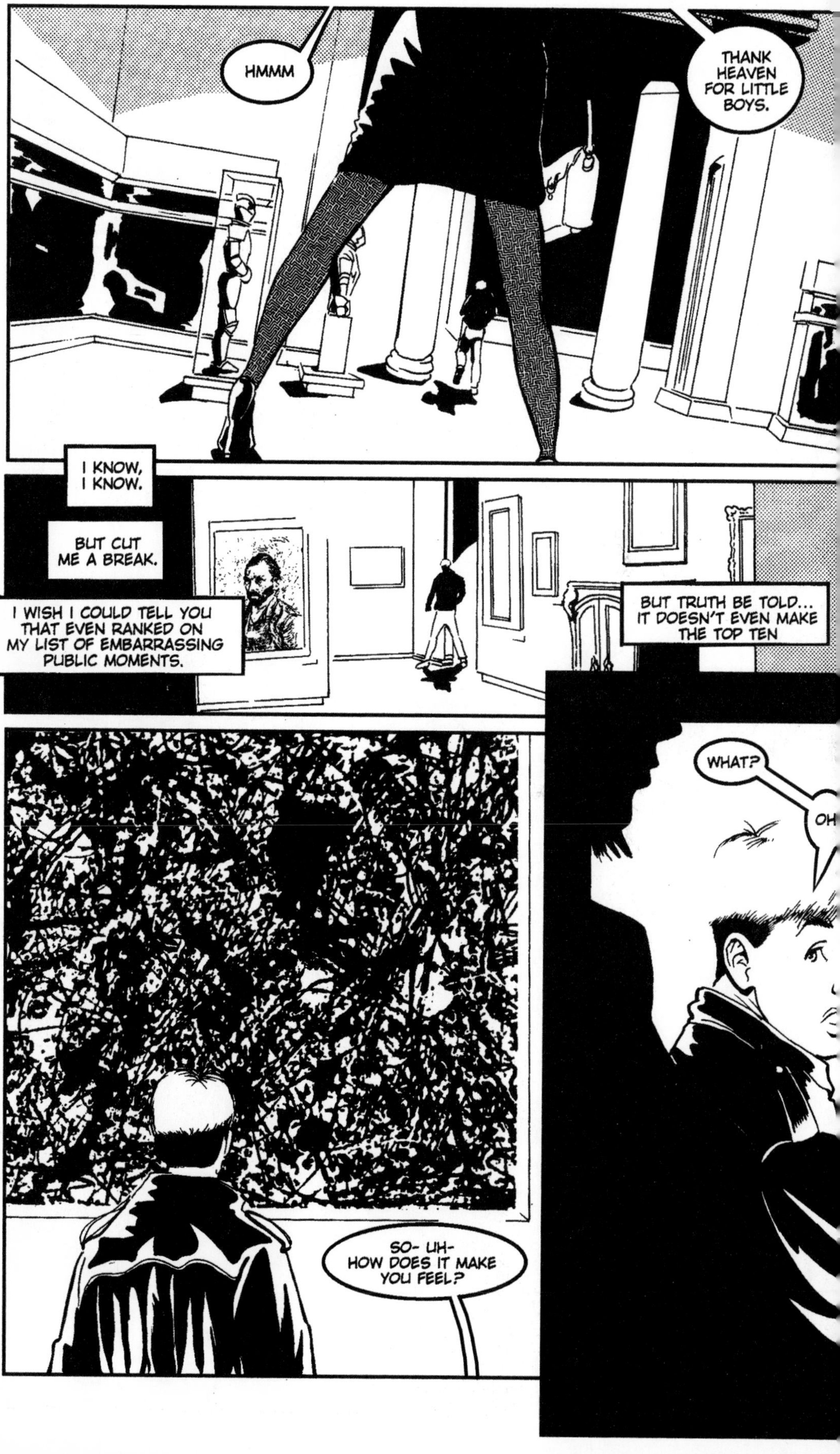
HMMM
THANK HEAVEN FOR LITTLE BOYS.
I KNOW, I KNOW.
BUT CUT ME A BREAK.
I WISH I COULD TELL YOU THAT EVEN RANKED ON MY LIST OF EMBARRASSING PUBLIC MOMENTS.
BUT TRUTH BE TOLD... IT DOESN'T EVEN MAKE THE TOP TEN
SO- UH- HOW DOES IT MAKE YOU FEEL?
WHAT?
OH

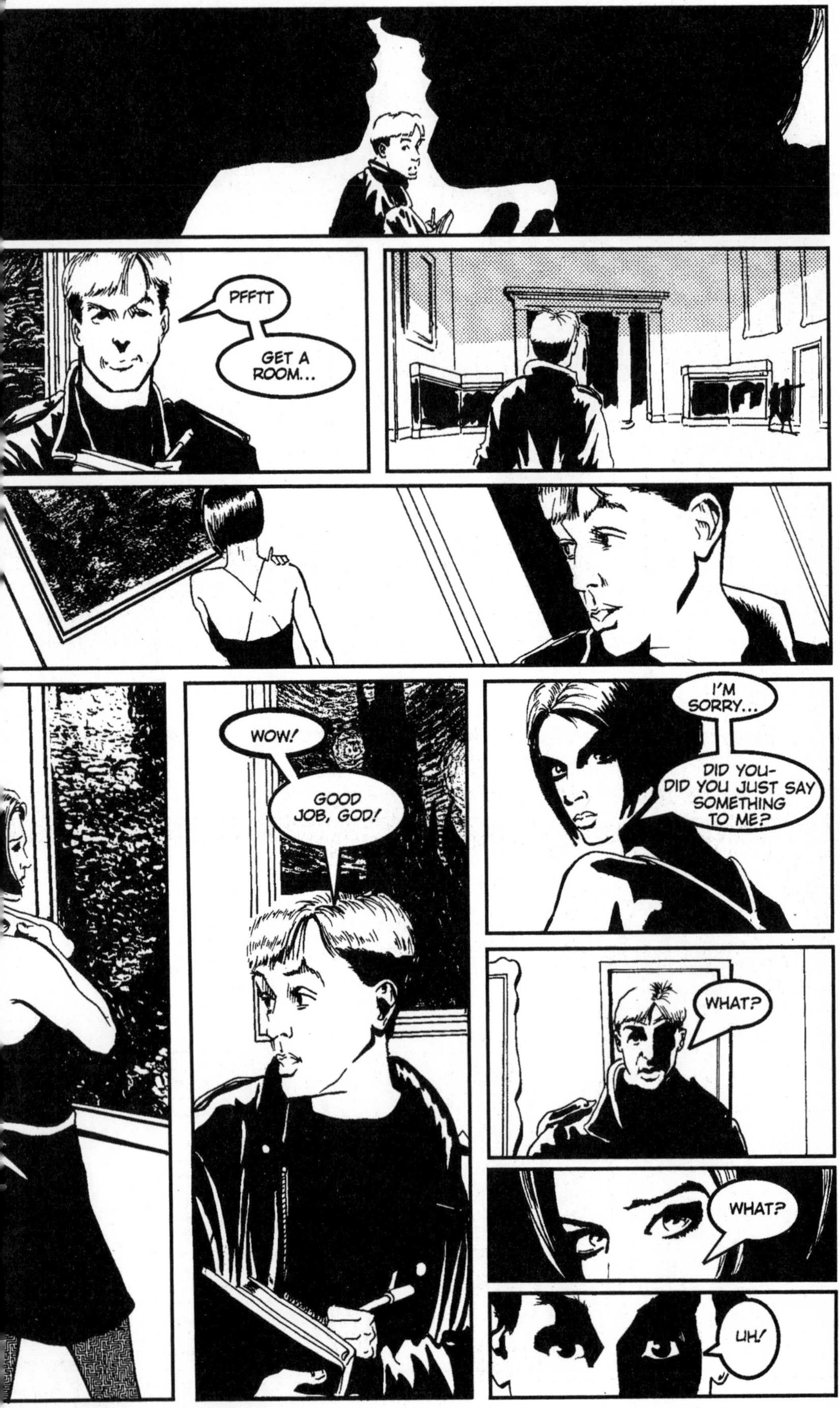
PFFTT
GET A ROOM...
WOW!
GOOD JOB, GOD!
I'M SORRY...
DID YOU- DID YOU JUST SAY SOMETHING TO ME?
WHAT?
WHAT?
UH!

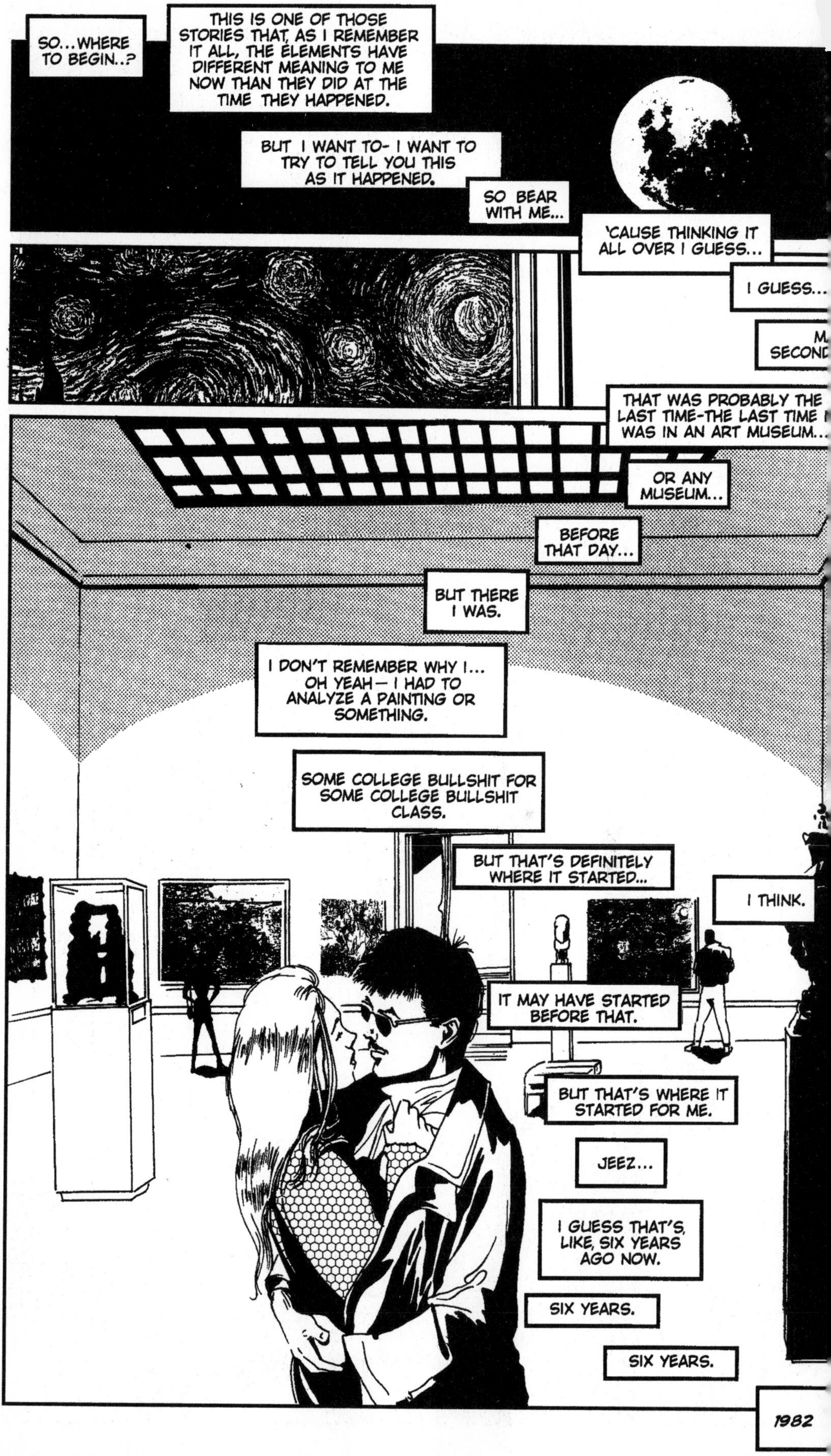

SO...WHERE TO BEGIN..?
THIS IS ONE OF THOSE STORIES THAT, AS I REMEMBER IT ALL, THE ELEMENTS HAVE DIFFERENT MEANING TO ME NOW THAN THEY DID AT THE TIME THEY HAPPENED.
BUT I WANT TO- I WANT TO TRY TO TELL YOU THIS AS IT HAPPENED.
SO BEAR WITH ME...
'CAUSE THINKING IT ALL OVER I GUESS...
I GUESS...
THAT WAS PROBABLY THE LAST TIME-THE LAST TIME
WAS IN AN ART MUSEUM...
OR ANY MUSEUM...
BEFORE THAT DAY...
BUT THERE I WAS.
I DON'T REMEMBER WHY I... OH YEAH— I HAD TO ANALYZE A PAINTING OR SOMETHING.
SOME COLLEGE BULLSHIT FOR SOME COLLEGE BULLSHIT CLASS.
BUT THAT'S DEFINITELY WHERE IT STARTED...
I THINK.
IT MAY HAVE STARTED BEFORE THAT.
BUT THAT'S WHERE IT STARTED FOR ME.
JEEZ...
I GUESS THAT'S, LIKE, SIX YEARS AGO NOW.
SIX YEARS.
SIX YEARS.
1982

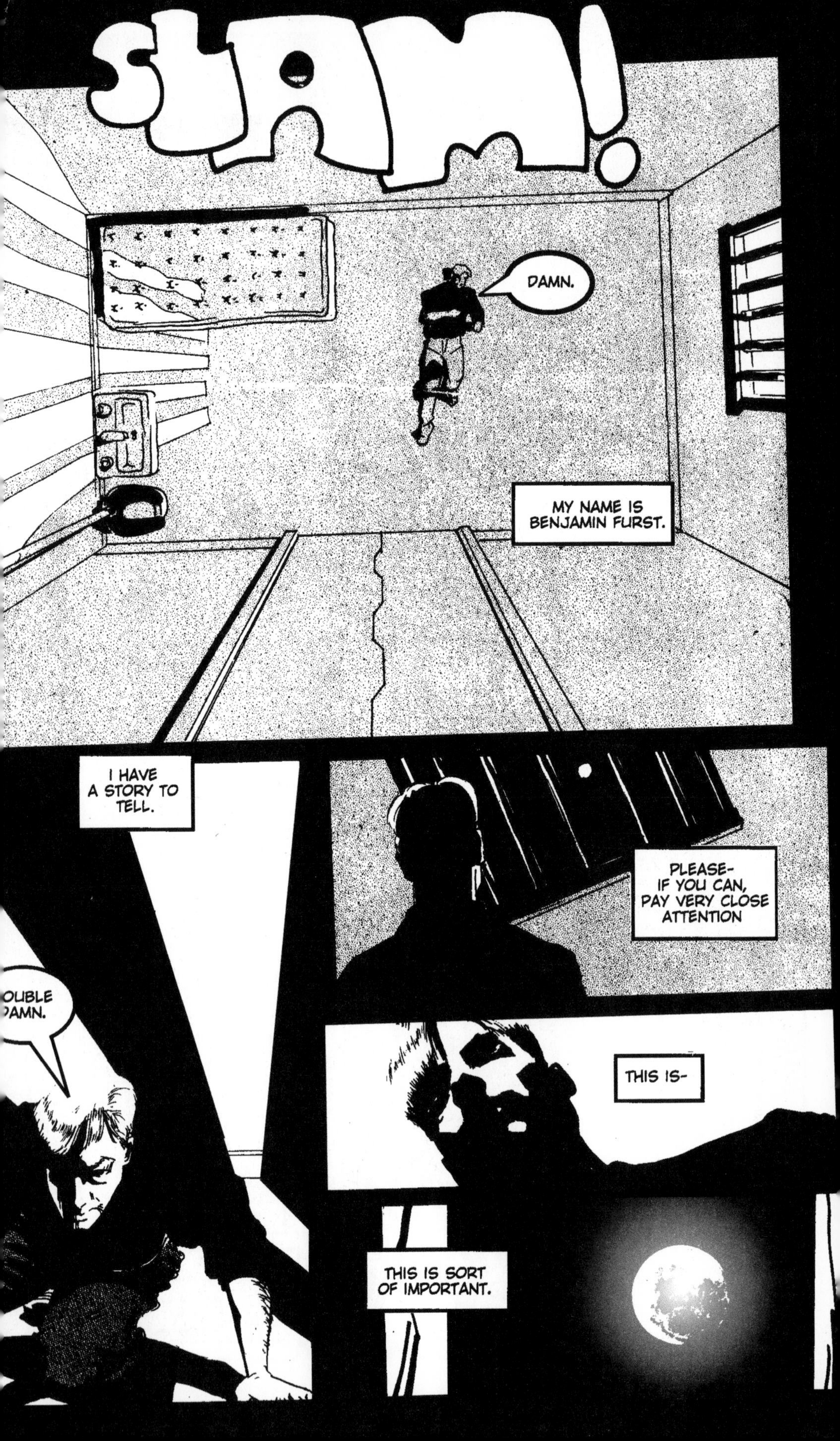
SLAM!
DAMN.
MY NAME IS BENJAMIN FURST.
I HAVE A STORY TO TELL.
PLEASE- IF YOU CAN, PAY VERY CLOSE ATTENTION
THIS IS-
THIS IS SORT OF IMPORTANT.

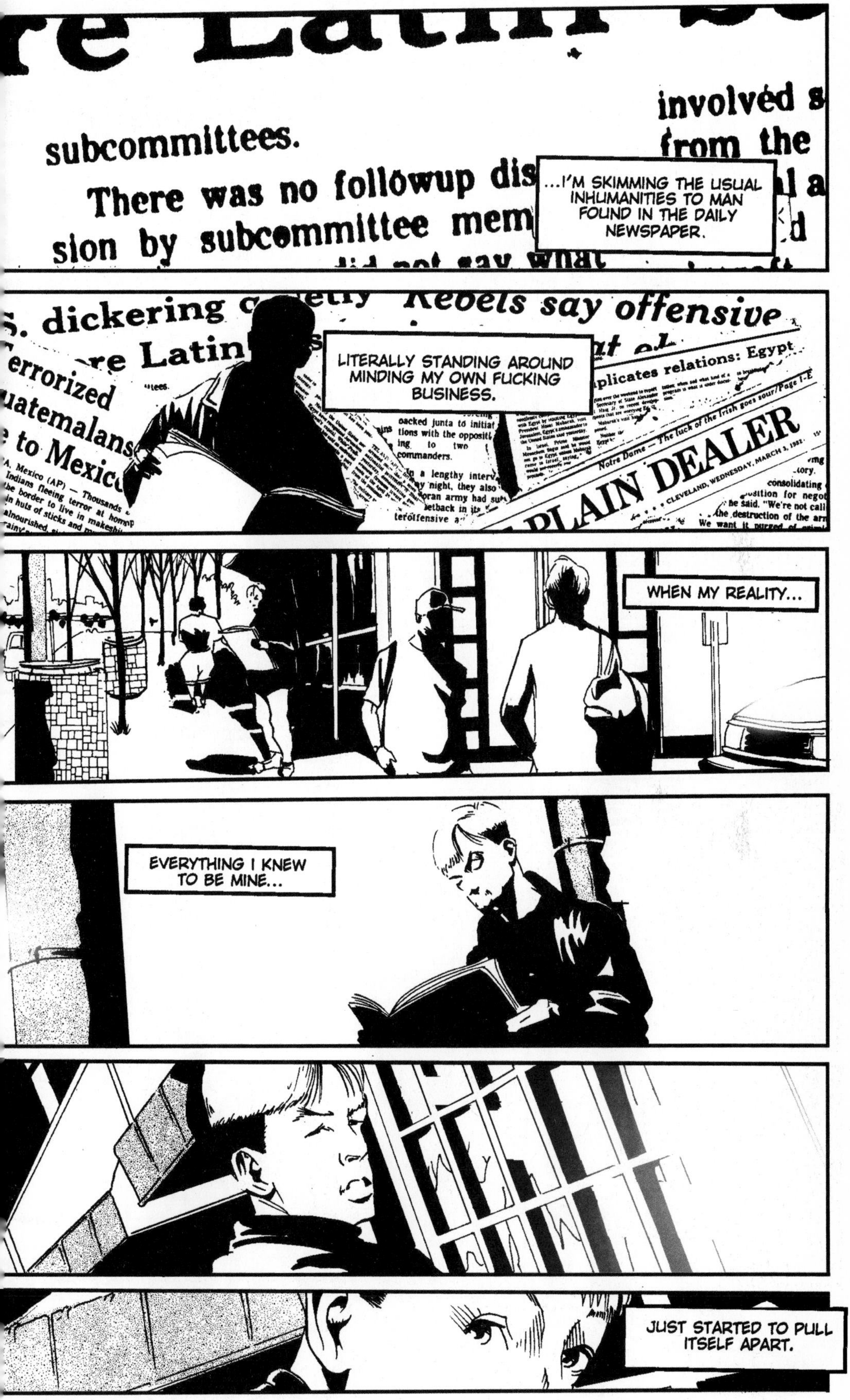
…I'M SKIMMING THE USUAL INHUMANITIES TO MAN FOUND IN THE DAILY NEWSPAPER.
LITERALLY STANDING AROUND MINDING MY OWN FUCKING BUSINESS.
PLAIN DEALER
WHEN MY REALITY…
EVERYTHING I KNEW TO BE MINE…
JUST STARTED TO PULL ITSELF APART.

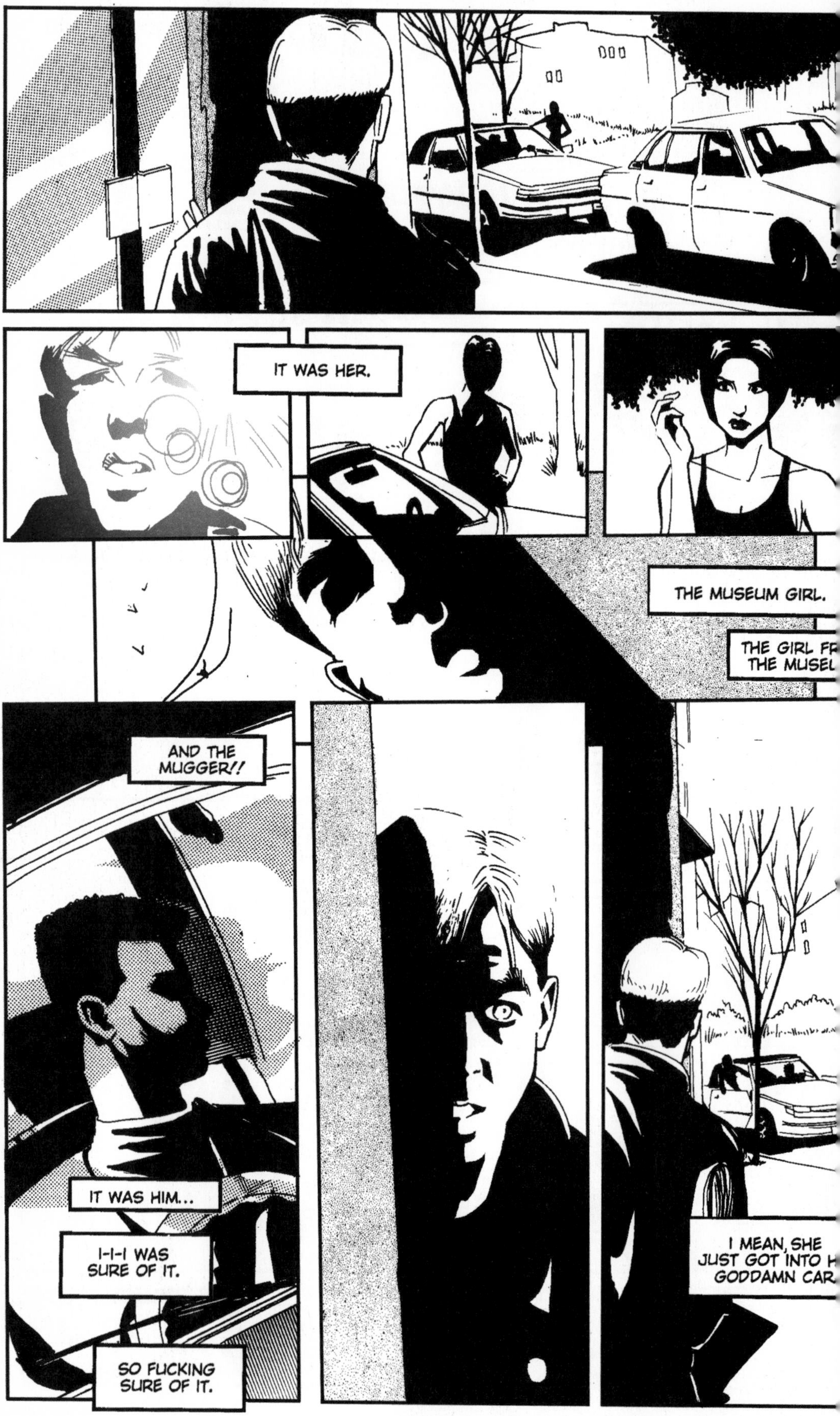
IT WAS HER.
THE MUSEUM GIRL.
THE GIRL FR
THE MUSEU
AND THE MUGGER!!
IT WAS HIM...
I-I-I WAS SURE OF IT.
SO FUCKING SURE OF IT.
I MEAN, SHE JUST GOT INTO H
GODDAMN CAR

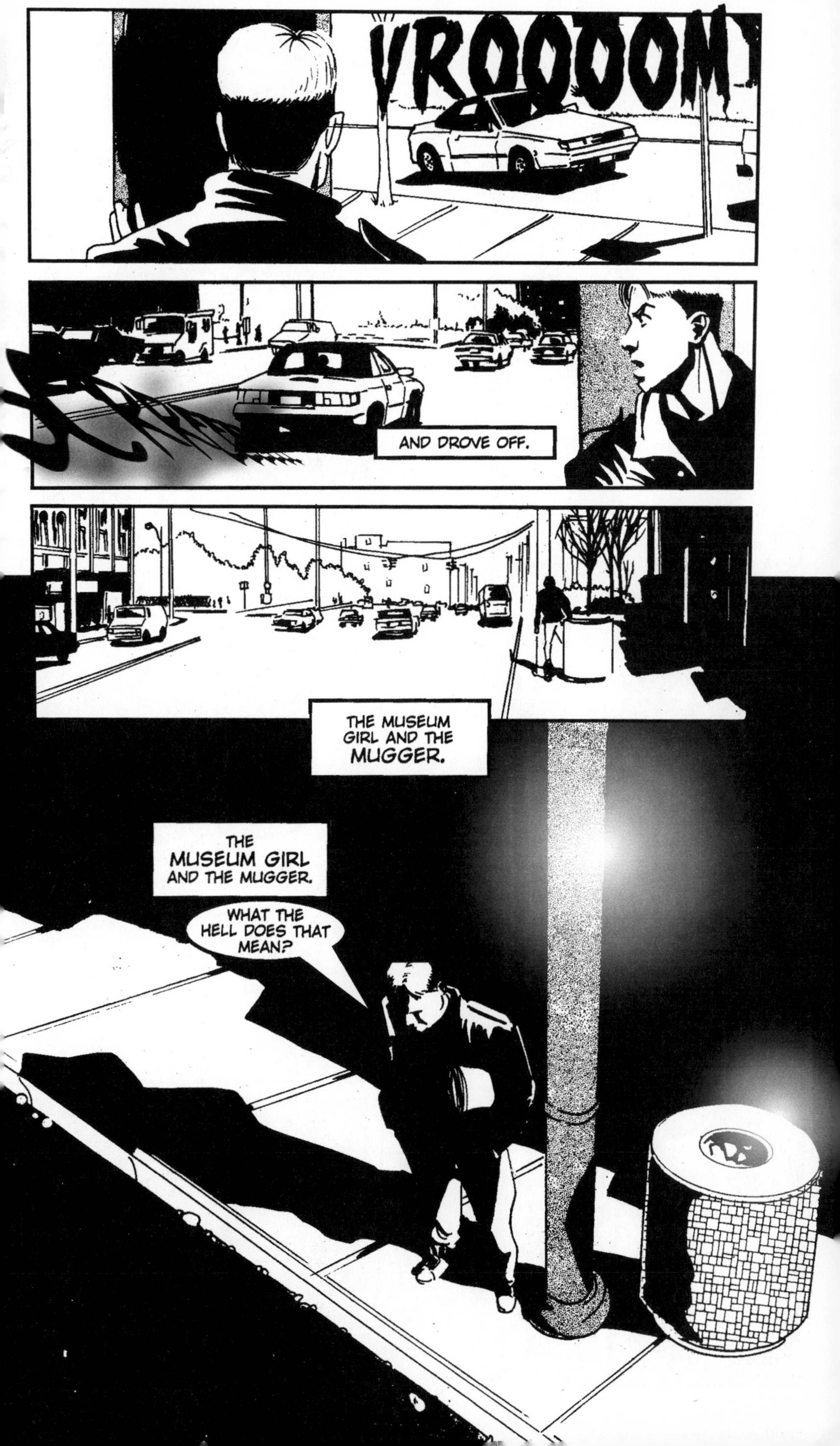
VROOOOM
AND DROVE OFF.
THE MUSEUM GIRL AND THE MUGGER.
THE MUSEUM GIRL AND THE MUGGER.
WHAT THE HELL DOES THAT MEAN?

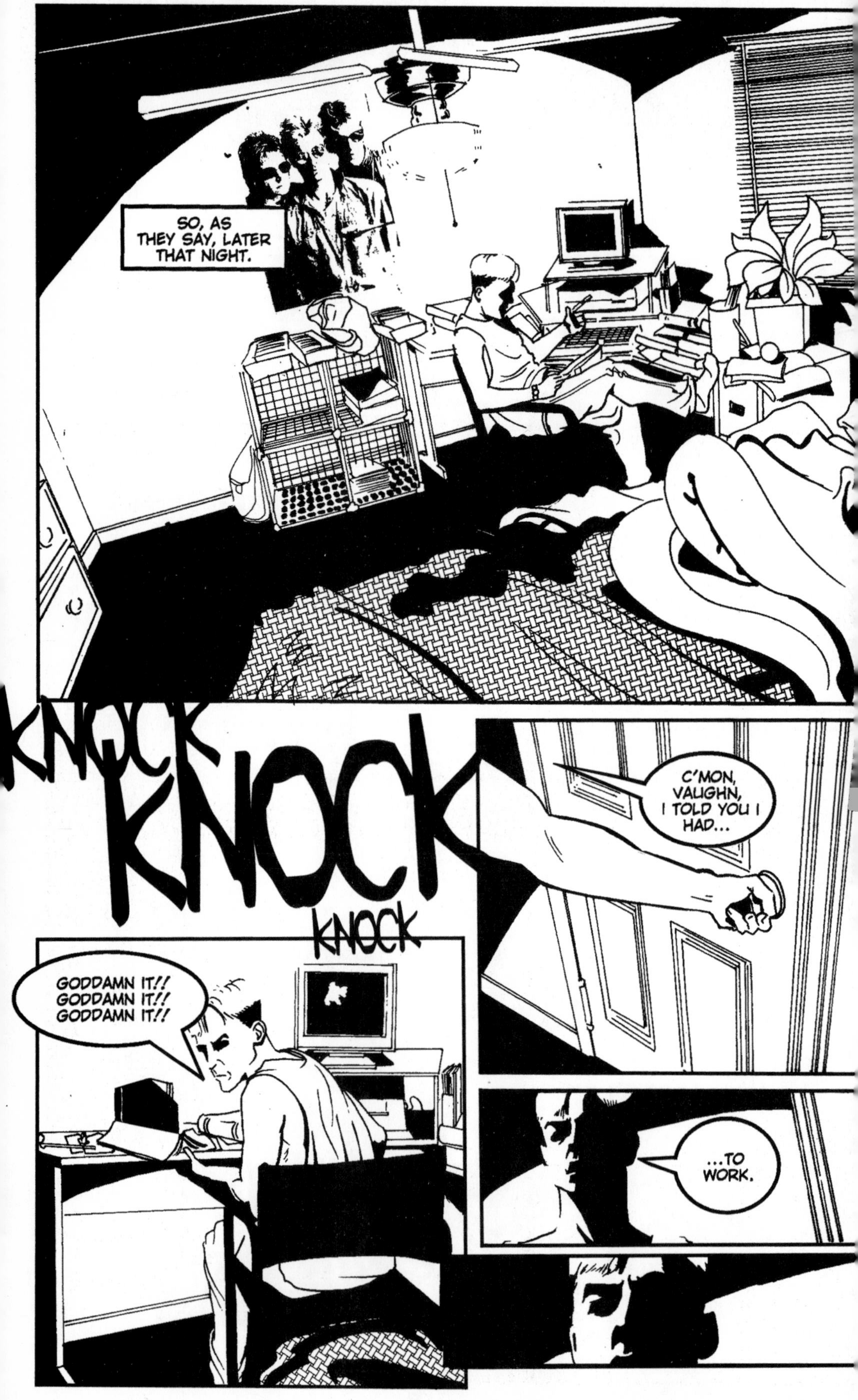
SO, AS THEY SAY, LATER THAT NIGHT.
KNOCK
KNOCK
KNOCK
C'MON, VAUGHN, I TOLD YOU I HAD...
GODDAMN IT!! GODDAMN IT!! GODDAMN IT!!
...TO WORK.

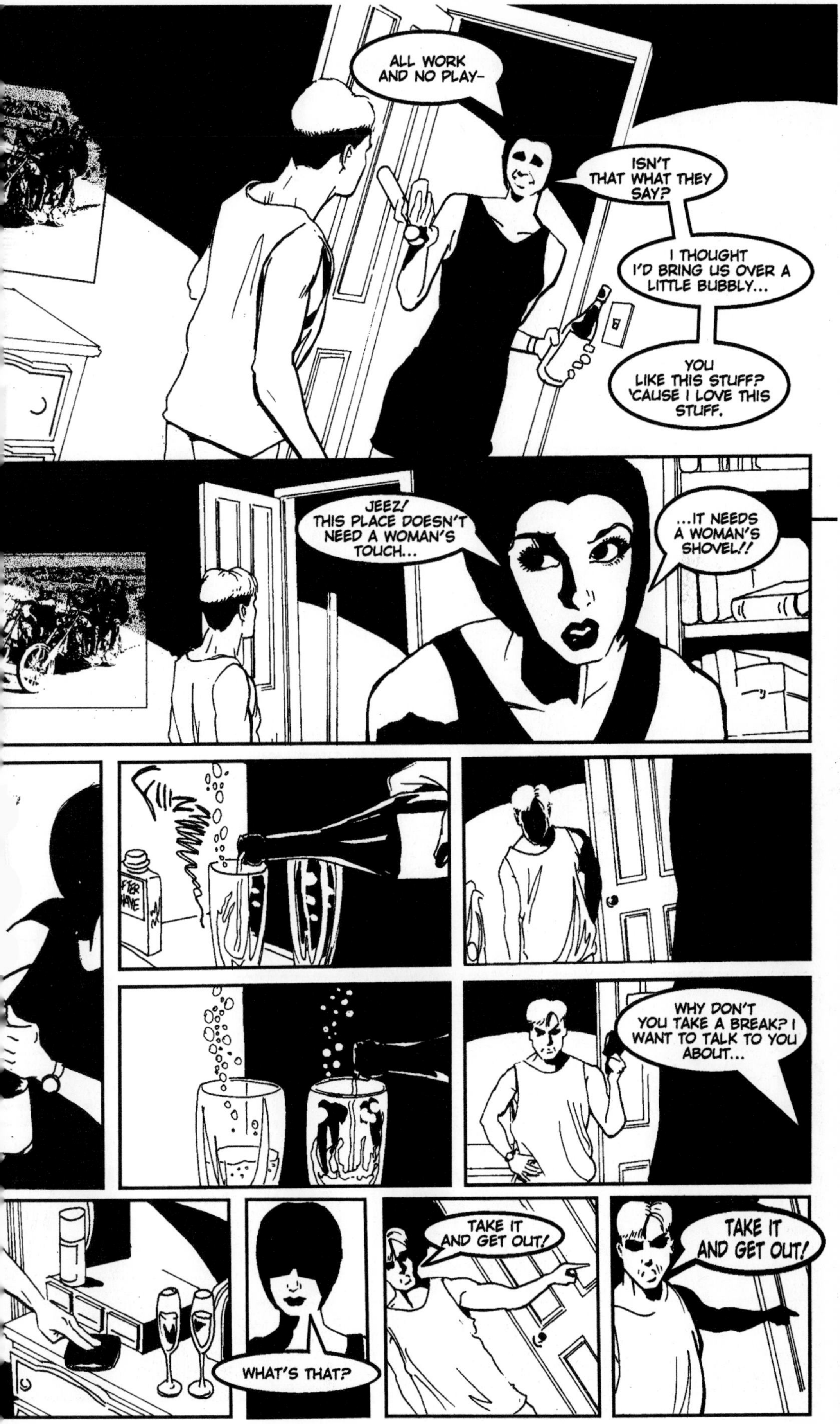
ALL WORK AND NO PLAY-
ISN'T THAT WHAT THEY SAY?
I THOUGHT I'D BRING US OVER A LITTLE BUBBLY...
YOU LIKE THIS STUFF? 'CAUSE I LOVE THIS STUFF.
JEEZ! THIS PLACE DOESN'T NEED A WOMAN'S TOUCH...
...IT NEEDS A WOMAN'S SHOVEL!!
AFTER SHAVE
WHY DON'T YOU TAKE A BREAK? I WANT TO TALK TO YOU ABOUT...
WHAT'S THAT?
TAKE IT AND GET OUT!
TAKE IT AND GET OUT!

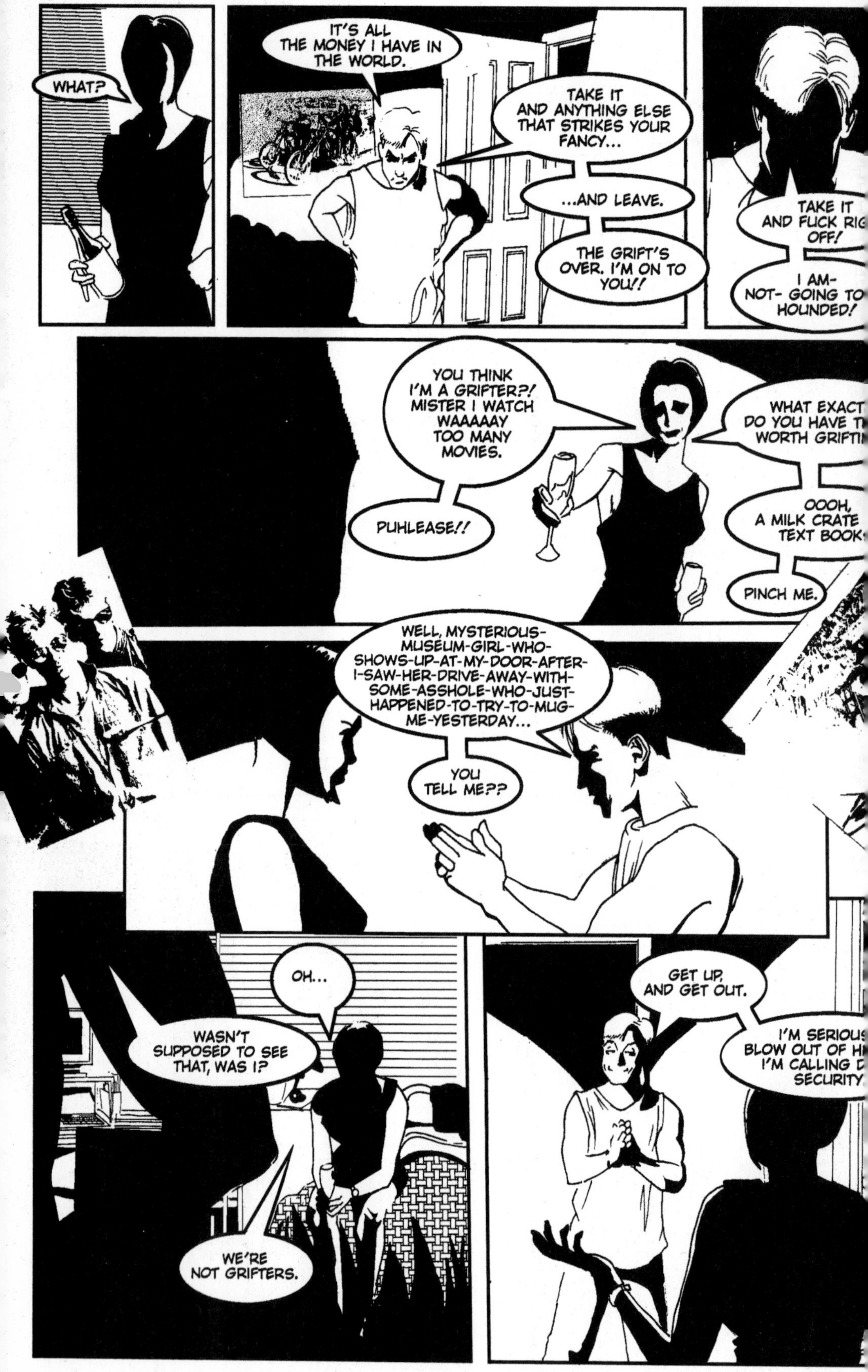
WHAT?
IT'S ALL THE MONEY I HAVE IN THE WORLD.
TAKE IT AND ANYTHING ELSE THAT STRIKES YOUR FANCY...
...AND LEAVE.
THE GRIFT'S OVER. I'M ON TO YOU!!
TAKE IT AND FUCK RIG OFF!
I AM- NOT- GOING TO HOUNDED!
YOU THINK I'M A GRIFTER?! MISTER I WATCH WAAAAAY TOO MANY MOVIES.
PUHLEASE!!
WHAT EXACT DO YOU HAVE T WORTH GRIFTI
OOOH, A MILK CRATE TEXT BOOK
PINCH ME.
WELL, MYSTERIOUS-MUSEUM-GIRL-WHO-SHOWS-UP-AT-MY-DOOR-AFTER-I-SAW-HER-DRIVE-AWAY-WITH-SOME-ASSHOLE-WHO-JUST-HAPPENED-TO-TRY-TO-MUG-ME-YESTERDAY...
YOU TELL ME??
OH...
WASN'T SUPPOSED TO SEE THAT, WAS I?
WE'RE NOT GRIFTERS.
GET UP, AND GET OUT.
I'M SERIOUS BLOW OUT OF H I'M CALLING D SECURITY

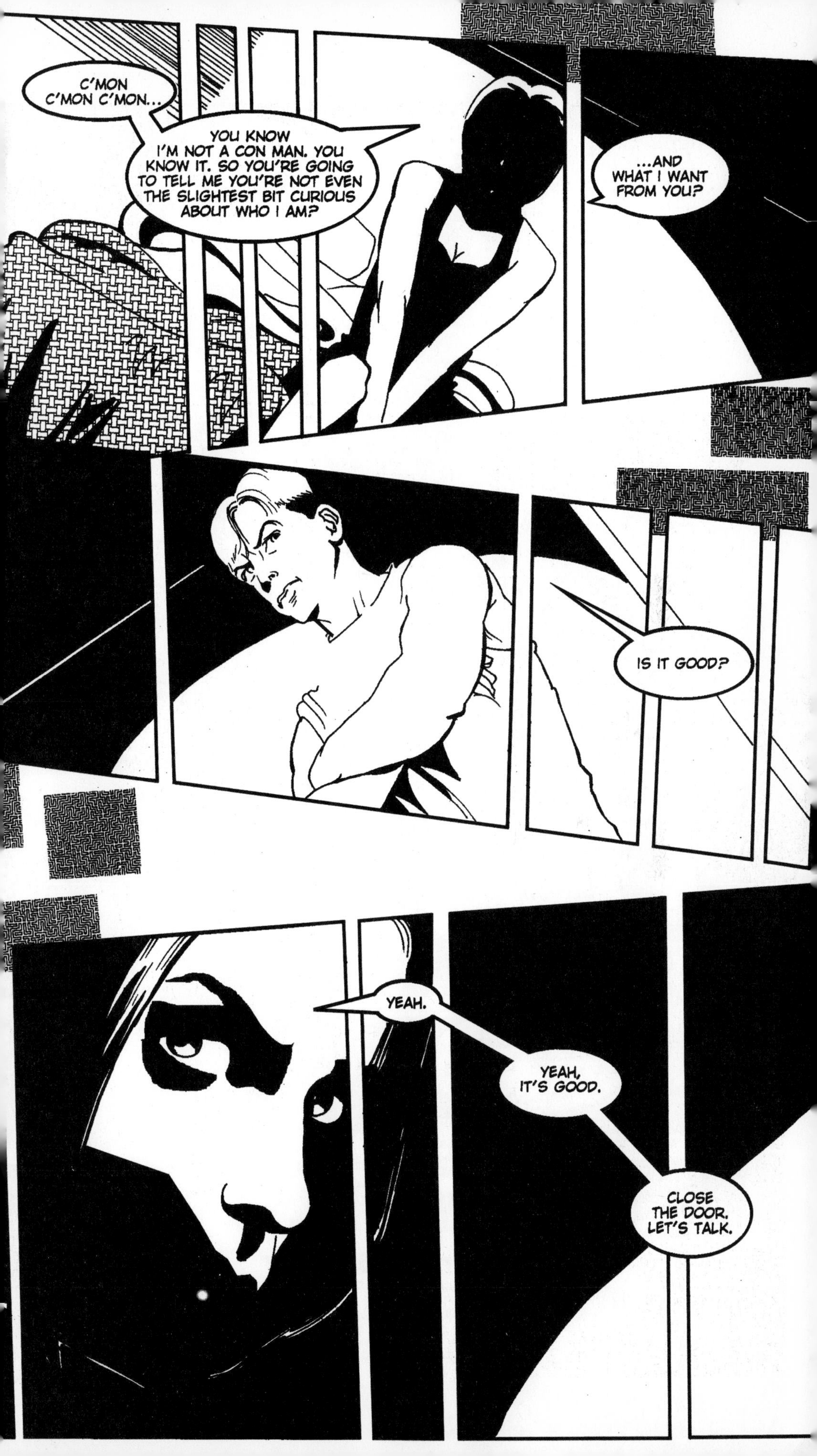
C'MON C'MON C'MON...
YOU KNOW I'M NOT A CON MAN. YOU KNOW IT. SO YOU'RE GOING TO TELL ME YOU'RE NOT EVEN THE SLIGHTEST BIT CURIOUS ABOUT WHO I AM?
...AND WHAT I WANT FROM YOU?
IS IT GOOD?
YEAH.
YEAH, IT'S GOOD.
CLOSE THE DOOR. LET'S TALK.

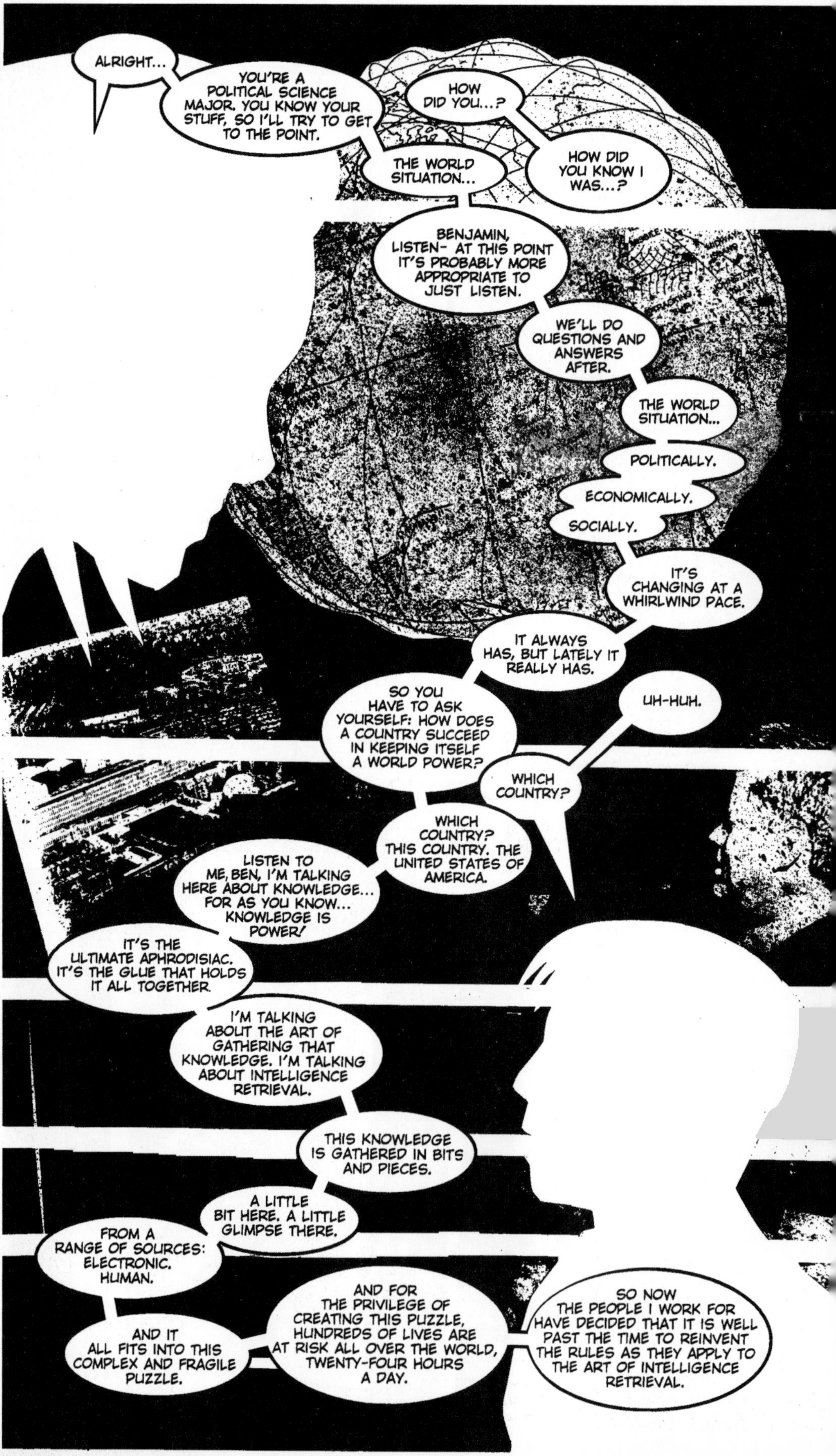
ALRIGHT...
YOU'RE A POLITICAL SCIENCE MAJOR. YOU KNOW YOUR STUFF, SO I'LL TRY TO GET TO THE POINT.
HOW DID YOU...?
HOW DID YOU KNOW I WAS...?
THE WORLD SITUATION...
BENJAMIN, LISTEN- AT THIS POINT IT'S PROBABLY MORE APPROPRIATE TO JUST LISTEN.
WE'LL DO QUESTIONS AND ANSWERS AFTER.
THE WORLD SITUATION...
POLITICALLY.
ECONOMICALLY.
SOCIALLY.
IT'S CHANGING AT A WHIRLWIND PACE.
IT ALWAYS HAS, BUT LATELY IT REALLY HAS.
SO YOU HAVE TO ASK YOURSELF: HOW DOES A COUNTRY SUCCEED IN KEEPING ITSELF A WORLD POWER?
UH-HUH.
WHICH COUNTRY?
WHICH COUNTRY? THIS COUNTRY. THE UNITED STATES OF AMERICA.
LISTEN TO ME, BEN, I'M TALKING HERE ABOUT KNOWLEDGE... FOR AS YOU KNOW... KNOWLEDGE IS POWER!
IT'S THE ULTIMATE APHRODISIAC. IT'S THE GLUE THAT HOLDS IT ALL TOGETHER.
I'M TALKING ABOUT THE ART OF GATHERING THAT KNOWLEDGE. I'M TALKING ABOUT INTELLIGENCE RETRIEVAL.
THIS KNOWLEDGE IS GATHERED IN BITS AND PIECES.
A LITTLE BIT HERE. A LITTLE GLIMPSE THERE.
FROM A RANGE OF SOURCES: ELECTRONIC. HUMAN.
AND IT ALL FITS INTO THIS COMPLEX AND FRAGILE PUZZLE.
AND FOR THE PRIVILEGE OF CREATING THIS PUZZLE, HUNDREDS OF LIVES ARE AT RISK ALL OVER THE WORLD, TWENTY-FOUR HOURS A DAY.
SO NOW THE PEOPLE I WORK FOR HAVE DECIDED THAT IT IS WELL PAST THE TIME TO REINVENT THE RULES AS THEY APPLY TO THE ART OF INTELLIGENCE RETRIEVAL.

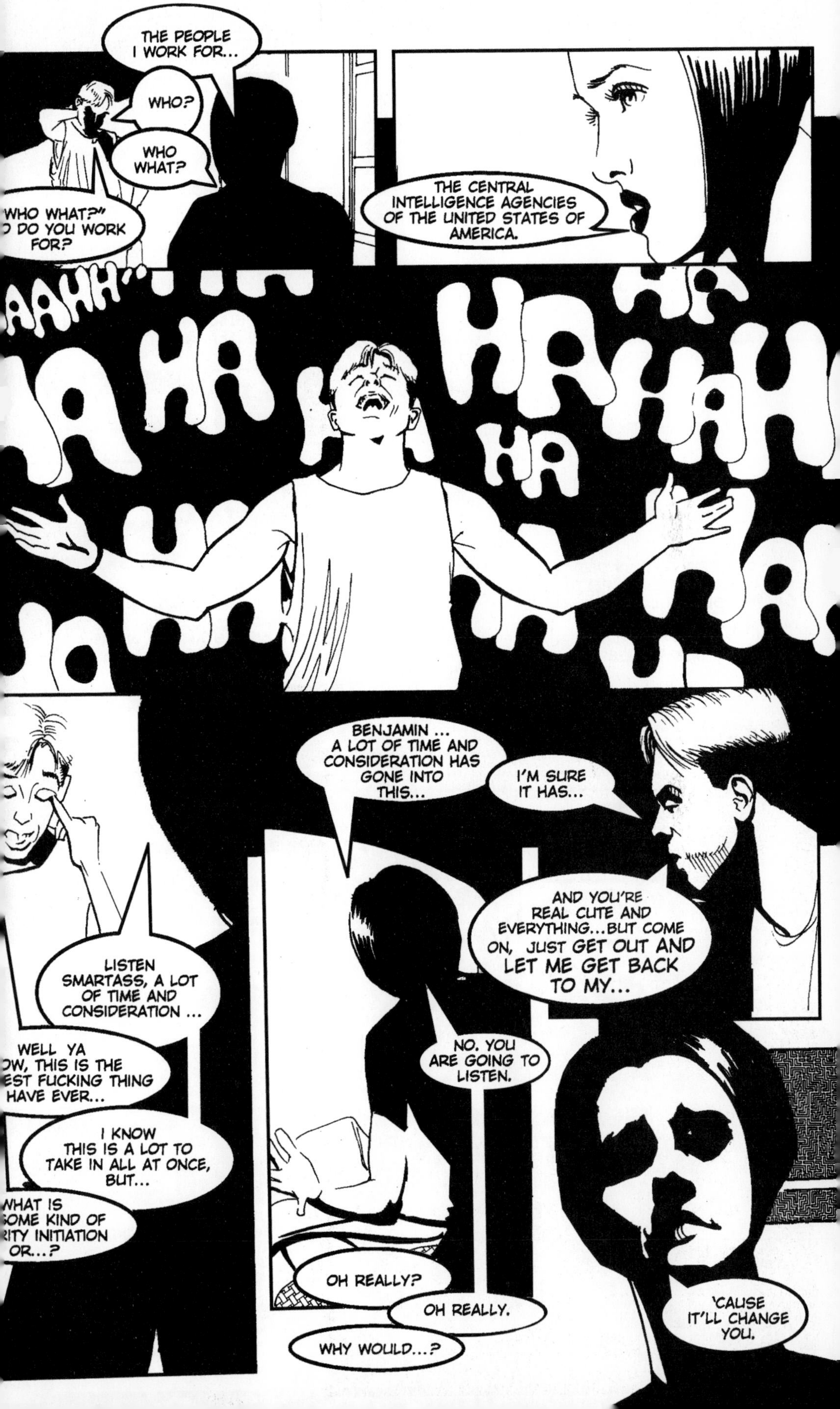

THE PEOPLE I WORK FOR...
WHO?
WHO WHAT?
WHO WHAT?" O DO YOU WORK FOR?
THE CENTRAL INTELLIGENCE AGENCIES OF THE UNITED STATES OF AMERICA.
AAHH
HA HA HA HA HA HA
BENJAMIN ... A LOT OF TIME AND CONSIDERATION HAS GONE INTO THIS...
I'M SURE IT HAS...
LISTEN SMARTASS, A LOT OF TIME AND CONSIDERATION ...
AND YOU'RE REAL CUTE AND EVERYTHING...BUT COME ON, JUST GET OUT AND LET ME GET BACK TO MY...
WELL YA OW, THIS IS THE EST FUCKING THING HAVE EVER...
NO. YOU ARE GOING TO LISTEN.
I KNOW THIS IS A LOT TO TAKE IN ALL AT ONCE, BUT...
WHAT IS OME KIND OF RITY INITIATION OR...?
OH REALLY?
OH REALLY.
WHY WOULD...?
'CAUSE IT'LL CHANGE YOU.

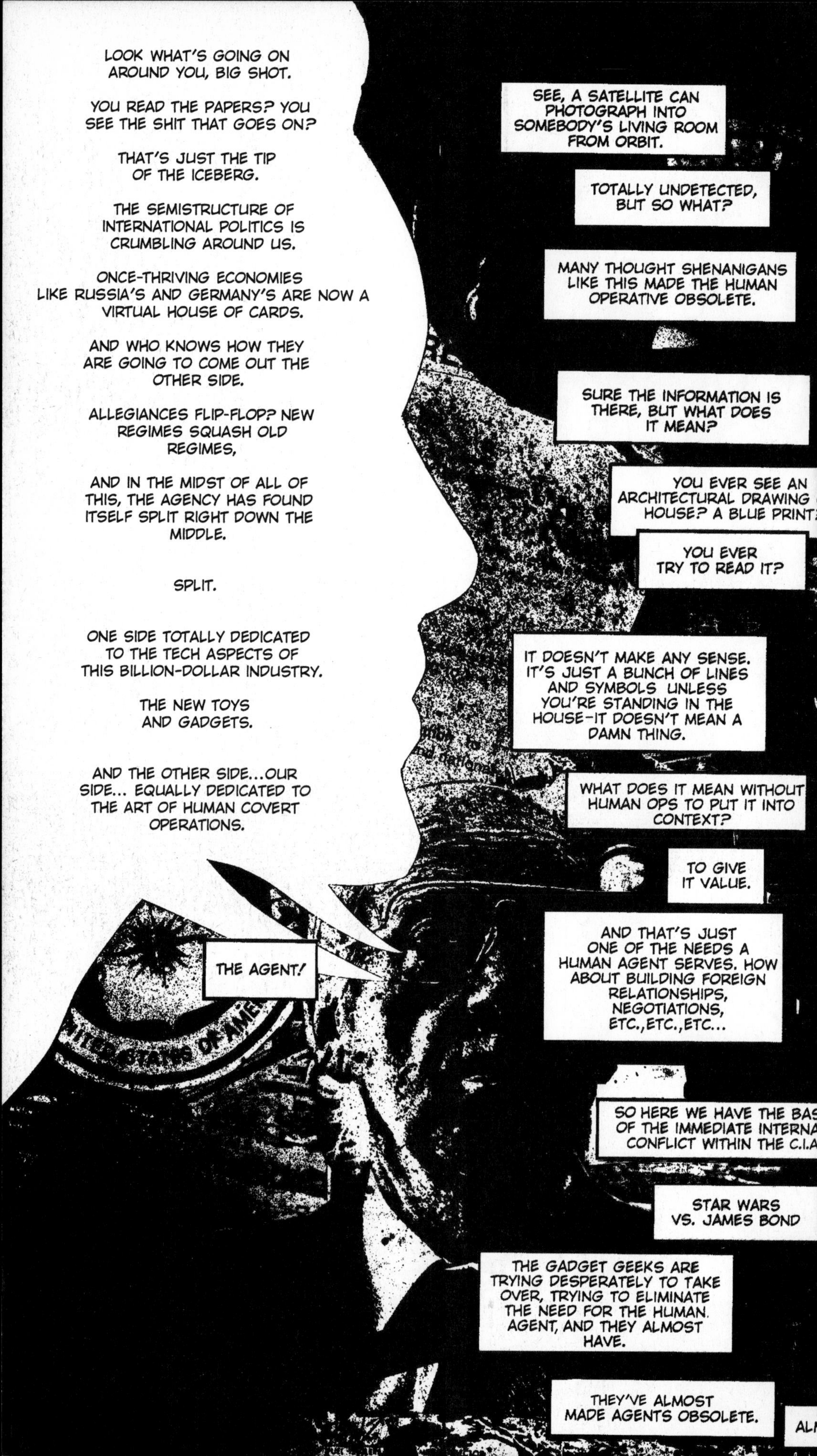
LOOK WHAT'S GOING ON AROUND YOU, BIG SHOT.
YOU READ THE PAPERS? YOU SEE THE SHIT THAT GOES ON?
THAT'S JUST THE TIP OF THE ICEBERG.
THE SEMISTRUCTURE OF INTERNATIONAL POLITICS IS CRUMBLING AROUND US.
ONCE-THRIVING ECONOMIES LIKE RUSSIA'S AND GERMANY'S ARE NOW A VIRTUAL HOUSE OF CARDS.
AND WHO KNOWS HOW THEY ARE GOING TO COME OUT THE OTHER SIDE.
ALLEGIANCES FLIP-FLOP? NEW REGIMES SQUASH OLD REGIMES,
AND IN THE MIDST OF ALL OF THIS, THE AGENCY HAS FOUND ITSELF SPLIT RIGHT DOWN THE MIDDLE.
SPLIT.
ONE SIDE TOTALLY DEDICATED TO THE TECH ASPECTS OF THIS BILLION-DOLLAR INDUSTRY.
THE NEW TOYS AND GADGETS.
AND THE OTHER SIDE...OUR SIDE... EQUALLY DEDICATED TO THE ART OF HUMAN COVERT OPERATIONS.
THE AGENT!
SEE, A SATELLITE CAN PHOTOGRAPH INTO SOMEBODY'S LIVING ROOM FROM ORBIT.
TOTALLY UNDETECTED, BUT SO WHAT?
MANY THOUGHT SHENANIGANS LIKE THIS MADE THE HUMAN OPERATIVE OBSOLETE.
SURE THE INFORMATION IS THERE, BUT WHAT DOES IT MEAN?
YOU EVER SEE AN ARCHITECTURAL DRAWING HOUSE? A BLUE PRINT
YOU EVER TRY TO READ IT?
IT DOESN'T MAKE ANY SENSE. IT'S JUST A BUNCH OF LINES AND SYMBOLS UNLESS YOU'RE STANDING IN THE HOUSE—IT DOESN'T MEAN A DAMN THING.
WHAT DOES IT MEAN WITHOUT HUMAN OPS TO PUT IT INTO CONTEXT?
TO GIVE IT VALUE.
AND THAT'S JUST ONE OF THE NEEDS A HUMAN AGENT SERVES. HOW ABOUT BUILDING FOREIGN RELATIONSHIPS, NEGOTIATIONS, ETC.,ETC.,ETC...
SO HERE WE HAVE THE BAS OF THE IMMEDIATE INTERNA CONFLICT WITHIN THE C.I.A
STAR WARS VS. JAMES BOND
THE GADGET GEEKS ARE TRYING DESPERATELY TO TAKE OVER, TRYING TO ELIMINATE THE NEED FOR THE HUMAN AGENT, AND THEY ALMOST HAVE.
THEY'VE ALMOST MADE AGENTS OBSOLETE.

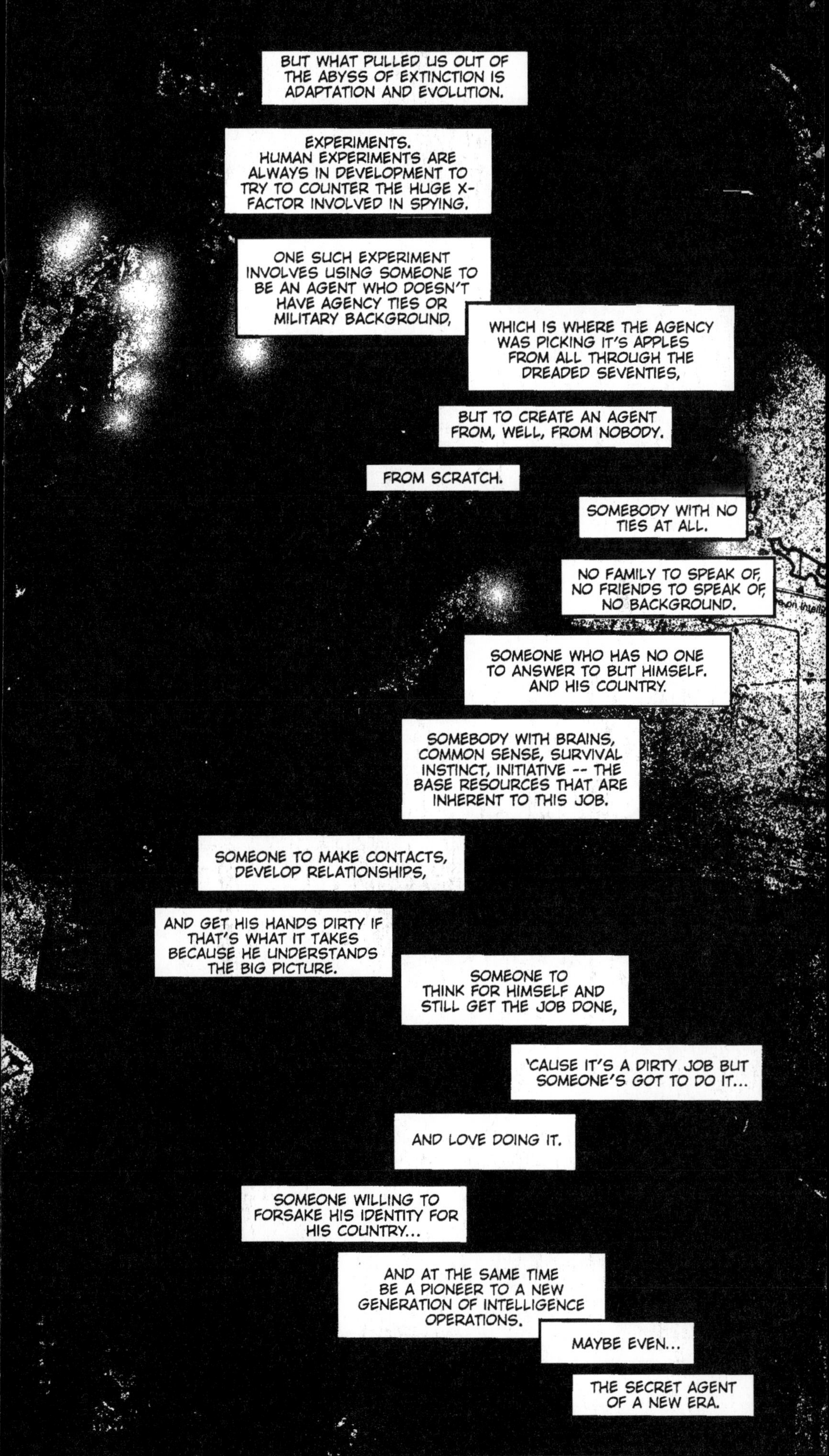
BUT WHAT PULLED US OUT OF THE ABYSS OF EXTINCTION IS ADAPTATION AND EVOLUTION.
EXPERIMENTS. HUMAN EXPERIMENTS ARE ALWAYS IN DEVELOPMENT TO TRY TO COUNTER THE HUGE X-FACTOR INVOLVED IN SPYING.
ONE SUCH EXPERIMENT INVOLVES USING SOMEONE TO BE AN AGENT WHO DOESN'T HAVE AGENCY TIES OR MILITARY BACKGROUND,
WHICH IS WHERE THE AGENCY WAS PICKING IT'S APPLES FROM ALL THROUGH THE DREADED SEVENTIES,
BUT TO CREATE AN AGENT FROM, WELL, FROM NOBODY.
FROM SCRATCH.
SOMEBODY WITH NO TIES AT ALL.
NO FAMILY TO SPEAK OF, NO FRIENDS TO SPEAK OF, NO BACKGROUND.
SOMEONE WHO HAS NO ONE TO ANSWER TO BUT HIMSELF. AND HIS COUNTRY.
SOMEBODY WITH BRAINS, COMMON SENSE, SURVIVAL INSTINCT, INITIATIVE -- THE BASE RESOURCES THAT ARE INHERENT TO THIS JOB.
SOMEONE TO MAKE CONTACTS, DEVELOP RELATIONSHIPS,
AND GET HIS HANDS DIRTY IF THAT'S WHAT IT TAKES BECAUSE HE UNDERSTANDS THE BIG PICTURE.
SOMEONE TO THINK FOR HIMSELF AND STILL GET THE JOB DONE,
'CAUSE IT'S A DIRTY JOB BUT SOMEONE'S GOT TO DO IT...
AND LOVE DOING IT.
SOMEONE WILLING TO FORSAKE HIS IDENTITY FOR HIS COUNTRY...
AND AT THE SAME TIME BE A PIONEER TO A NEW GENERATION OF INTELLIGENCE OPERATIONS.
MAYBE EVEN...
THE SECRET AGENT OF A NEW ERA.

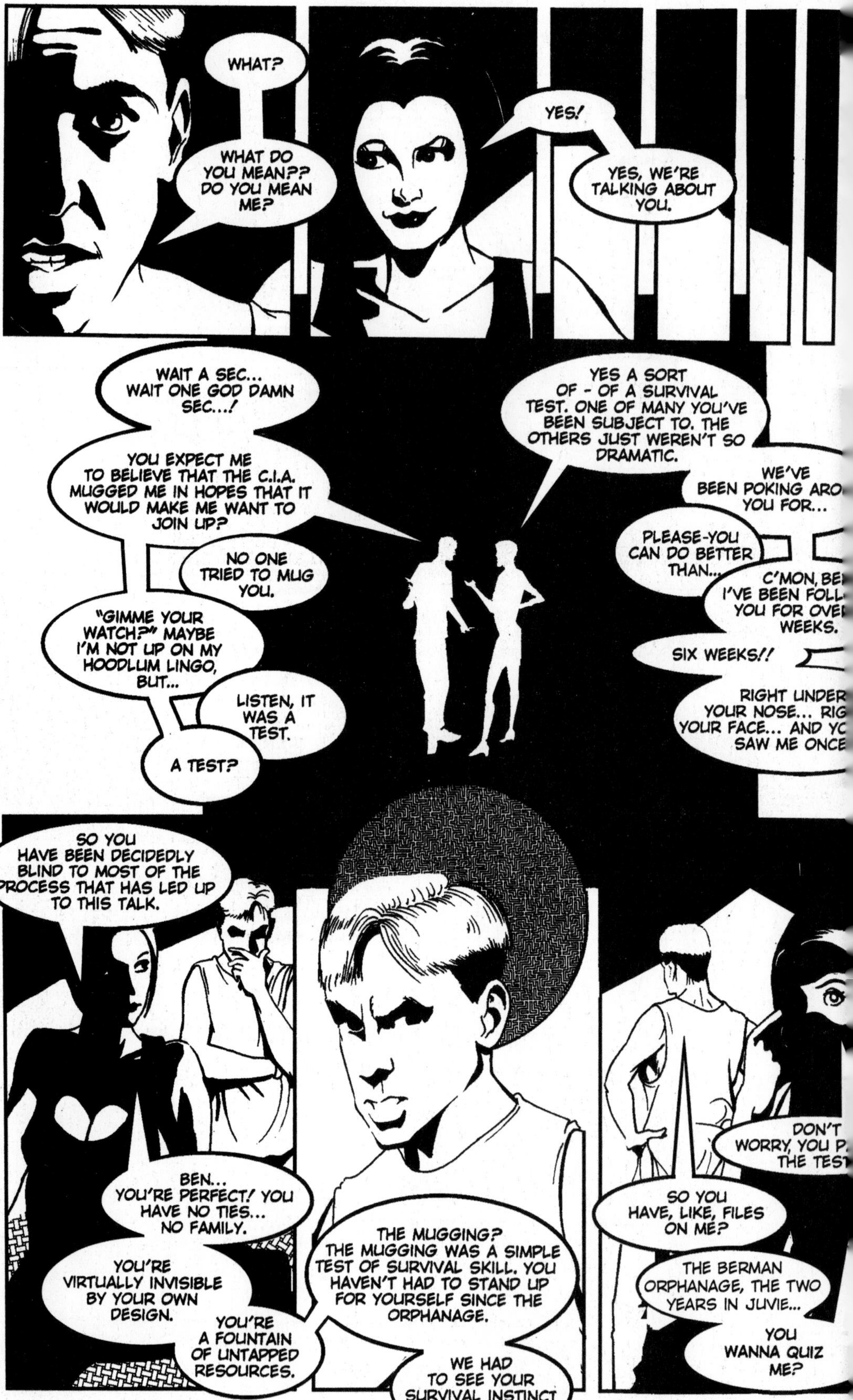
WHAT?
WHAT DO YOU MEAN?? DO YOU MEAN ME?
YES!
YES, WE'RE TALKING ABOUT YOU.
WAIT A SEC... WAIT ONE GOD DAMN SEC...!
YOU EXPECT ME TO BELIEVE THAT THE C.I.A. MUGGED ME IN HOPES THAT IT WOULD MAKE ME WANT TO JOIN UP?
NO ONE TRIED TO MUG YOU.
"GIMME YOUR WATCH?" MAYBE I'M NOT UP ON MY HOODLUM LINGO, BUT...
LISTEN, IT WAS A TEST.
A TEST?
YES A SORT OF - OF A SURVIVAL TEST. ONE OF MANY YOU'VE BEEN SUBJECT TO. THE OTHERS JUST WEREN'T SO DRAMATIC.
WE'VE BEEN POKING ARO YOU FOR...
PLEASE-YOU CAN DO BETTER THAN...
C'MON, BE I'VE BEEN FOLL YOU FOR OVE WEEKS.
SIX WEEKS!!
RIGHT UNDER YOUR NOSE... RIG YOUR FACE... AND YO SAW ME ONCE
SO YOU HAVE BEEN DECIDEDLY BLIND TO MOST OF THE PROCESS THAT HAS LED UP TO THIS TALK.
BEN... YOU'RE PERFECT! YOU HAVE NO TIES... NO FAMILY.
YOU'RE VIRTUALLY INVISIBLE BY YOUR OWN DESIGN.
YOU'RE A FOUNTAIN OF UNTAPPED RESOURCES.
THE MUGGING? THE MUGGING WAS A SIMPLE TEST OF SURVIVAL SKILL. YOU HAVEN'T HAD TO STAND UP FOR YOURSELF SINCE THE ORPHANAGE.
WE HAD TO SEE YOUR SURVIVAL INSTINCT AT WORK!
DON'T WORRY, YOU P THE TES
SO YOU HAVE, LIKE, FILES ON ME?
THE BERMAN ORPHANAGE, THE TWO YEARS IN JUVIE...
YOU WANNA QUIZ ME?

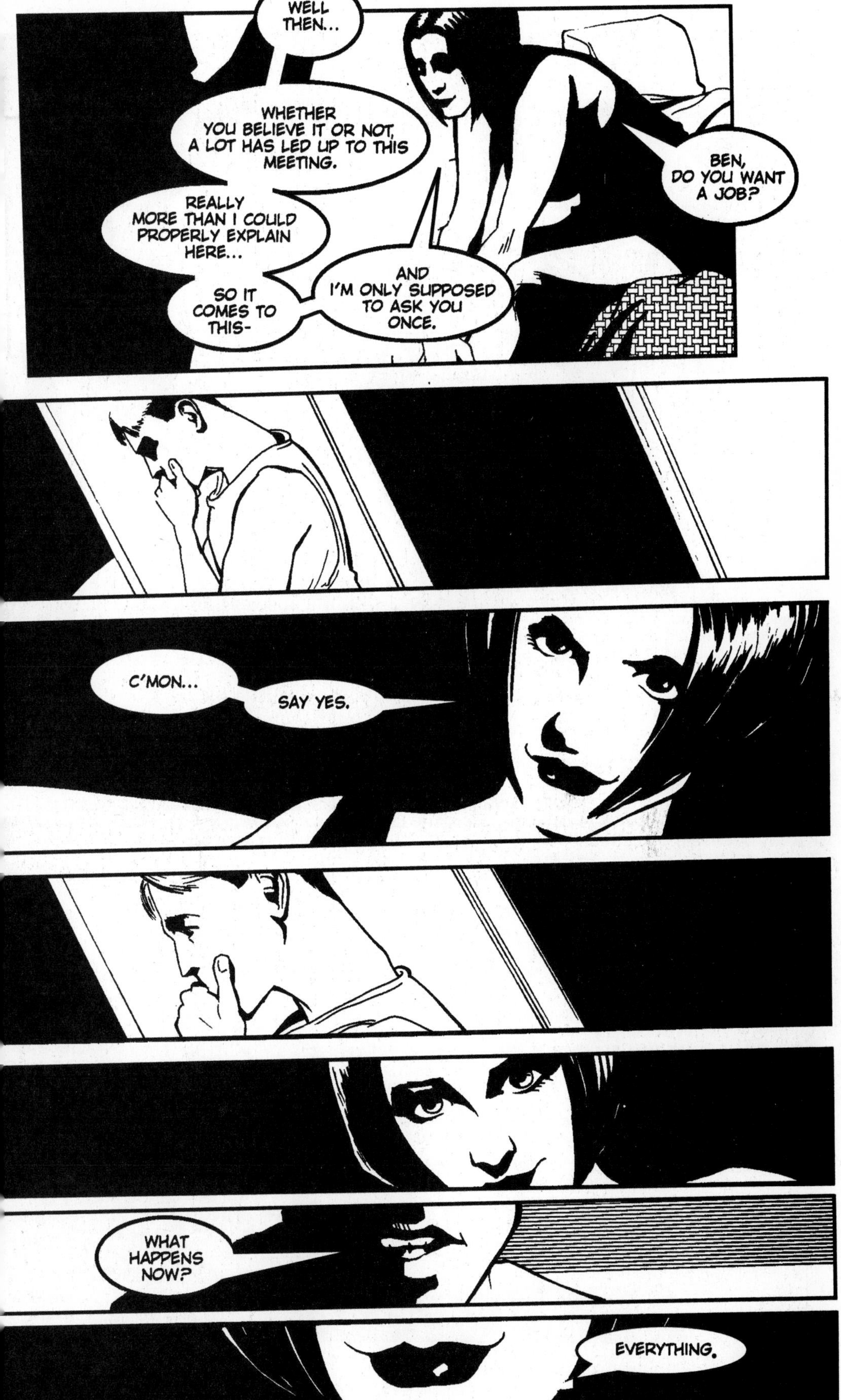
WELL THEN...
WHETHER YOU BELIEVE IT OR NOT, A LOT HAS LED UP TO THIS MEETING.
REALLY MORE THAN I COULD PROPERLY EXPLAIN HERE...
SO IT COMES TO THIS-
AND I'M ONLY SUPPOSED TO ASK YOU ONCE.
BEN, DO YOU WANT A JOB?
C'MON...
SAY YES.
WHAT HAPPENS NOW?
EVERYTHING.

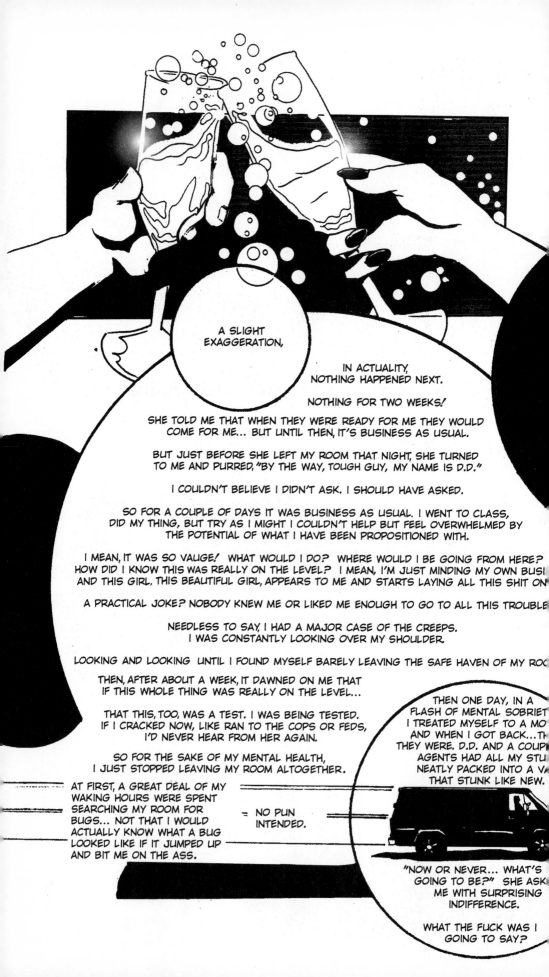

A SLIGHT EXAGGERATION,

IN ACTUALITY, NOTHING HAPPENED NEXT.

NOTHING FOR TWO WEEKS!

SHE TOLD ME THAT WHEN THEY WERE READY FOR ME THEY WOULD COME FOR ME... BUT UNTIL THEN, IT'S BUSINESS AS USUAL.

BUT JUST BEFORE SHE LEFT MY ROOM THAT NIGHT, SHE TURNED TO ME AND PURRED, "BY THE WAY, TOUGH GUY, MY NAME IS D.D."

I COULDN'T BELIEVE I DIDN'T ASK. I SHOULD HAVE ASKED.

SO FOR A COUPLE OF DAYS IT WAS BUSINESS AS USUAL. I WENT TO CLASS, DID MY THING, BUT TRY AS I MIGHT I COULDN'T HELP BUT FEEL OVERWHELMED BY THE POTENTIAL OF WHAT I HAVE BEEN PROPOSITIONED WITH.

I MEAN, IT WAS SO VAUGE! WHAT WOULD I DO? WHERE WOULD I BE GOING FROM HERE? HOW DID I KNOW THIS WAS REALLY ON THE LEVEL? I MEAN, I'M JUST MINDING MY OWN BUSI AND THIS GIRL, THIS BEAUTIFUL GIRL, APPEARS TO ME AND STARTS LAYING ALL THIS SHIT ON

A PRACTICAL JOKE? NOBODY KNEW ME OR LIKED ME ENOUGH TO GO TO ALL THIS TROUBLE

NEEDLESS TO SAY, I HAD A MAJOR CASE OF THE CREEPS. I WAS CONSTANTLY LOOKING OVER MY SHOULDER.

LOOKING AND LOOKING UNTIL I FOUND MYSELF BARELY LEAVING THE SAFE HAVEN OF MY ROO

THEN, AFTER ABOUT A WEEK, IT DAWNED ON ME THAT IF THIS WHOLE THING WAS REALLY ON THE LEVEL...

THAT THIS, TOO, WAS A TEST. I WAS BEING TESTED. IF I CRACKED NOW, LIKE RAN TO THE COPS OR FEDS, I'D NEVER HEAR FROM HER AGAIN.

SO FOR THE SAKE OF MY MENTAL HEALTH, I JUST STOPPED LEAVING MY ROOM ALTOGETHER.

AT FIRST, A GREAT DEAL OF MY WAKING HOURS WERE SPENT SEARCHING MY ROOM FOR BUGS... NOT THAT I WOULD ACTUALLY KNOW WHAT A BUG LOOKED LIKE IF IT JUMPED UP AND BIT ME ON THE ASS.

= NO PUN INTENDED.

THEN ONE DAY, IN A FLASH OF MENTAL SOBRIET I TREATED MYSELF TO A MO AND WHEN I GOT BACK...TH THEY WERE. D.D. AND A COUP AGENTS HAD ALL MY STU NEATLY PACKED INTO A V/ THAT STUNK LIKE NEW.

"NOW OR NEVER... WHAT'S GOING TO BE?" SHE ASK ME WITH SURPRISING INDIFFERENCE.

WHAT THE FUCK WAS I GOING TO SAY?

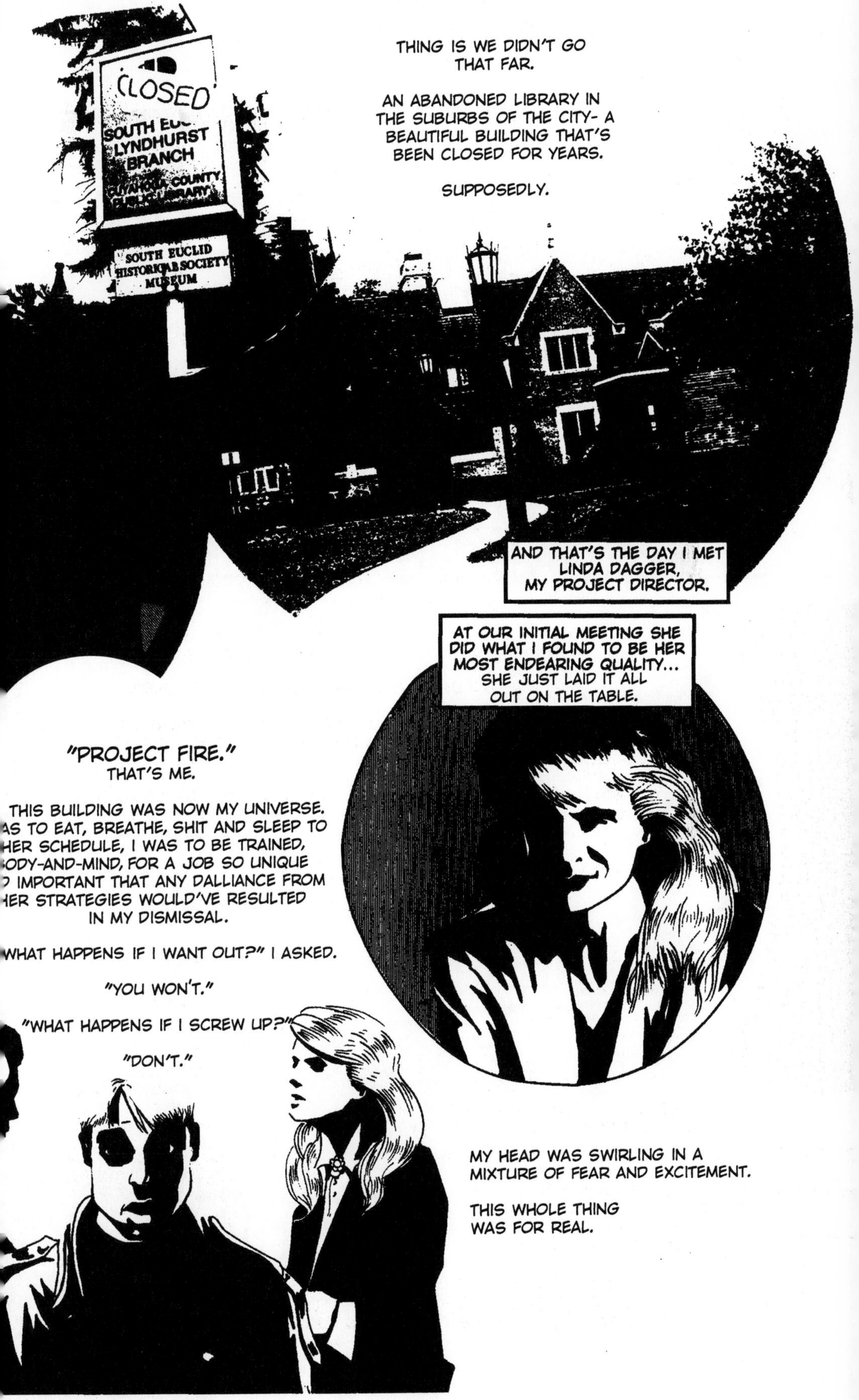

CLOSED
SOUTH EUCLID LYNDHURST BRANCH
CUYAHOGA COUNTY PUBLIC LIBRARY
SOUTH EUCLID HISTORICAL SOCIETY MUSEUM
THING IS WE DIDN'T GO THAT FAR.
AN ABANDONED LIBRARY IN THE SUBURBS OF THE CITY- A BEAUTIFUL BUILDING THAT'S BEEN CLOSED FOR YEARS.
SUPPOSEDLY.
AND THAT'S THE DAY I MET LINDA DAGGER, MY PROJECT DIRECTOR.
AT OUR INITIAL MEETING SHE DID WHAT I FOUND TO BE HER MOST ENDEARING QUALITY... SHE JUST LAID IT ALL OUT ON THE TABLE.
"PROJECT FIRE." THAT'S ME.
THIS BUILDING WAS NOW MY UNIVERSE. AS TO EAT, BREATHE, SHIT AND SLEEP TO HER SCHEDULE, I WAS TO BE TRAINED, ODY-AND-MIND, FOR A JOB SO UNIQUE IMPORTANT THAT ANY DALLIANCE FROM HER STRATEGIES WOULD'VE RESULTED IN MY DISMISSAL.
WHAT HAPPENS IF I WANT OUT?" I ASKED.
"YOU WON'T."
"WHAT HAPPENS IF I SCREW UP?"
"DON'T."
MY HEAD WAS SWIRLING IN A MIXTURE OF FEAR AND EXCITEMENT.
THIS WHOLE THING WAS FOR REAL.

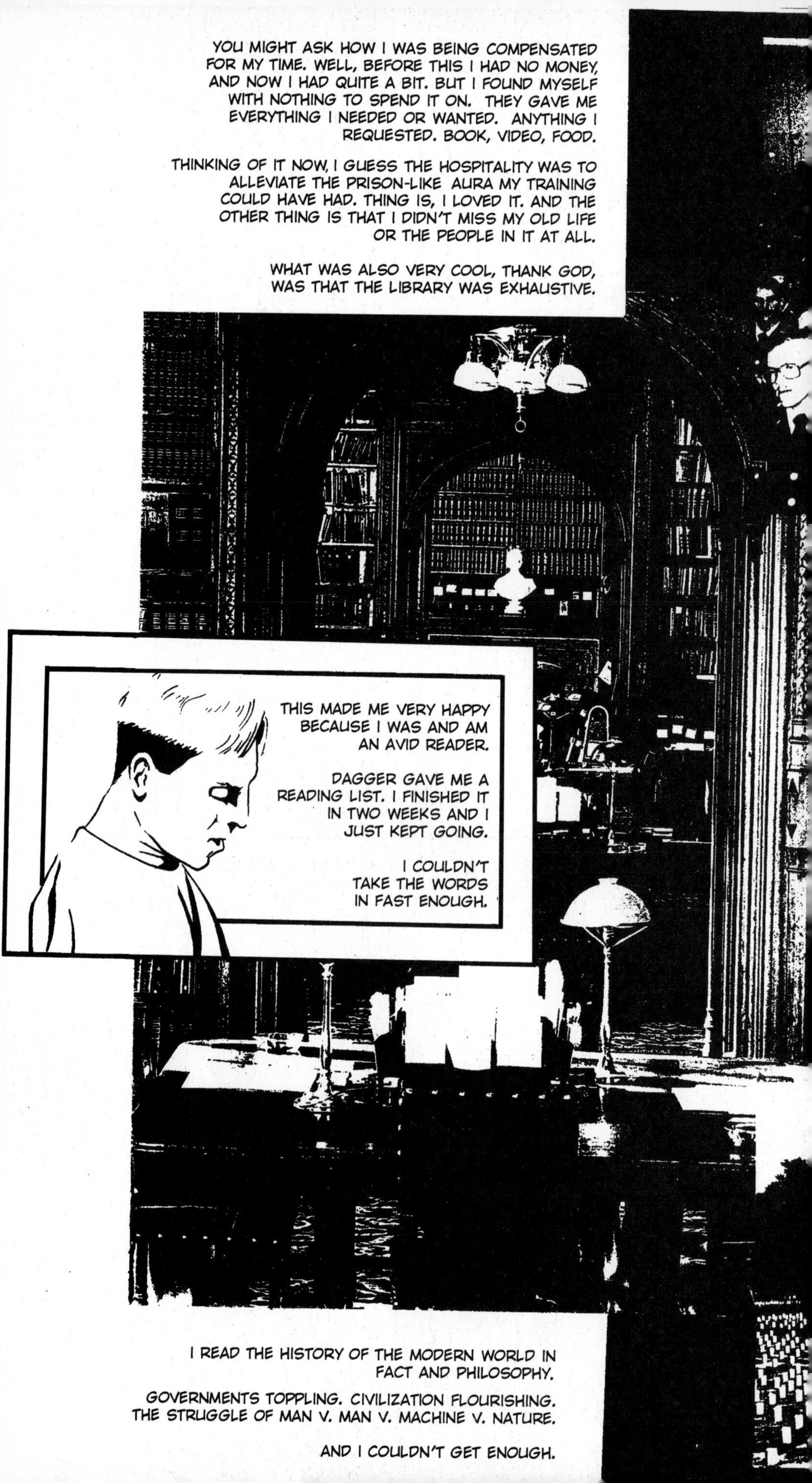
YOU MIGHT ASK HOW I WAS BEING COMPENSATED FOR MY TIME. WELL, BEFORE THIS I HAD NO MONEY, AND NOW I HAD QUITE A BIT. BUT I FOUND MYSELF WITH NOTHING TO SPEND IT ON. THEY GAVE ME EVERYTHING I NEEDED OR WANTED. ANYTHING I REQUESTED. BOOK, VIDEO, FOOD.
THINKING OF IT NOW, I GUESS THE HOSPITALITY WAS TO ALLEVIATE THE PRISON-LIKE AURA MY TRAINING COULD HAVE HAD. THING IS, I LOVED IT. AND THE OTHER THING IS THAT I DIDN'T MISS MY OLD LIFE OR THE PEOPLE IN IT AT ALL.
WHAT WAS ALSO VERY COOL, THANK GOD, WAS THAT THE LIBRARY WAS EXHAUSTIVE.
THIS MADE ME VERY HAPPY BECAUSE I WAS AND AM AN AVID READER.
DAGGER GAVE ME A READING LIST. I FINISHED IT IN TWO WEEKS AND I JUST KEPT GOING.
I COULDN'T TAKE THE WORDS IN FAST ENOUGH.
I READ THE HISTORY OF THE MODERN WORLD IN FACT AND PHILOSOPHY.
GOVERNMENTS TOPPLING. CIVILIZATION FLOURISHING. THE STRUGGLE OF MAN V. MAN V. MACHINE V. NATURE.
AND I COULDN'T GET ENOUGH.

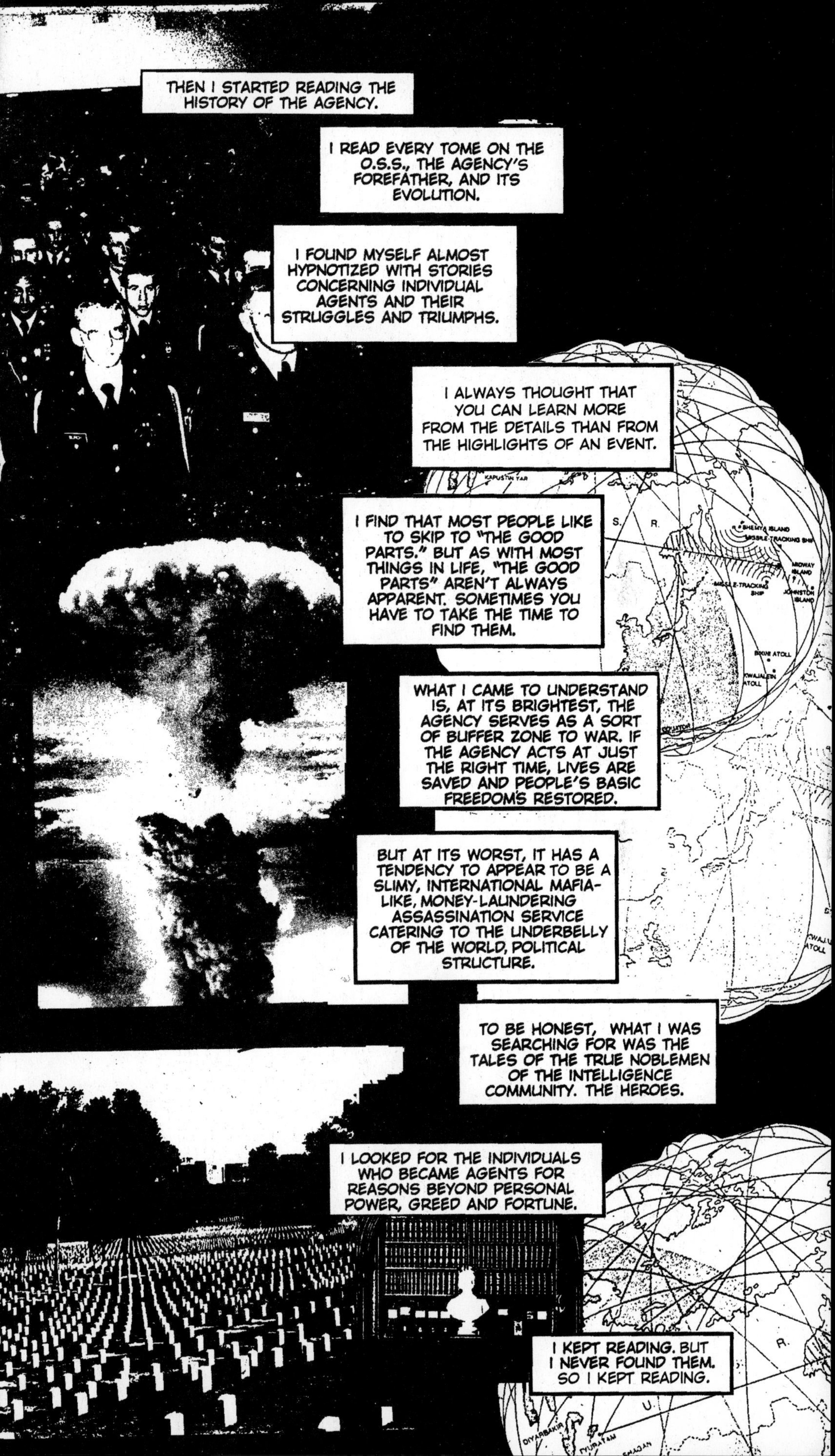
THEN I STARTED READING THE HISTORY OF THE AGENCY.
I READ EVERY TOME ON THE O.S.S., THE AGENCY'S FOREFATHER, AND ITS EVOLUTION.
I FOUND MYSELF ALMOST HYPNOTIZED WITH STORIES CONCERNING INDIVIDUAL AGENTS AND THEIR STRUGGLES AND TRIUMPHS.
I ALWAYS THOUGHT THAT YOU CAN LEARN MORE FROM THE DETAILS THAN FROM THE HIGHLIGHTS OF AN EVENT.
I FIND THAT MOST PEOPLE LIKE TO SKIP TO "THE GOOD PARTS." BUT AS WITH MOST THINGS IN LIFE, "THE GOOD PARTS" AREN'T ALWAYS APPARENT. SOMETIMES YOU HAVE TO TAKE THE TIME TO FIND THEM.
WHAT I CAME TO UNDERSTAND IS, AT ITS BRIGHTEST, THE AGENCY SERVES AS A SORT OF BUFFER ZONE TO WAR. IF THE AGENCY ACTS AT JUST THE RIGHT TIME, LIVES ARE SAVED AND PEOPLE'S BASIC FREEDOMS RESTORED.
BUT AT ITS WORST, IT HAS A TENDENCY TO APPEAR TO BE A SLIMY, INTERNATIONAL MAFIA-LIKE, MONEY-LAUNDERING ASSASSINATION SERVICE CATERING TO THE UNDERBELLY OF THE WORLD, POLITICAL STRUCTURE.
TO BE HONEST, WHAT I WAS SEARCHING FOR WAS THE TALES OF THE TRUE NOBLEMEN OF THE INTELLIGENCE COMMUNITY. THE HEROES.
I LOOKED FOR THE INDIVIDUALS WHO BECAME AGENTS FOR REASONS BEYOND PERSONAL POWER, GREED AND FORTUNE.
I KEPT READING. BUT I NEVER FOUND THEM. SO I KEPT READING.

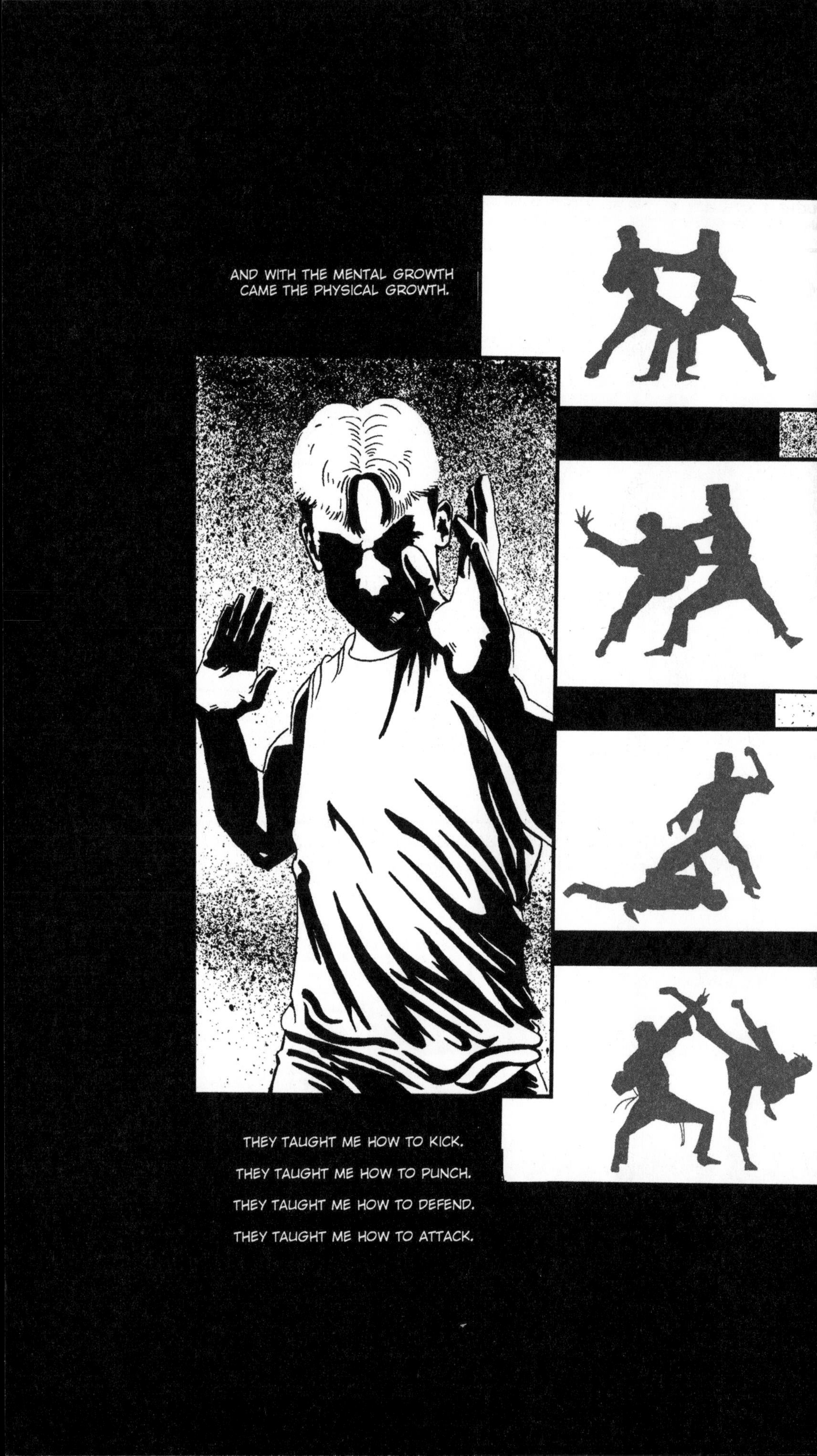
AND WITH THE MENTAL GROWTH CAME THE PHYSICAL GROWTH.
THEY TAUGHT ME HOW TO KICK.
THEY TAUGHT ME HOW TO PUNCH.
THEY TAUGHT ME HOW TO DEFEND.
THEY TAUGHT ME HOW TO ATTACK.

AME A PRETTY GOOD MARKSMAN, TOO. LISTEN TO THIS- SO I WOULD GET USED TO THE IDEA OF SHOOTING PERSON IF I HAD TOO, I SPENT A WHOLE WEEK SHOOTING AT CADAVERS.

UGHT IT WAS VULGAR AND SILLY THAT THEY WERE ACTUALLY SHIPPING IN BODIES FOR ME TO SHOOT AT. N, THIS WAS SOMEBODY'S JOB: GETTING ME BODIES.

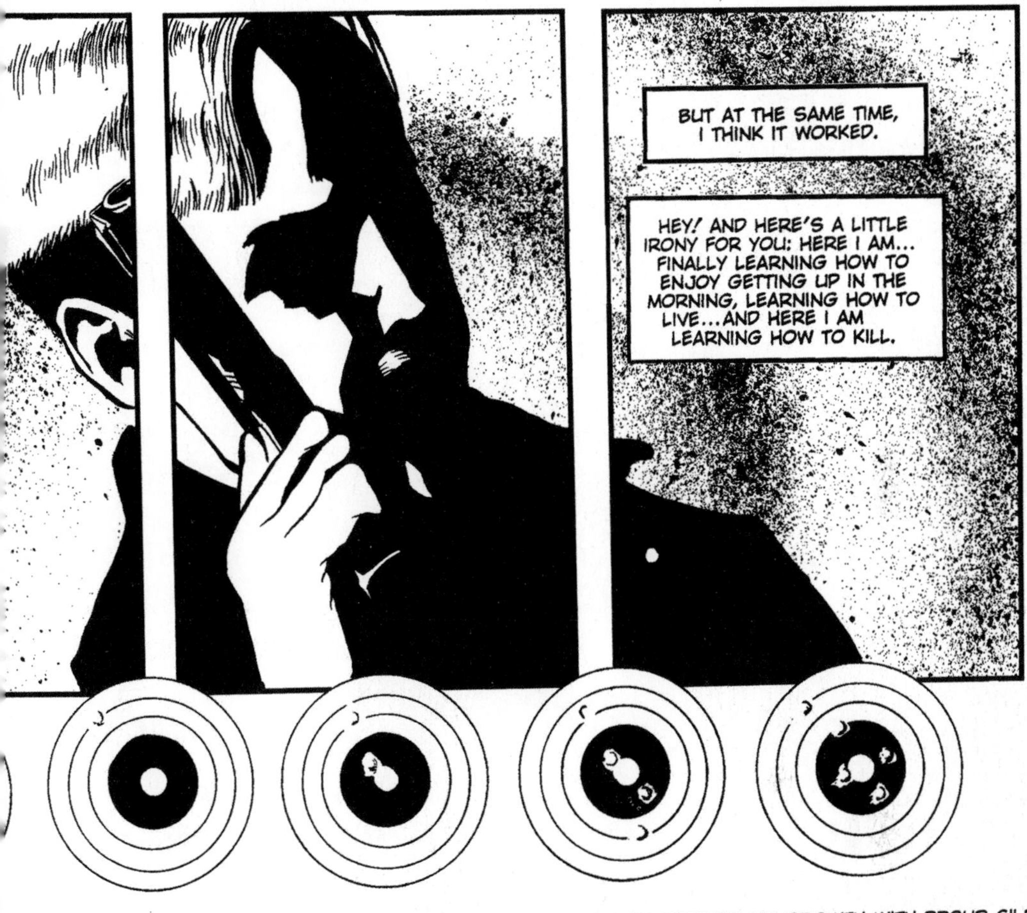
BUT AT THE SAME TIME, I THINK IT WORKED.
HEY! AND HERE'S A LITTLE IRONY FOR YOU: HERE I AM... FINALLY LEARNING HOW TO ENJOY GETTING UP IN THE MORNING, LEARNING HOW TO LIVE... AND HERE I AM LEARNING HOW TO KILL.

UGHOUT MY TWO YEARS AND THREE MONTHS OF TRAINING, DAGGER WATCHED MY GROWTH WITH PROUD SILENCE. I WAS SNEAKING INTO THE LIBRARY AFTER HOURS. SHE KNEW I GREW RESTLESS TO START MY CAREER. ON MY HIRD BIRTHDAY, I DISMANTLED THE PROJECT'S SECURITY SYSTEM... NOT TO BE AN ASSHOLE OR ANYTHING, JUST SOMETHING TO DO. DAGGER DIDN'T KNOW WHETHER TO KISS ME OR KILL ME, AND, YOU KNOW, I KIND OF LIKED

S EVERYBODY ELSE AT THE PROJECT WAS CONCERNED, WELL, THEY CREATED THIS DISTANT VENEER. NOBODY TY, BUT THEY WEREN'T EXACTLY FRIENDLY. THEY WERE JUST PROFESSIONAL. WHICH, FRANKLY, WAS FINE BY ME.

'T SEE D.D. FOR FOUR OR FIVE MONTHS AT A TIME, OR I'D SEE HER EVERY DAY FOR SIX MONTHS. THAT SPUNKY SS DEMEANOR SHE DISPLAYED DURING MY INITIATION HAD ALL BUT DISAPPEARED. UPON MY ARRIVAL SHE VERY INTERNAL. HARD TO READ. THE ODDEST THING I CAN SAY ABOUT HER WAS THAT I REALLY COULDN'T EVER OLD SHE WAS. THE DAMNDEST THING.

ELL YOU WHY I WOULD THINK OF HER SO MUCH. I MEAN, THERE WAS ZILCH CHEMISTRY. I MEAN, SHE'S DAMN VE BUT... OH, WHO WAS I KIDDING, IT WAS BECAUSE SHE WAS THE ONLY GIRLWITHIN A HUNDRED MILES OF ME. ESS IT DOESN'T MATTER NOW.

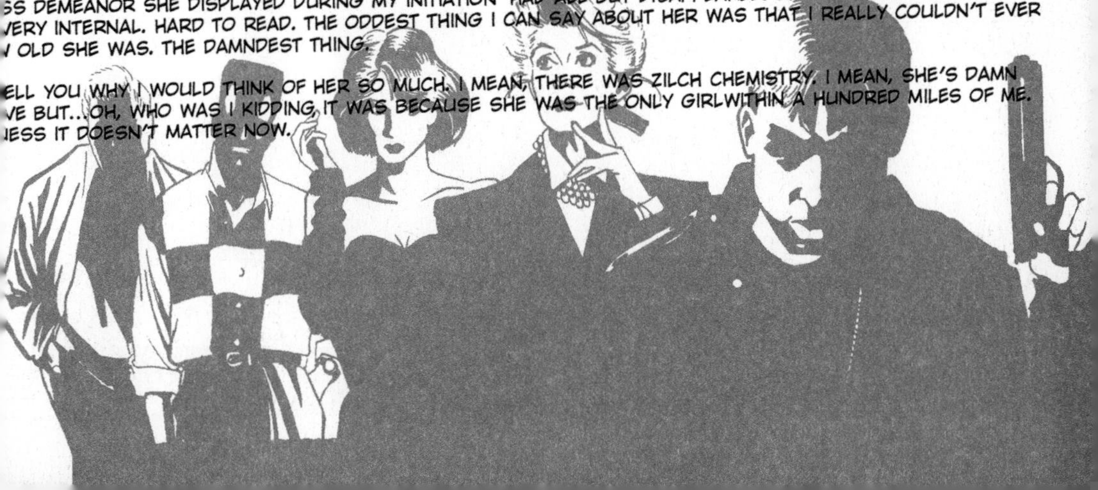

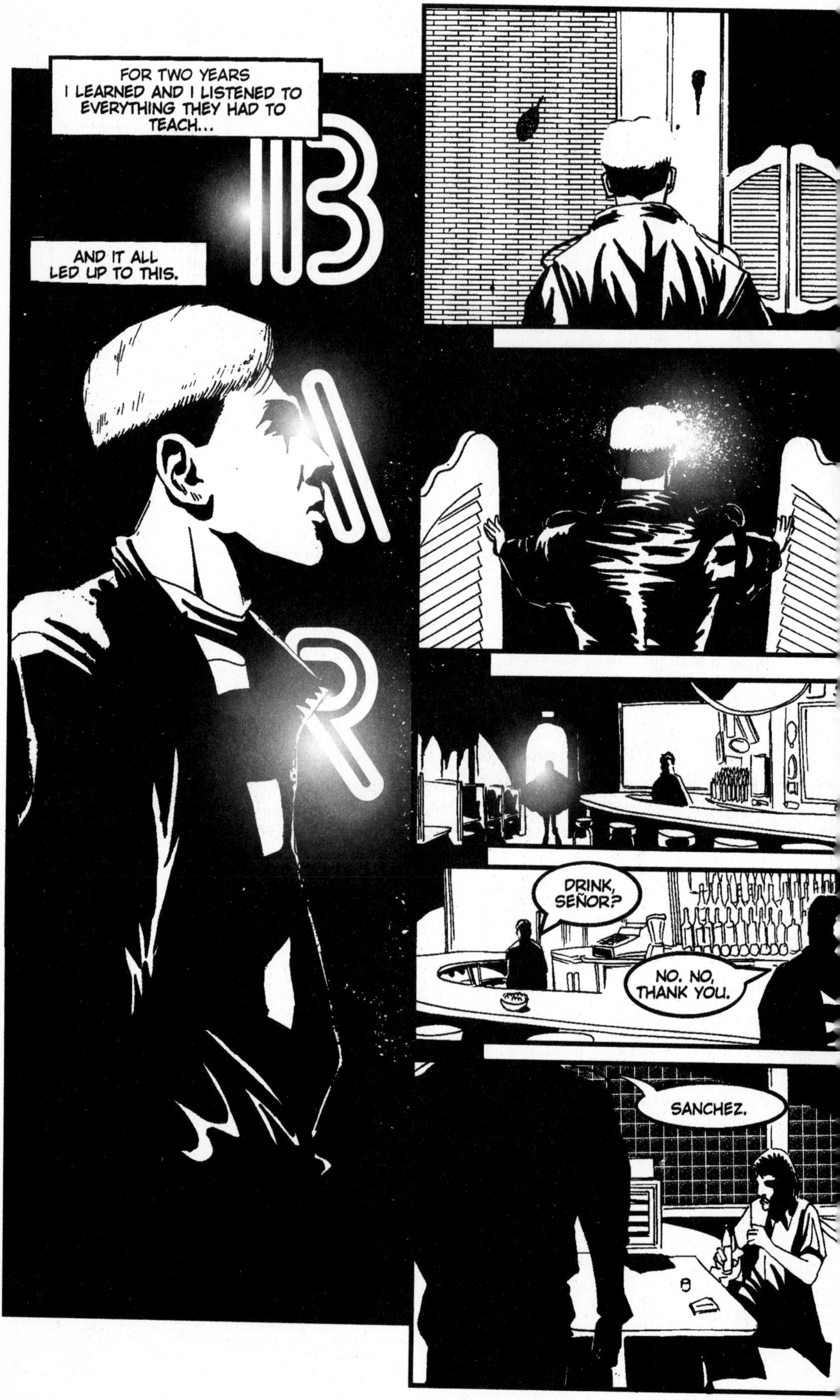
FOR TWO YEARS I LEARNED AND I LISTENED TO EVERYTHING THEY HAD TO TEACH...
AND IT ALL LED UP TO THIS.
DRINK, SEÑOR?
NO. NO, THANK YOU.
SANCHEZ.

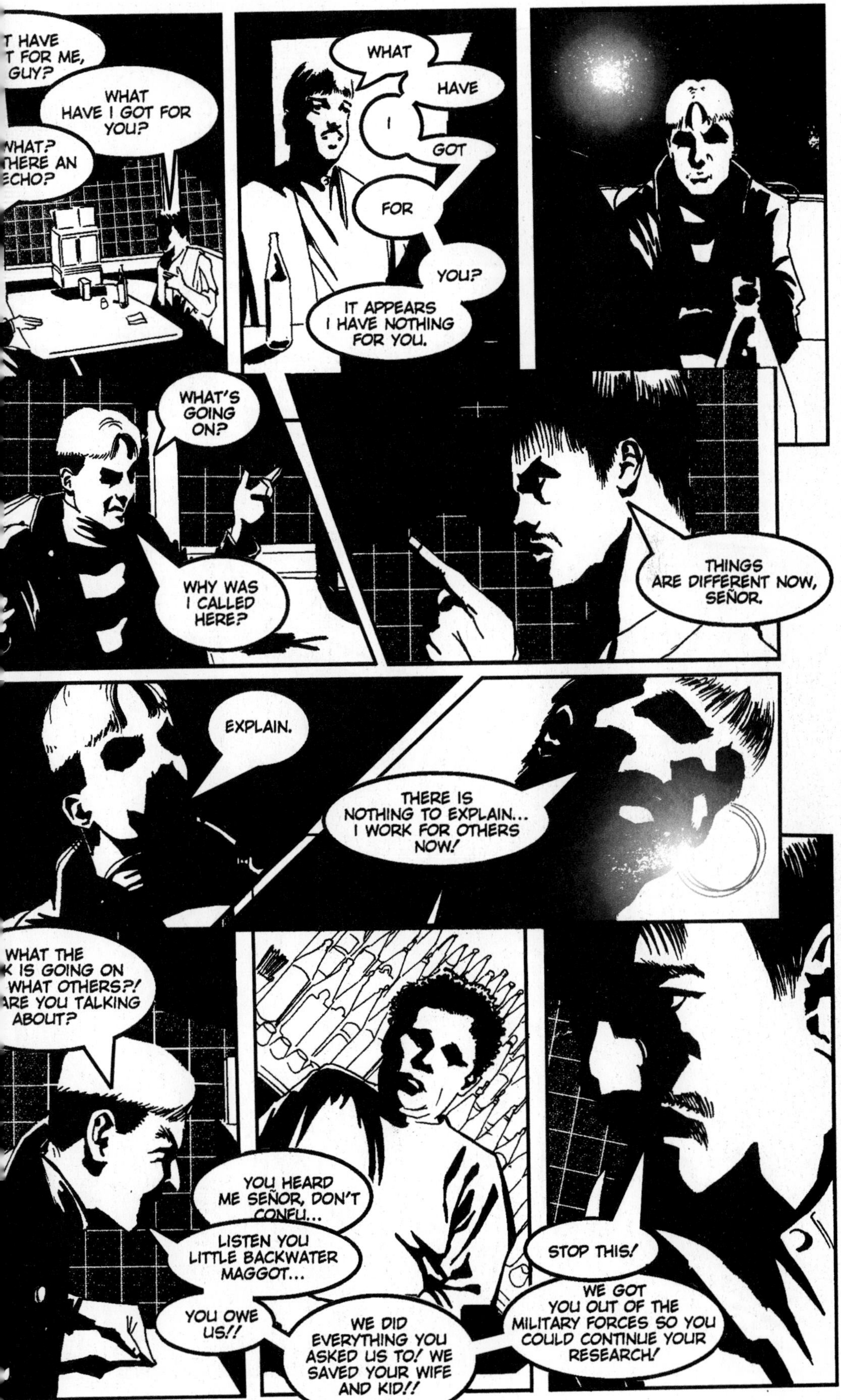

T HAVE
T FOR ME,
GUY?
WHAT HAVE I GOT FOR YOU?
WHAT?
THERE AN
ECHO?
WHAT
HAVE
I
GOT
FOR
YOU?
IT APPEARS I HAVE NOTHING FOR YOU.
WHAT'S GOING ON?
WHY WAS I CALLED HERE?
THINGS ARE DIFFERENT NOW, SEÑOR.
EXPLAIN.
THERE IS NOTHING TO EXPLAIN... I WORK FOR OTHERS NOW!
WHAT THE
K IS GOING ON
WHAT OTHERS?!
ARE YOU TALKING
ABOUT?
YOU HEARD ME SEÑOR, DON'T CONFU...
LISTEN YOU LITTLE BACKWATER MAGGOT...
YOU OWE US!!
WE DID EVERYTHING YOU ASKED US TO! WE SAVED YOUR WIFE AND KID!!
STOP THIS!
WE GOT YOU OUT OF THE MILITARY FORCES SO YOU COULD CONTINUE YOUR RESEARCH!

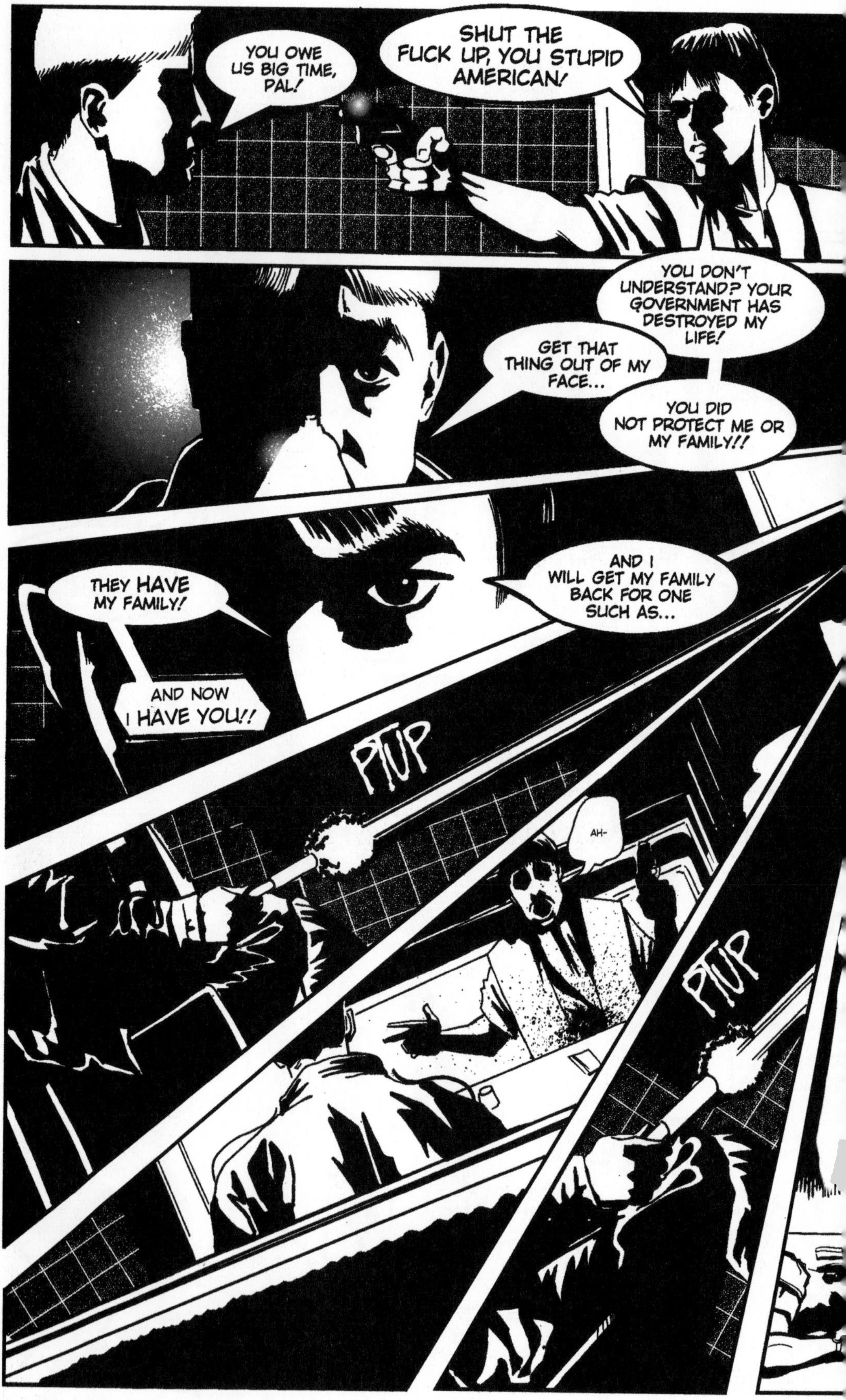
YOU OWE US BIG TIME, PAL!
SHUT THE FUCK UP, YOU STUPID AMERICAN!
YOU DON'T UNDERSTAND? YOUR GOVERNMENT HAS DESTROYED MY LIFE!
GET THAT THING OUT OF MY FACE...
YOU DID NOT PROTECT ME OR MY FAMILY!!
THEY HAVE MY FAMILY!
AND I WILL GET MY FAMILY BACK FOR ONE SUCH AS...
AND NOW I HAVE YOU!!
PTUP
AH-
PTUP

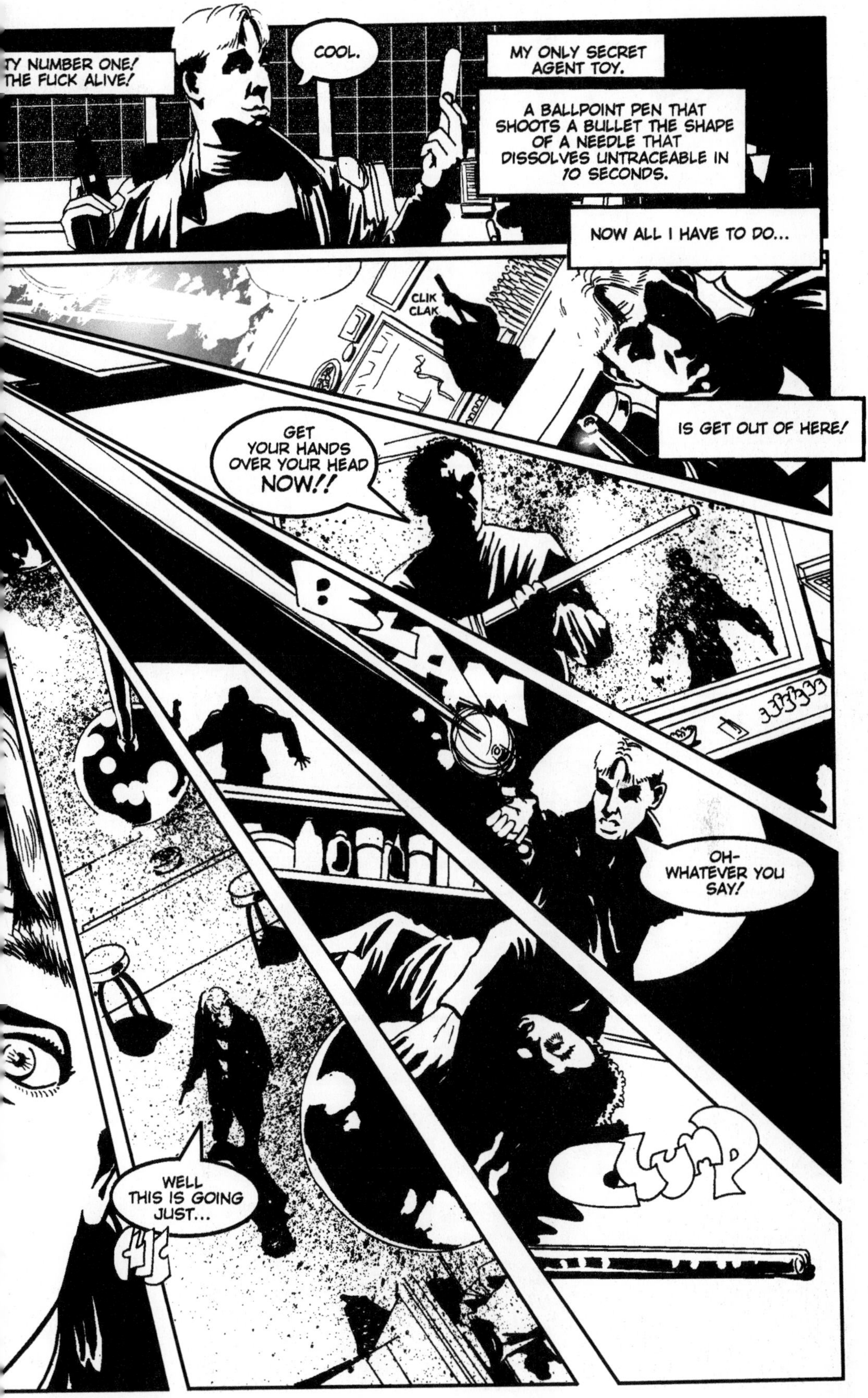
TY NUMBER ONE! THE FUCK ALIVE!
COOL.
MY ONLY SECRET AGENT TOY.
A BALLPOINT PEN THAT SHOOTS A BULLET THE SHAPE OF A NEEDLE THAT DISSOLVES UNTRACEABLE IN 10 SECONDS.
NOW ALL I HAVE TO DO...
CLIK CLAK
IS GET OUT OF HERE!
GET YOUR HANDS OVER YOUR HEAD NOW!!
OH- WHATEVER YOU SAY!
CLUMP
WELL THIS IS GOING JUST...

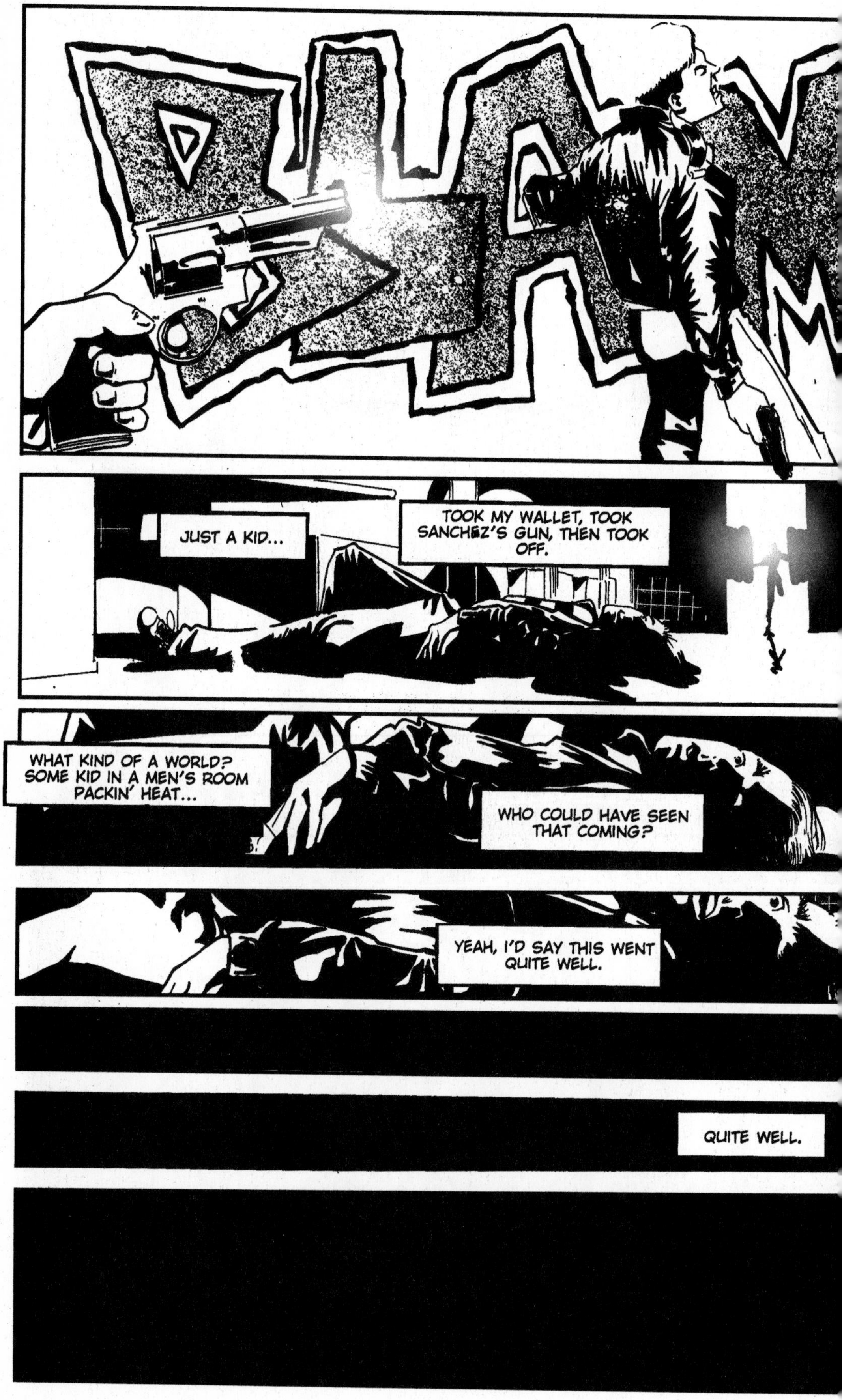
JUST A KID...
TOOK MY WALLET, TOOK SANCHEZ'S GUN, THEN TOOK OFF.
WHAT KIND OF A WORLD? SOME KID IN A MEN'S ROOM PACKIN' HEAT...
WHO COULD HAVE SEEN THAT COMING?
YEAH, I'D SAY THIS WENT QUITE WELL.
QUITE WELL.

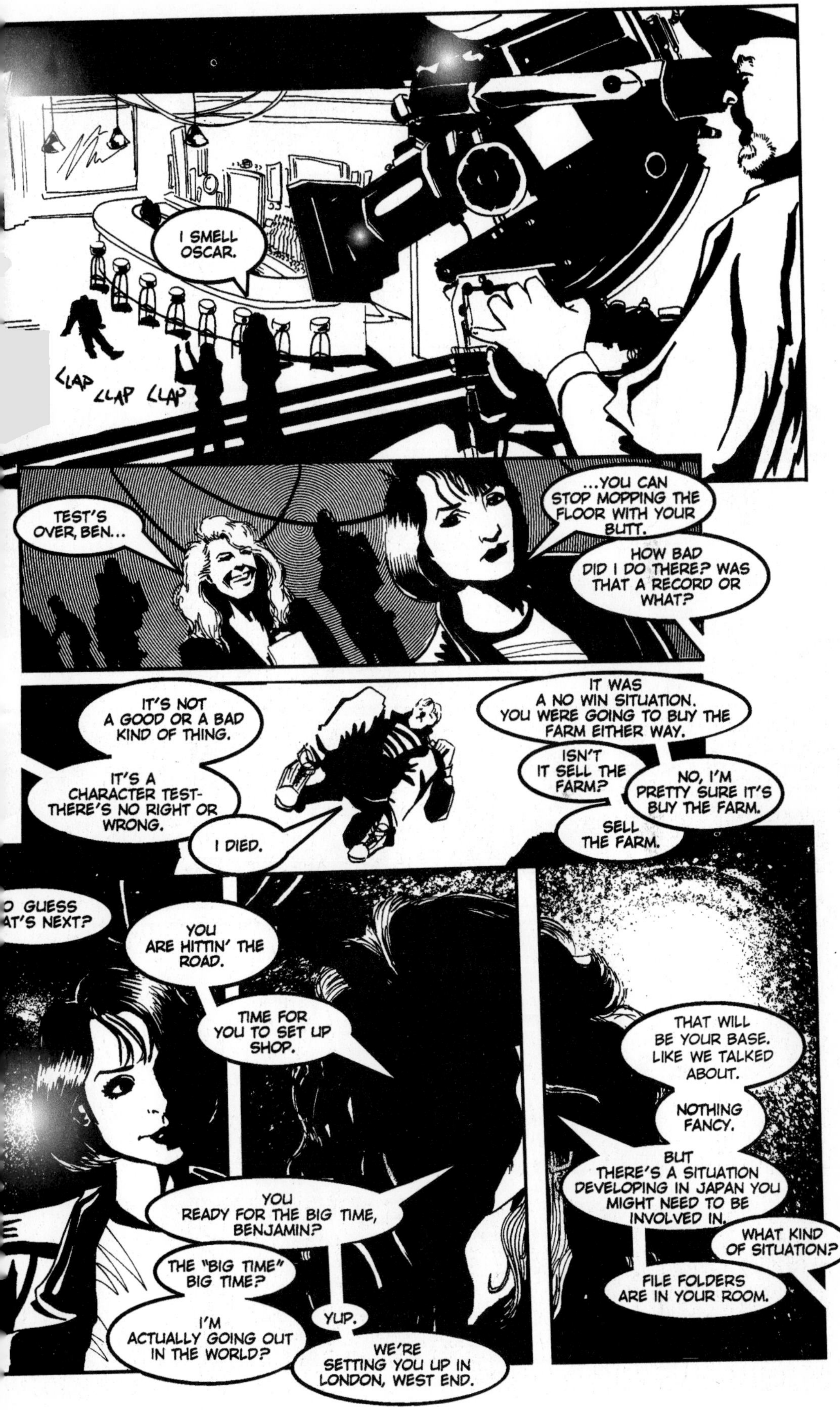
I SMELL OSCAR.
CLAP CLAP CLAP
TEST'S OVER, BEN...
...YOU CAN STOP MOPPING THE FLOOR WITH YOUR BUTT.
HOW BAD DID I DO THERE? WAS THAT A RECORD OR WHAT?
IT'S NOT A GOOD OR A BAD KIND OF THING.
IT'S A CHARACTER TEST- THERE'S NO RIGHT OR WRONG.
I DIED.
IT WAS A NO WIN SITUATION. YOU WERE GOING TO BUY THE FARM EITHER WAY.
ISN'T IT SELL THE FARM?
NO, I'M PRETTY SURE IT'S BUY THE FARM.
SELL THE FARM.
O GUESS AT'S NEXT?
YOU ARE HITTIN' THE ROAD.
TIME FOR YOU TO SET UP SHOP.
YOU READY FOR THE BIG TIME, BENJAMIN?
THE "BIG TIME" BIG TIME?
I'M ACTUALLY GOING OUT IN THE WORLD?
YUP.
WE'RE SETTING YOU UP IN LONDON, WEST END.
THAT WILL BE YOUR BASE. LIKE WE TALKED ABOUT.
NOTHING FANCY.
BUT THERE'S A SITUATION DEVELOPING IN JAPAN YOU MIGHT NEED TO BE INVOLVED IN.
WHAT KIND OF SITUATION?
FILE FOLDERS ARE IN YOUR ROOM.

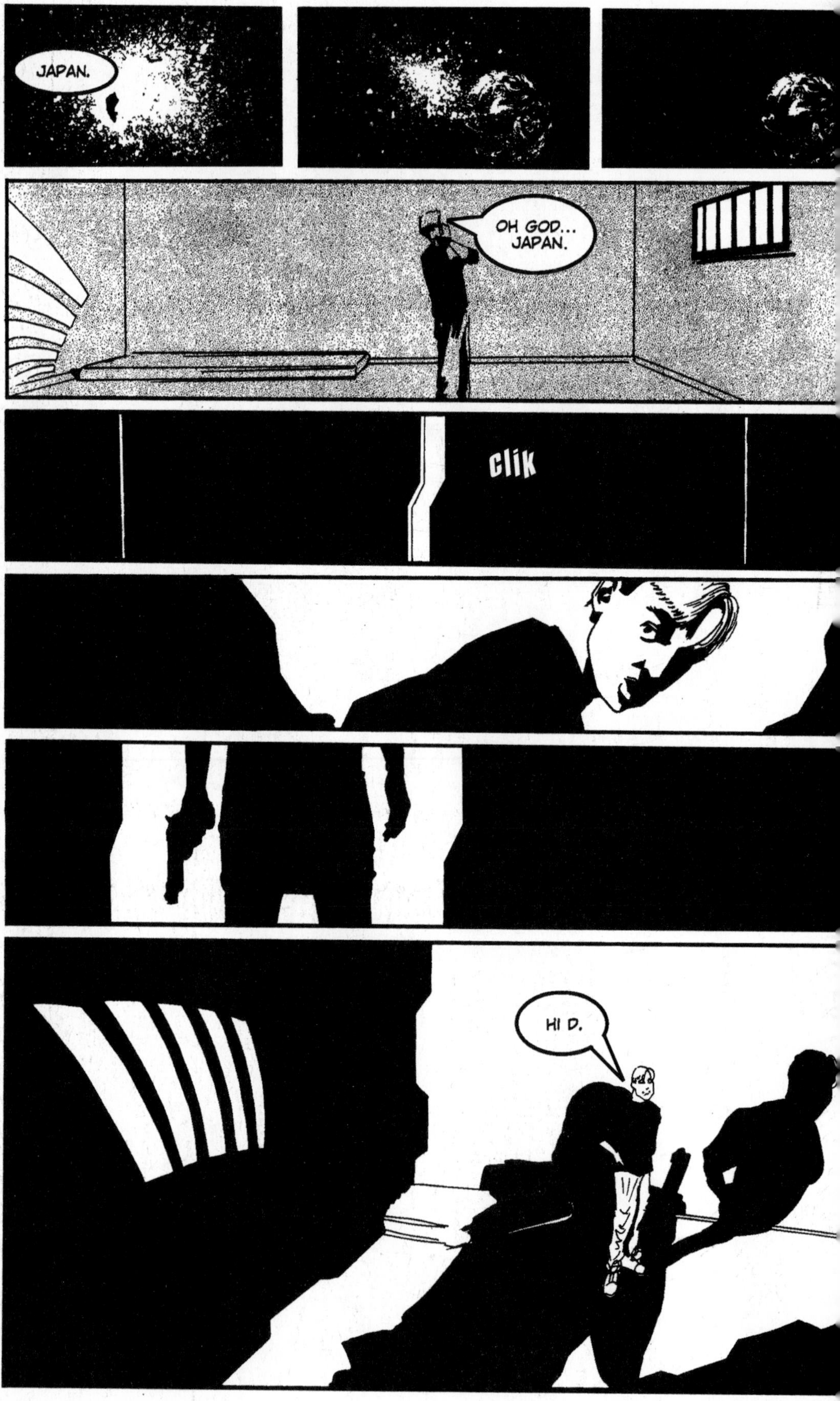
JAPAN.
OH GOD... JAPAN.
CLIK
HI D.

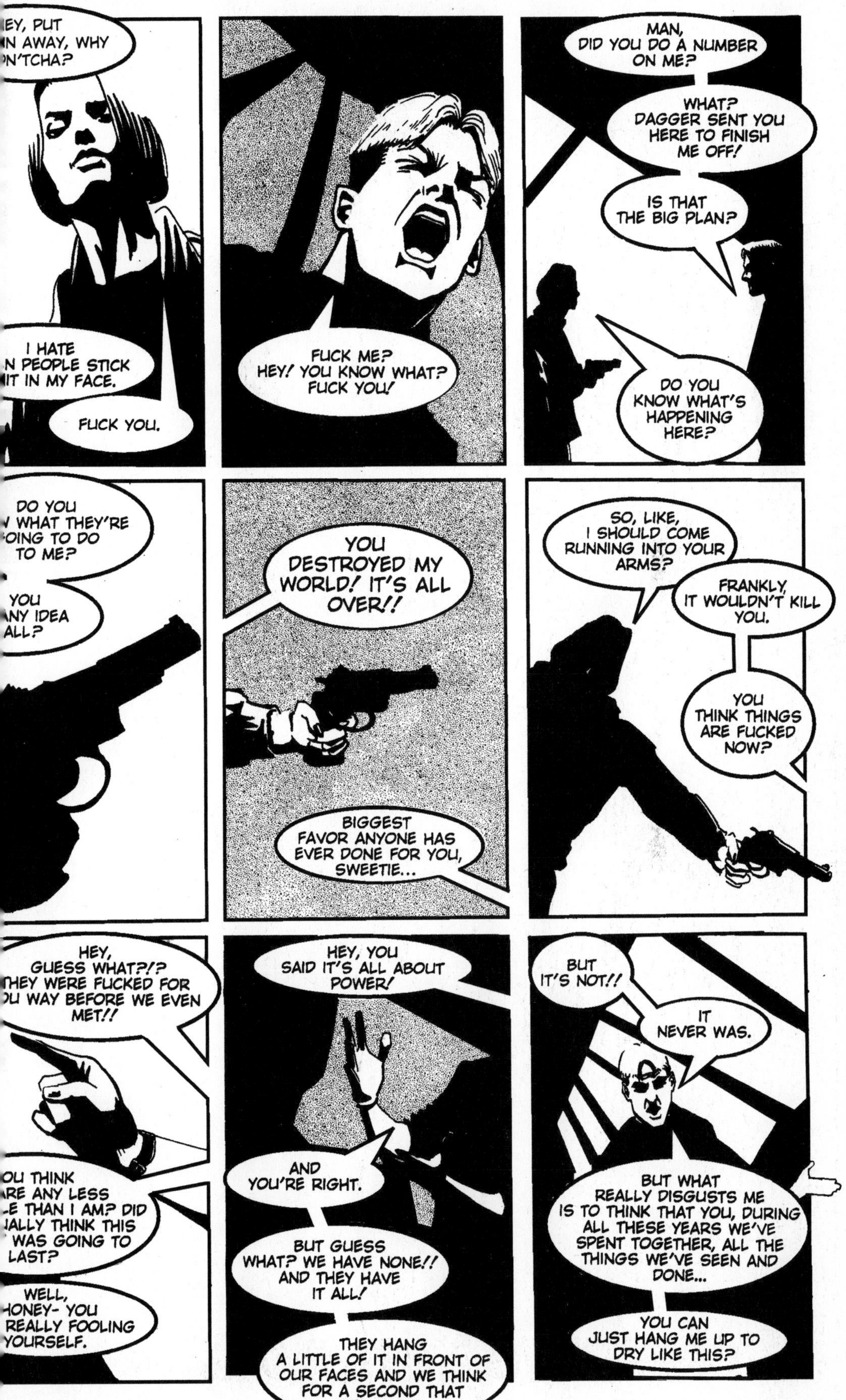

EY, PUT
N AWAY, WHY
N'TCHA?
I HATE
N PEOPLE STICK
IT IN MY FACE.
FUCK YOU.
FUCK ME? HEY! YOU KNOW WHAT? FUCK YOU!
MAN, DID YOU DO A NUMBER ON ME?
WHAT? DAGGER SENT YOU HERE TO FINISH ME OFF!
IS THAT THE BIG PLAN?
DO YOU KNOW WHAT'S HAPPENING HERE?
DO YOU
WHAT THEY'RE
OING TO DO
TO ME?
YOU
NY IDEA
ALL?
YOU DESTROYED MY WORLD! IT'S ALL OVER!!
BIGGEST FAVOR ANYONE HAS EVER DONE FOR YOU, SWEETIE...
SO, LIKE, I SHOULD COME RUNNING INTO YOUR ARMS?
FRANKLY, IT WOULDN'T KILL YOU.
YOU THINK THINGS ARE FUCKED NOW?
HEY,
GUESS WHAT?!?
THEY WERE FUCKED FOR
OU WAY BEFORE WE EVEN
MET!!
OU THINK
RE ANY LESS
E THAN I AM? DID
ALLY THINK THIS
WAS GOING TO
LAST?
WELL,
HONEY- YOU
REALLY FOOLING
YOURSELF.
HEY, YOU SAID IT'S ALL ABOUT POWER!
AND YOU'RE RIGHT.
BUT GUESS WHAT? WE HAVE NONE!! AND THEY HAVE IT ALL!
THEY HANG A LITTLE OF IT IN FRONT OF OUR FACES AND WE THINK FOR A SECOND THAT IT'S OURS.
BUT IT'S NOT!!
IT NEVER WAS.
BUT WHAT REALLY DISGUSTS ME IS TO THINK THAT YOU, DURING ALL THESE YEARS WE'VE SPENT TOGETHER, ALL THE THINGS WE'VE SEEN AND DONE...
YOU CAN JUST HANG ME UP TO DRY LIKE THIS?

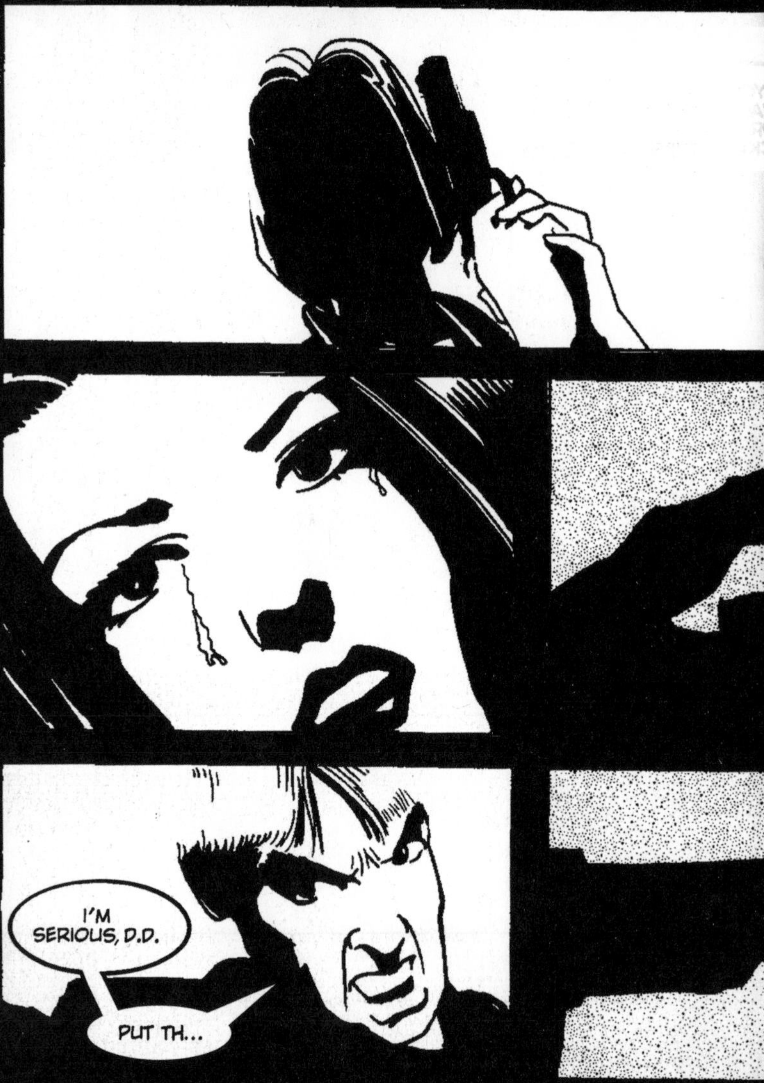
I'M SERIOUS, D.D.
PUT TH...

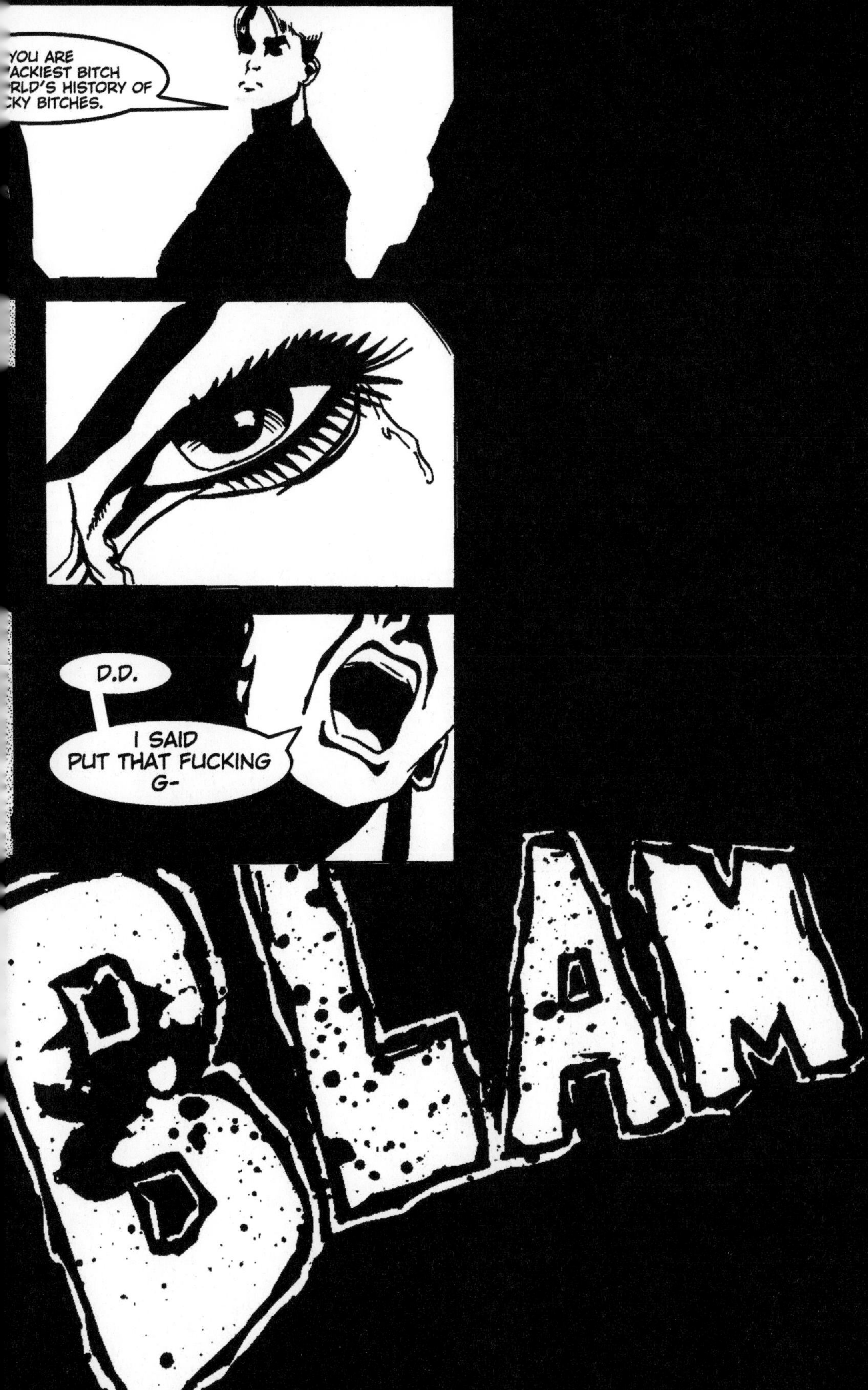
YOU ARE ACKIEST BITCH RLD'S HISTORY OF CKY BITCHES.
D.D.
I SAID PUT THAT FUCKING G-
BLAM

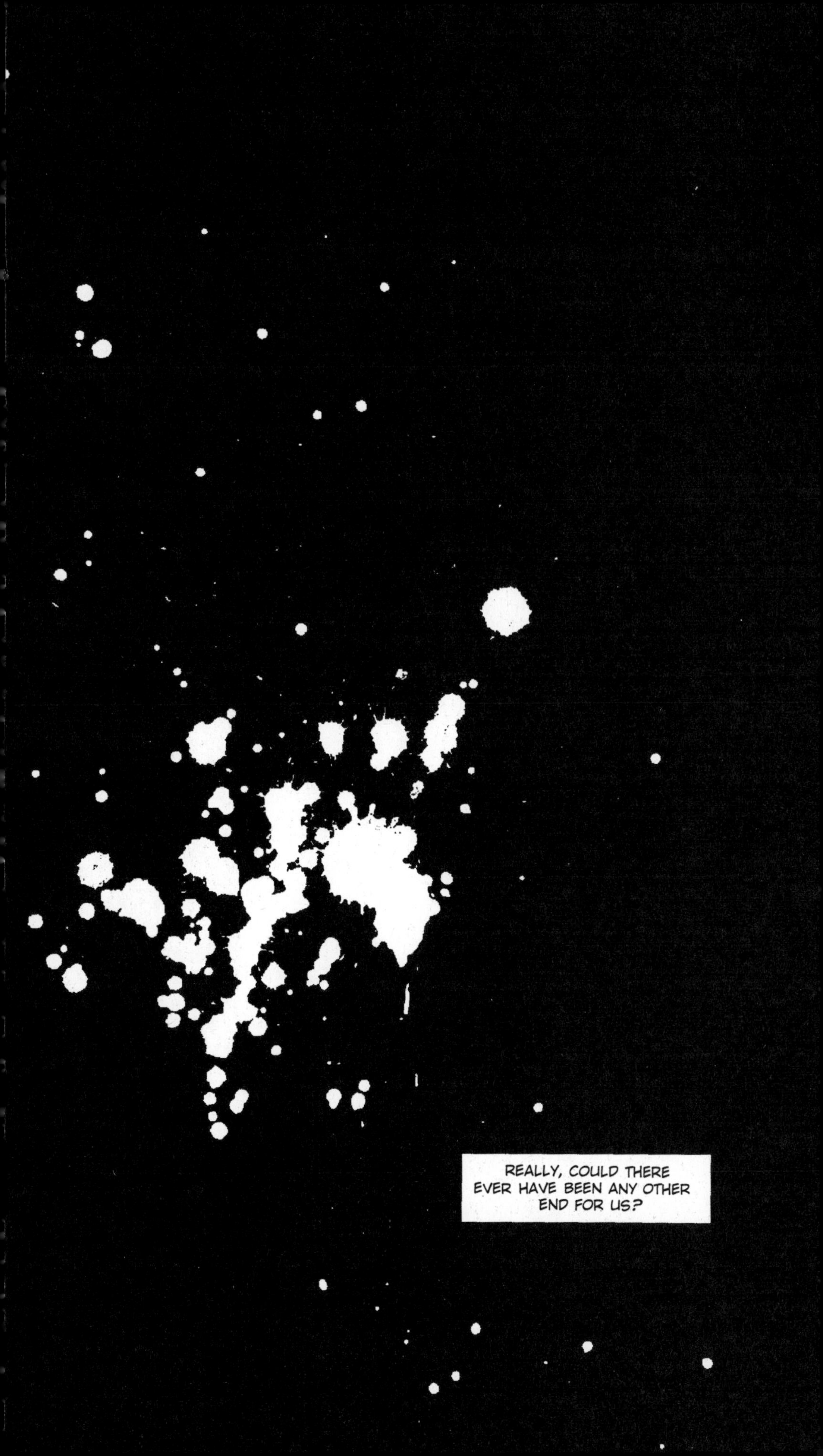
REALLY, COULD THERE EVER HAVE BEEN ANY OTHER END FOR US?

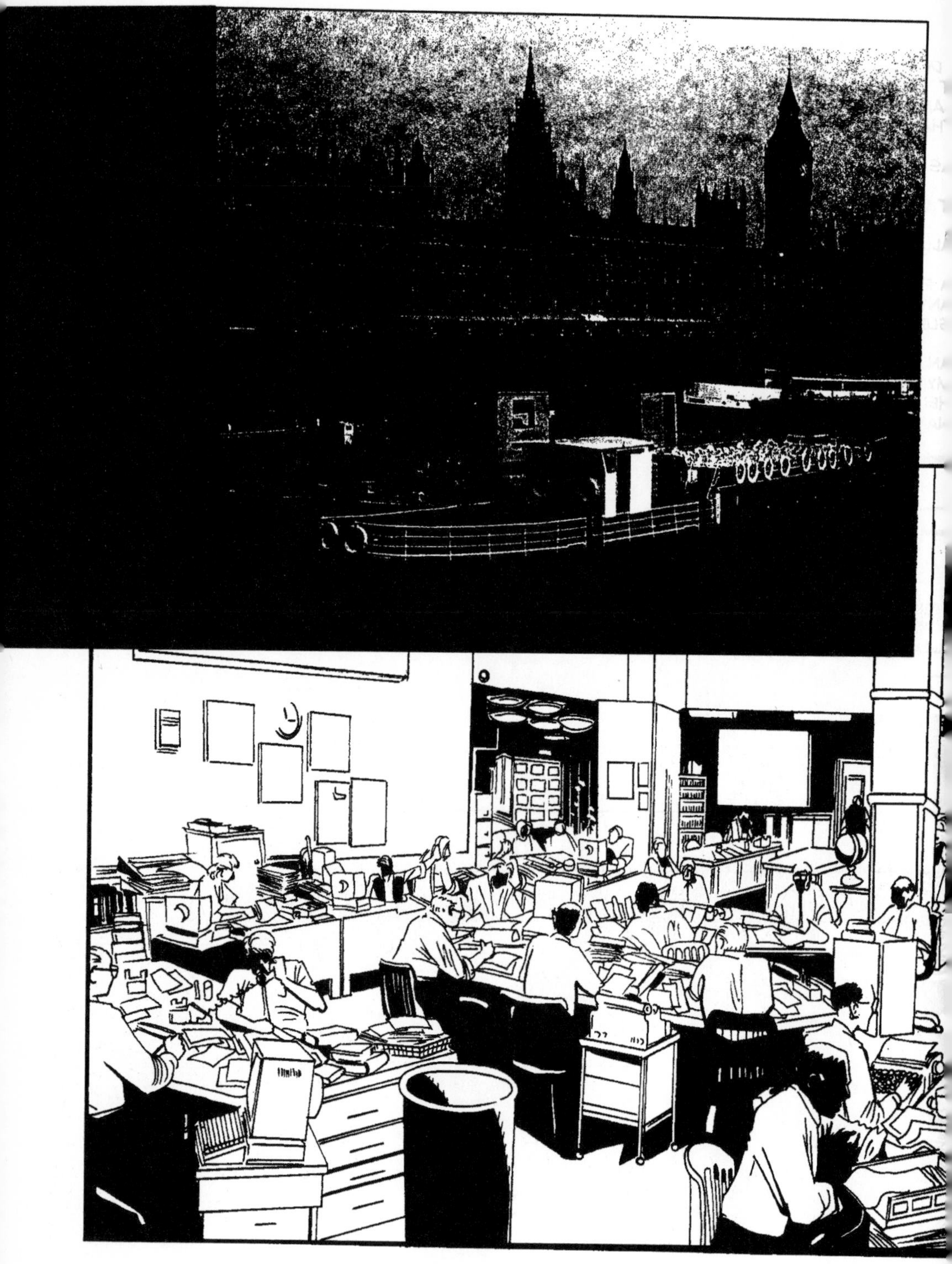

DON'T KNOW WHAT I THOUGHT MY LIFE WOULD BE LIKE... NO, THAT'S NOT TRUE. I-I THOUGHT
' WAS GOING TO BE JAMES BOND. DON'T LAUGH. I DID. I KNOW THAT'S TOTALLY GEEKY AND
AME, BUT IT WAS MY ONLY POOL OF REFERENCE. THE REALITY, HOWEVER, WAS A DRILL
HAT BECAME WAY TOO FAMILIAR WAY TOO FUCKING FAST.

.S PROMISED, I WAS SET UP IN A NEW ENVIRONMENT. A COVER.

' WAS JACK-NO, NO, IT WAS JAKE DONALDSON. THAT WAS MY NAME THEN.

.LL GOOD ESPIONAGE COVERS COME INTACT WITH A MENIAL JOB AT THE LONDON TIMES!

PRETTY COOL PLACE TO BE SET UP IN ACTUALLY. OF COURSE I HAD TO SUPPRESS
NY EXCITEMENT OR DISDAIN I FELT FOR ANYTHING WHEN ON ASSIGNMENT, OBJECTIVITY
UPPOSEDLY BEING A KEY TO PROFESSIONAL RETREIVAL.

ND WHAT WAS MY ASSIGNMENT? I HAD NO FUCKING IDEA. GOING IN I NEVER KNEW WHAT
Y OBJECTIVE WAS. I KNEW MY COVER AND I KNEW TO WAIT. DID THIS MAKE ME HAPPY?
ELL NO! ACTUALLY IT MADE ME QUITE UNEASY, SO I JUST CONCENTRATED ON BEING A GUY
AMED JAKE WHO ANSWERED TO...

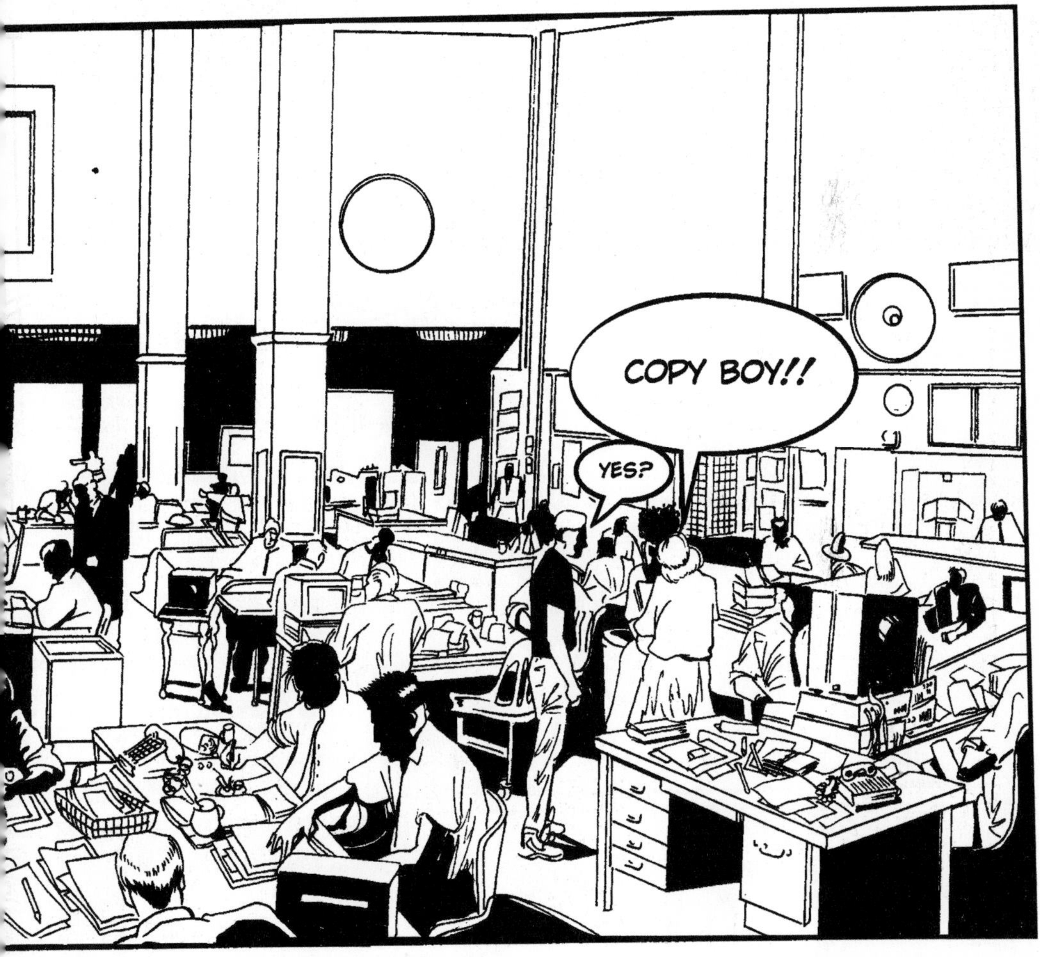
COPY BOY!!
YES?

THERE'S A LONG AGENCY TRADITION OF AGENT PLACEMENT IN MAJOR MEDIA ORGANIZATIONS-
Y'KNOW TV, NEWSPAPERS, RADIO. IT AMAZES ME HOW EASY IT IS TO SLIDE SOMEBODY
INTO A PLACE LIKE THIS.

IT'S IDEAL FOR ESPIONAGE MANEUVERING BECAUSE SO MUCH INFORMATION MOVES
THROUGH THESE PLACES THAT IT'S ALMOST IMPOSSIBLE TO DETECT SOMETHING
OUT OF THE ORDINARY.

HEY, IF IT WORKED FOR SUPERMAN...

AND EVERY NIGHT I LAY IN MY INCONSPICUOUS LITTLE ROOM.

TO MATCH MY INCONSPICUOUS LITTLE LIFE.

GENERALLY YOU AVOID GOING OUT. IT KEEPS YOU OUT OF TROUBLE.

ACCIDENTAL TROUBLE. SHIT YOU CAN'T POSSIBLY SEE COMING.

I'M A BIG BELIEVER TO REDUCE THE X-

BRITISH TV SUCKS SO BAD. ALL THE GOOD STUFF HAS ALREADY MADE IT TO AMERICA.

JAKE DONALDSON WAS AVID ARTHURIAN LORE E

SOME LIGHT READING.

IT BORED ME SHITLESS! WI CAN'T THE AGENT PICK HIS COVER'S LIKES AND DISLIKE

THE REAL TORTURE OF THIS MONTH LONG SIT-OUT IS THAT YOU'RE LEFT TO THE PRISON-LIKE CONFINES OF YOUR OWN MIND.

I SAT THERE PICKING O SPECTACULAR EVENT? HAD SHAPED THE CO THAT HAD LED ME T

CONSTANTLY RELIVING EVERY SECOND OF MY NEW LIFE, AND, NO MATTER HOW HARD I TRY TO FORGET, NO MATTER HARD I TRIED TO PUSH IT DOWN.

SOME OF IT JUST H ME. LIKE...

JAPAN.

MY FIRST MISSION.

MED ILLOGICAL AND
HT ODD TO SEND A
LIKE MYSELF ON A
MISSION LIKE THIS,

ME OUT OF LONDON,
O JAPAN AND BACK.

SE I LEARNED EARLY
N MY TRAINING THAT
ONING ORDERS WAS
TABOO, AND I DIDN'T
WAS SENDING THE
DOWN. SO WHO WAS
GOING TO BITCH TO?

OULD HAVE KEPT MY
OUTH SHUT. I REALLY
WOULD HAVE.

AGGER PRESSED ME.

YOU'RE CLEAR ON
YOUR ORDERS?"

"YES, I AM."

"ANY QUESTIONS,
UNCLEAR DETAILS?

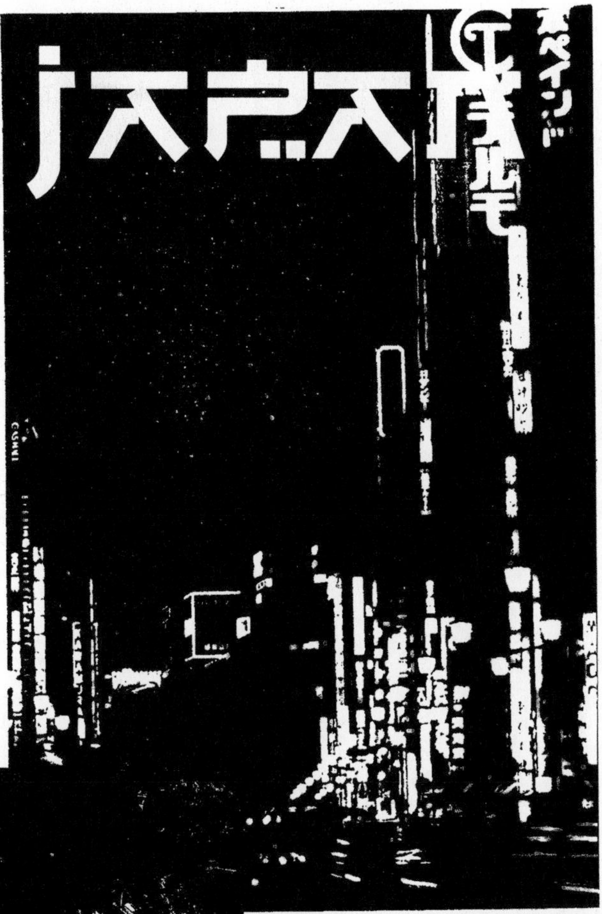
JAPAN

"ANY RESERVATIONS?"

"REALLY I UNDERSTAND
THAT IT'S NOT MY PLACE...
AND THAT'S FINE.
JUST LE..."

"NO, I INSIST.
IT'S GOOD
FOR THE SOUL."

WELL, I DID VOICE MY
OPINION, AS
DIPLOMATICALLY
AS I COULD...

SHE STARED AT ME
WITH EMOTIONLESS
SILENCE. HER FACE
WAS ABSOLUTLY
UNREADABLE.

"WELL, GET USED
TO IT, OR FUCK ON
OUT OF HERE. IT'S
AS SIMPLE AS THAT."

"WELL, THAT'S
PLEASANT."

"NOT MY JOB TO BE
PLEASANT. IT'S MY
JOB TO TELL IT HOW
IT IS. AND THAT IS HOW
IT IS. FOR ME AND FOR
YOU."

I LEFT THE NEXT
MORNING, VOWING
NEVER TO GET
SUCKERED INTO ONE
OF THOSE EXCHANGES
WITH HER AGAIN.

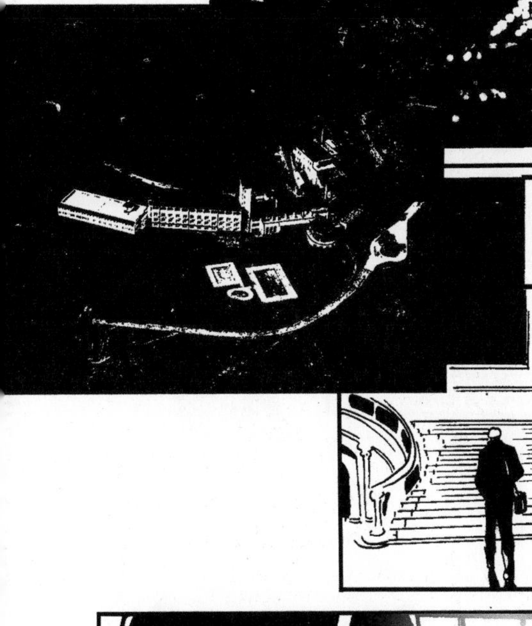

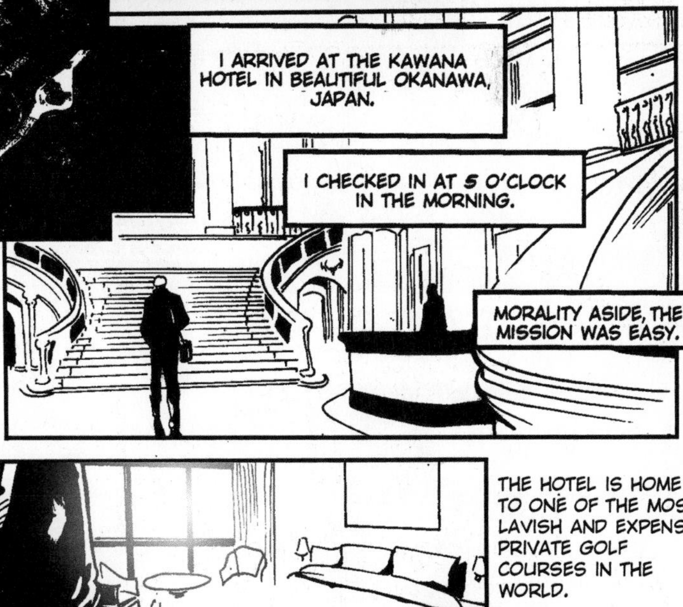
I ARRIVED AT THE KAWANA HOTEL IN BEAUTIFUL OKANAWA, JAPAN.
I CHECKED IN AT 5 O'CLOCK IN THE MORNING.
MORALITY ASIDE, THE MISSION WAS EASY.

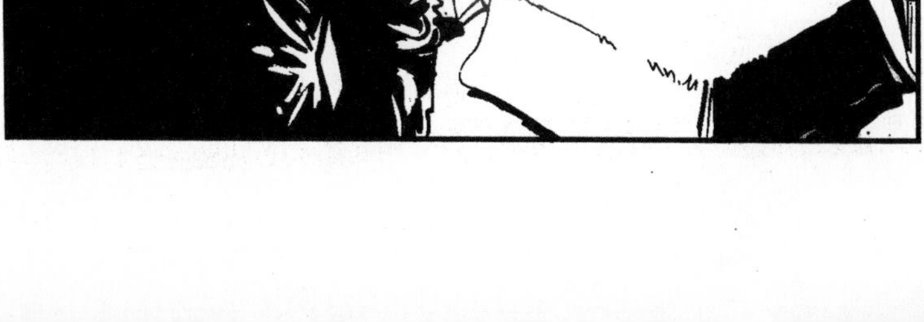

THE HOTEL IS HOME
TO ONE OF THE MOST
LAVISH AND EXPENSIVE
PRIVATE GOLF
COURSES IN THE
WORLD.

MY ROOM HAD A
PERFECT VIEW OF
MOST OF
THE GREEN.

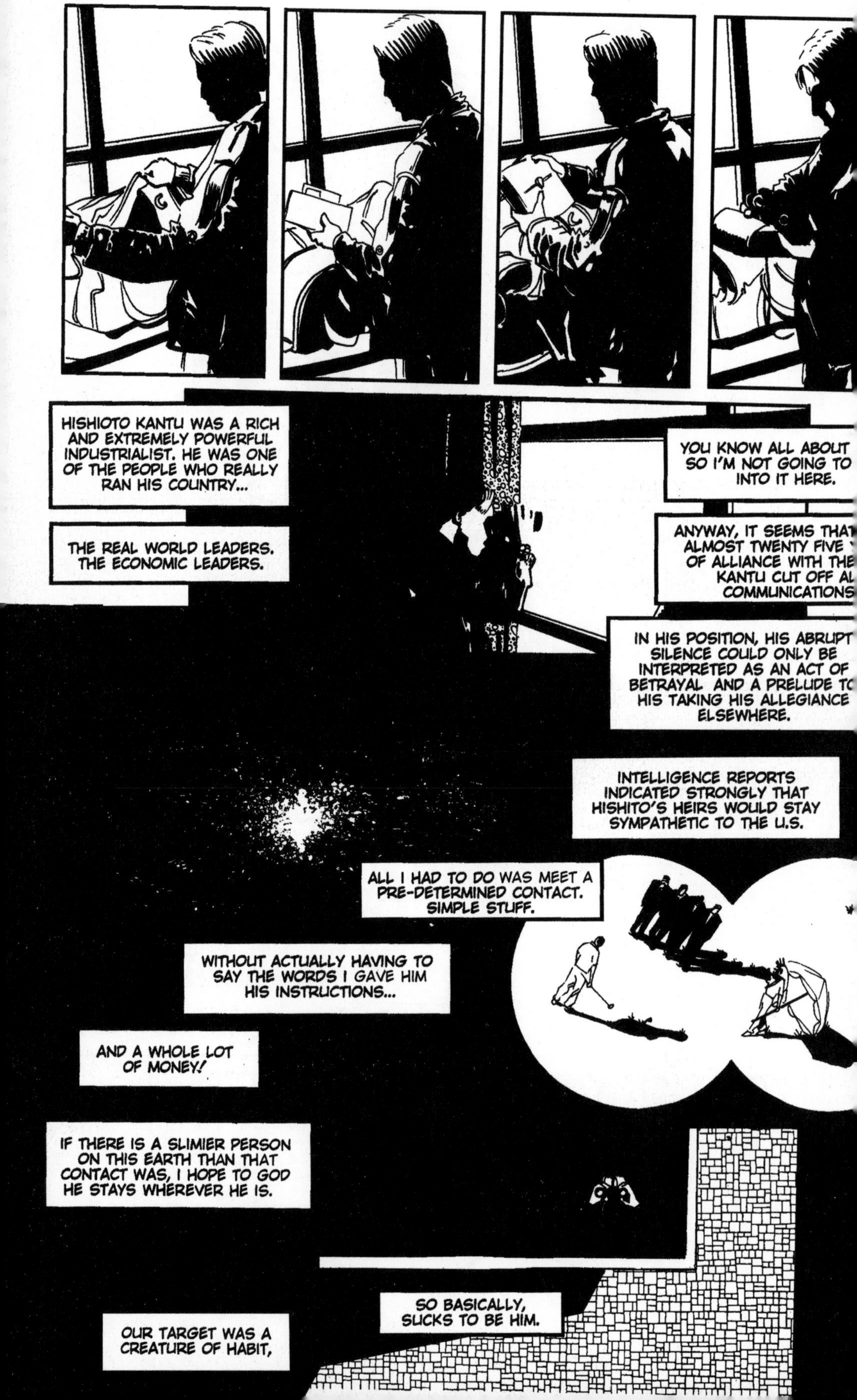
HISHIOTO KANTU WAS A RICH AND EXTREMELY POWERFUL INDUSTRIALIST. HE WAS ONE OF THE PEOPLE WHO REALLY RAN HIS COUNTRY...
THE REAL WORLD LEADERS. THE ECONOMIC LEADERS.
YOU KNOW ALL ABOUT SO I'M NOT GOING TO INTO IT HERE.
ANYWAY, IT SEEMS THAT ALMOST TWENTY FIVE OF ALLIANCE WITH THE KANTU CUT OFF AL COMMUNICATIONS
IN HIS POSITION, HIS ABRUPT SILENCE COULD ONLY BE INTERPRETED AS AN ACT OF BETRAYAL AND A PRELUDE TO HIS TAKING HIS ALLEGIANCE ELSEWHERE.
INTELLIGENCE REPORTS INDICATED STRONGLY THAT HISHITO'S HEIRS WOULD STAY SYMPATHETIC TO THE U.S.
ALL I HAD TO DO WAS MEET A PRE-DETERMINED CONTACT. SIMPLE STUFF.
WITHOUT ACTUALLY HAVING TO SAY THE WORDS I GAVE HIM HIS INSTRUCTIONS...
AND A WHOLE LOT OF MONEY!
IF THERE IS A SLIMIER PERSON ON THIS EARTH THAN THAT CONTACT WAS, I HOPE TO GOD HE STAYS WHEREVER HE IS.
SO BASICALLY, SUCKS TO BE HIM.
OUR TARGET WAS A CREATURE OF HABIT,

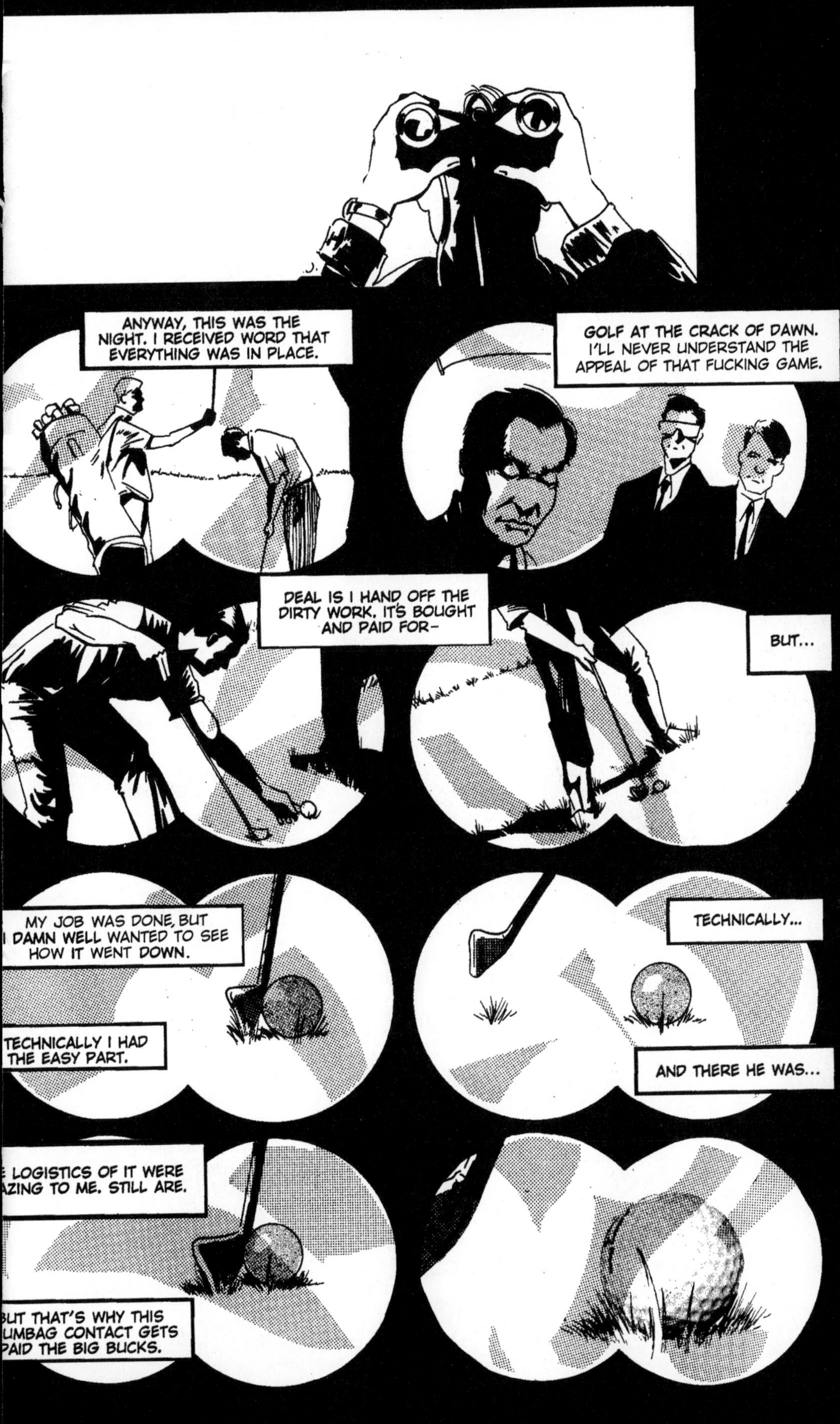
ANYWAY, THIS WAS THE NIGHT. I RECEIVED WORD THAT EVERYTHING WAS IN PLACE.
GOLF AT THE CRACK OF DAWN. I'LL NEVER UNDERSTAND THE APPEAL OF THAT FUCKING GAME.
DEAL IS I HAND OFF THE DIRTY WORK. IT'S BOUGHT AND PAID FOR–
BUT...
MY JOB WAS DONE, BUT I DAMN WELL WANTED TO SEE HOW IT WENT DOWN.
TECHNICALLY I HAD THE EASY PART.
TECHNICALLY...
AND THERE HE WAS...
LOGISTICS OF IT WERE AZING TO ME. STILL ARE.
BUT THAT'S WHY THIS UMBAG CONTACT GETS PAID THE BIG BUCKS.

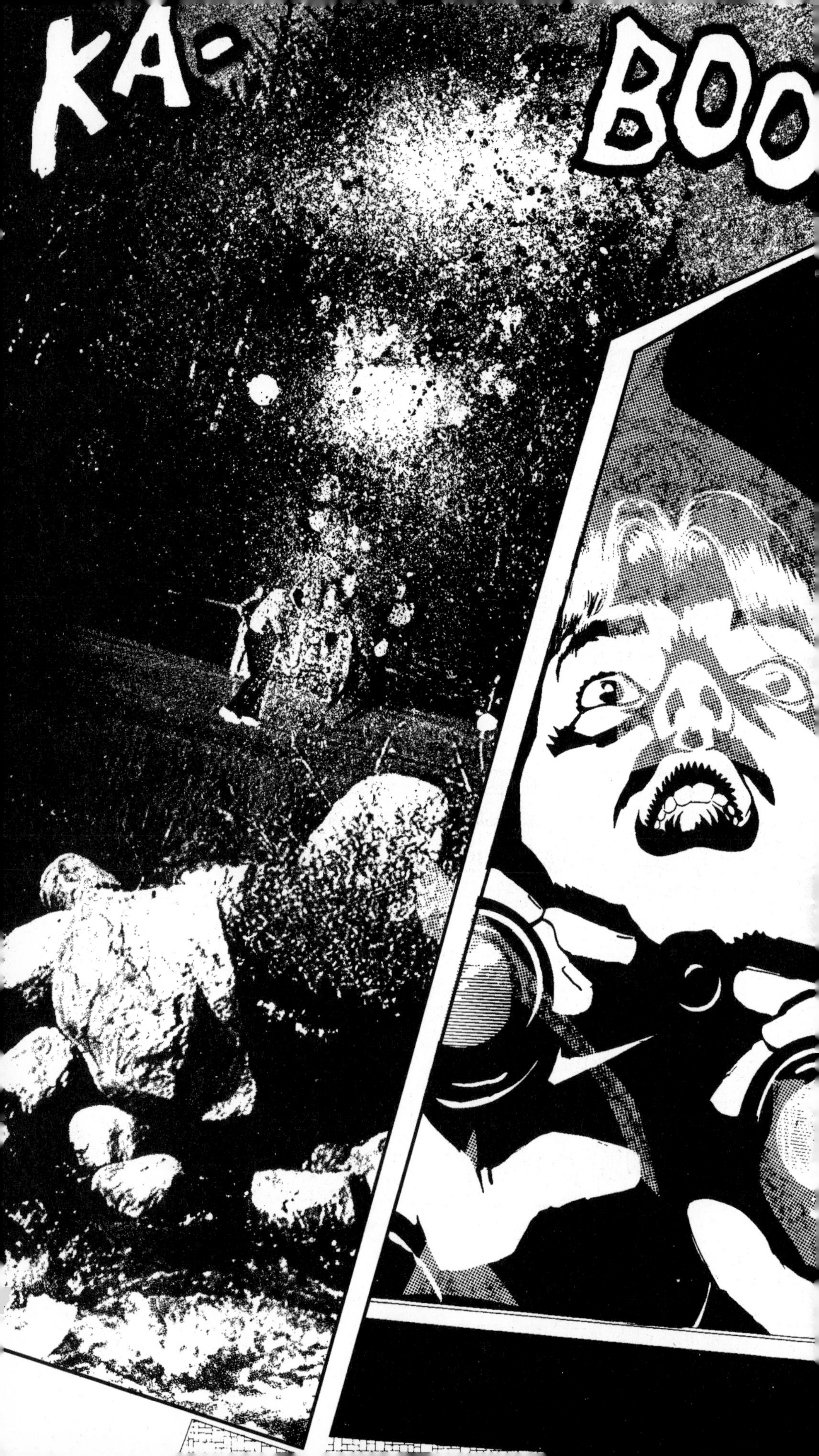
KA-
BOO

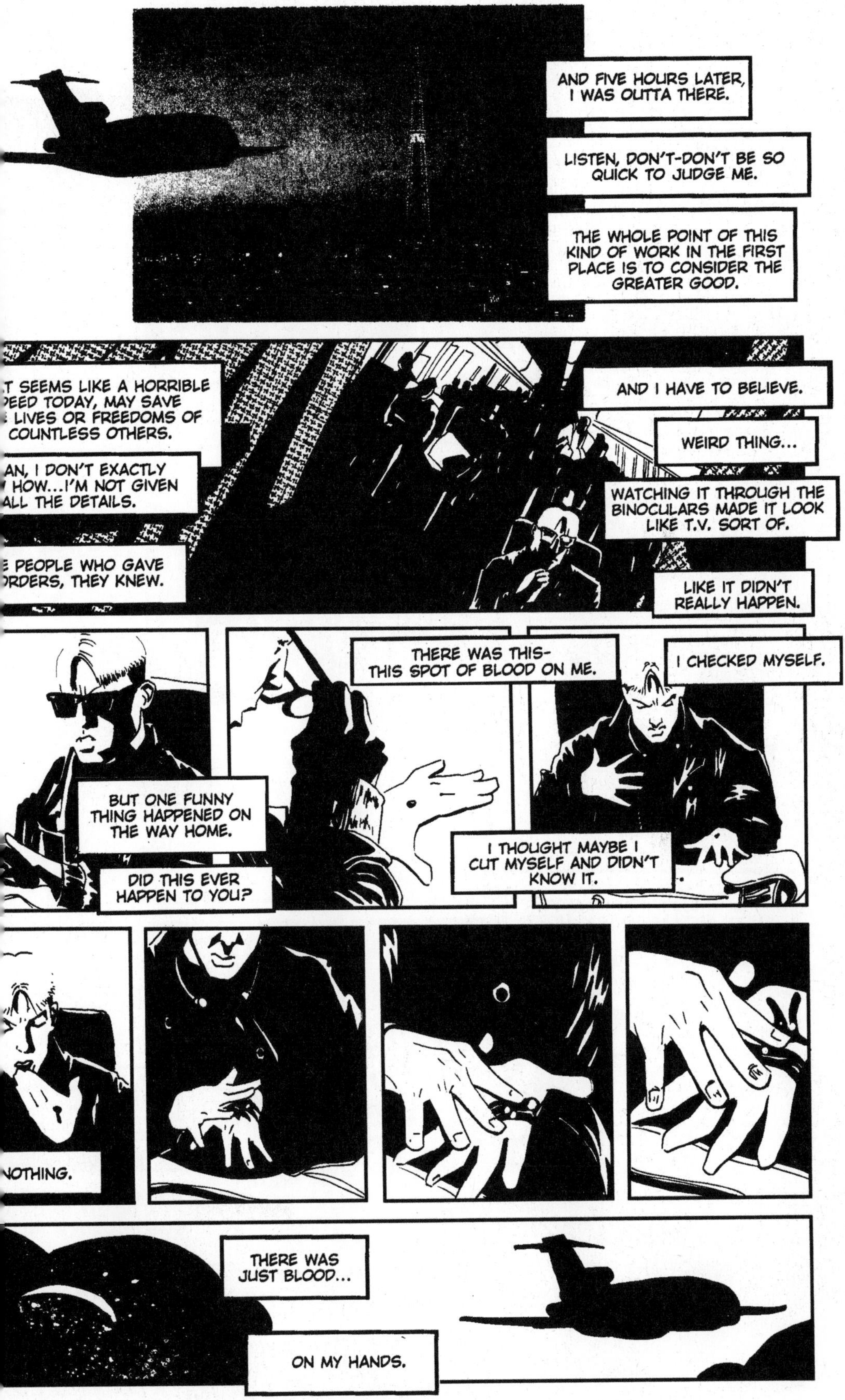
AND FIVE HOURS LATER, I WAS OUTTA THERE.
LISTEN, DON'T-DON'T BE SO QUICK TO JUDGE ME.
THE WHOLE POINT OF THIS KIND OF WORK IN THE FIRST PLACE IS TO CONSIDER THE GREATER GOOD.
T SEEMS LIKE A HORRIBLE PEED TODAY, MAY SAVE LIVES OR FREEDOMS OF COUNTLESS OTHERS.
AN, I DON'T EXACTLY HOW...I'M NOT GIVEN ALL THE DETAILS.
E PEOPLE WHO GAVE ORDERS, THEY KNEW.
AND I HAVE TO BELIEVE.
WEIRD THING...
WATCHING IT THROUGH THE BINOCULARS MADE IT LOOK LIKE T.V. SORT OF.
LIKE IT DIDN'T REALLY HAPPEN.
BUT ONE FUNNY THING HAPPENED ON THE WAY HOME.
DID THIS EVER HAPPEN TO YOU?
THERE WAS THIS-THIS SPOT OF BLOOD ON ME.
I THOUGHT MAYBE I CUT MYSELF AND DIDN'T KNOW IT.
I CHECKED MYSELF.
NOTHING.
THERE WAS JUST BLOOD...
ON MY HANDS.

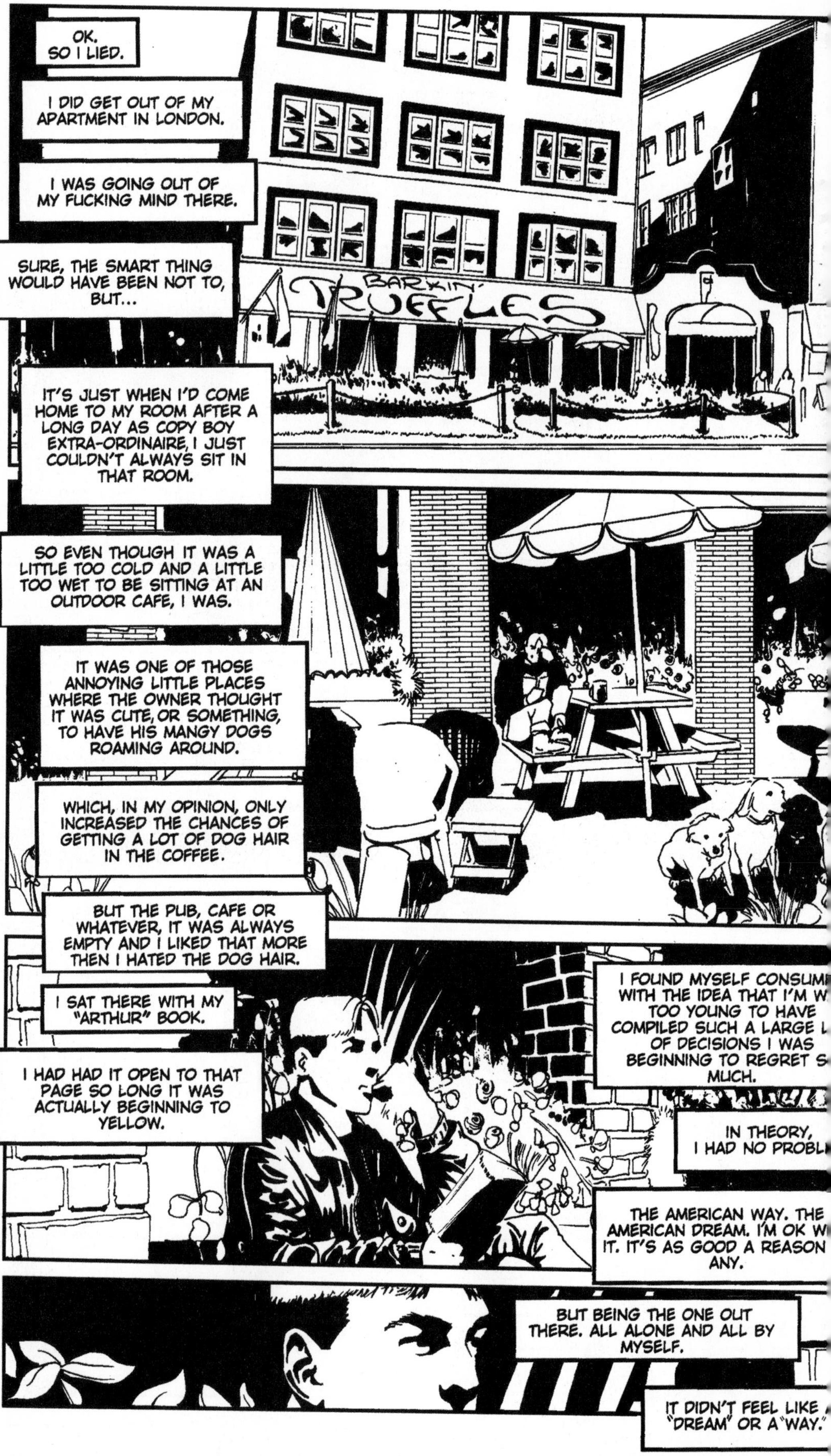

OK.
SO I LIED.
I DID GET OUT OF MY APARTMENT IN LONDON.
I WAS GOING OUT OF MY FUCKING MIND THERE.
SURE, THE SMART THING WOULD HAVE BEEN NOT TO, BUT...
BARKIN' TRUFFLES
IT'S JUST WHEN I'D COME HOME TO MY ROOM AFTER A LONG DAY AS COPY BOY EXTRA-ORDINAIRE, I JUST COULDN'T ALWAYS SIT IN THAT ROOM.
SO EVEN THOUGH IT WAS A LITTLE TOO COLD AND A LITTLE TOO WET TO BE SITTING AT AN OUTDOOR CAFE, I WAS.
IT WAS ONE OF THOSE ANNOYING LITTLE PLACES WHERE THE OWNER THOUGHT IT WAS CUTE, OR SOMETHING, TO HAVE HIS MANGY DOGS ROAMING AROUND.
WHICH, IN MY OPINION, ONLY INCREASED THE CHANCES OF GETTING A LOT OF DOG HAIR IN THE COFFEE.
BUT THE PUB, CAFE OR WHATEVER, IT WAS ALWAYS EMPTY AND I LIKED THAT MORE THEN I HATED THE DOG HAIR.
I SAT THERE WITH MY "ARTHUR" BOOK.
I HAD HAD IT OPEN TO THAT PAGE SO LONG IT WAS ACTUALLY BEGINNING TO YELLOW.
I FOUND MYSELF CONSUM WITH THE IDEA THAT I'M W TOO YOUNG TO HAVE COMPILED SUCH A LARGE L OF DECISIONS I WAS BEGINNING TO REGRET S MUCH.
IN THEORY, I HAD NO PROBL
THE AMERICAN WAY. THE AMERICAN DREAM. I'M OK W IT. IT'S AS GOOD A REASON ANY.
BUT BEING THE ONE OUT THERE. ALL ALONE AND ALL BY MYSELF.
IT DIDN'T FEEL LIKE "DREAM" OR A "WAY."

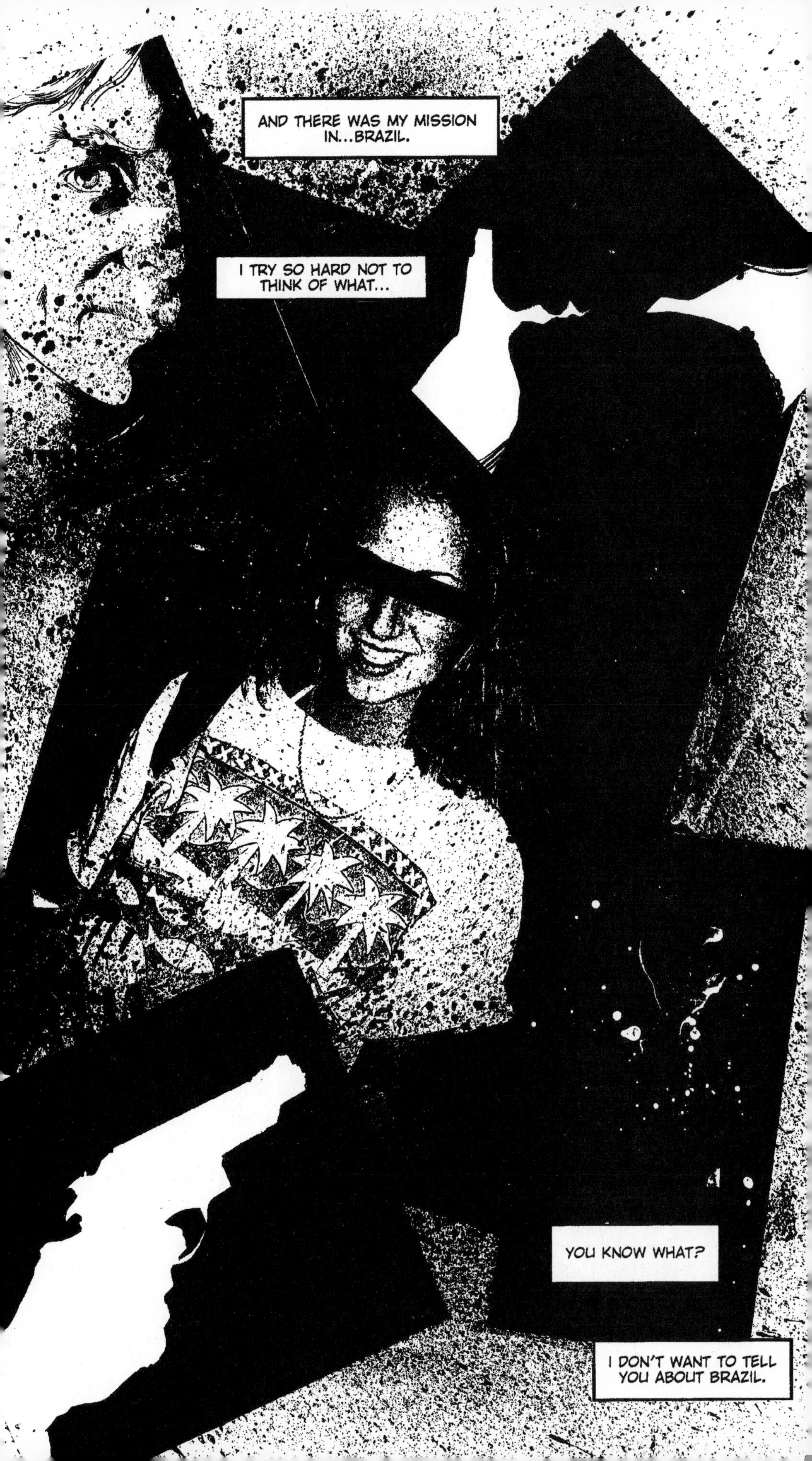
AND THERE WAS MY MISSION IN...BRAZIL.
I TRY SO HARD NOT TO THINK OF WHAT...
YOU KNOW WHAT?
I DON'T WANT TO TELL YOU ABOUT BRAZIL.

DID YOU HEAR ME?

I SAID— WOULD YOU LIKE ANOTHER COFFEE, LUV??

UH– NO, I'M NOT DONE STARING AT THIS ONE YET.

OOOOH, LISTEN TO YOU. AN AMERICAN ARE YOU?

UH-HUH.

STUDENT?

NO.

VACATION?

S-SORT OF, UH-LISTEN...

Y'KNOW, I SEE YOU HERE ALMOST EVERY DAY, AND I...

HEY, I'M SURE YOU'RE A LOVELY GIRL...

AND I KNOW YOU'RE JUST TRYING TO BE FRIENDLY...

BUT I CAME HERE TO SIT QUIETLY AND READ MY BOOK.

NOW, I'LL BUY MORE COFFEE IF THAT WILL MAKE YOU HAPPY.

BUT RE, ALL I WANT.. LIKE TO DO HERE

Y'KNOW – JUST SIT.

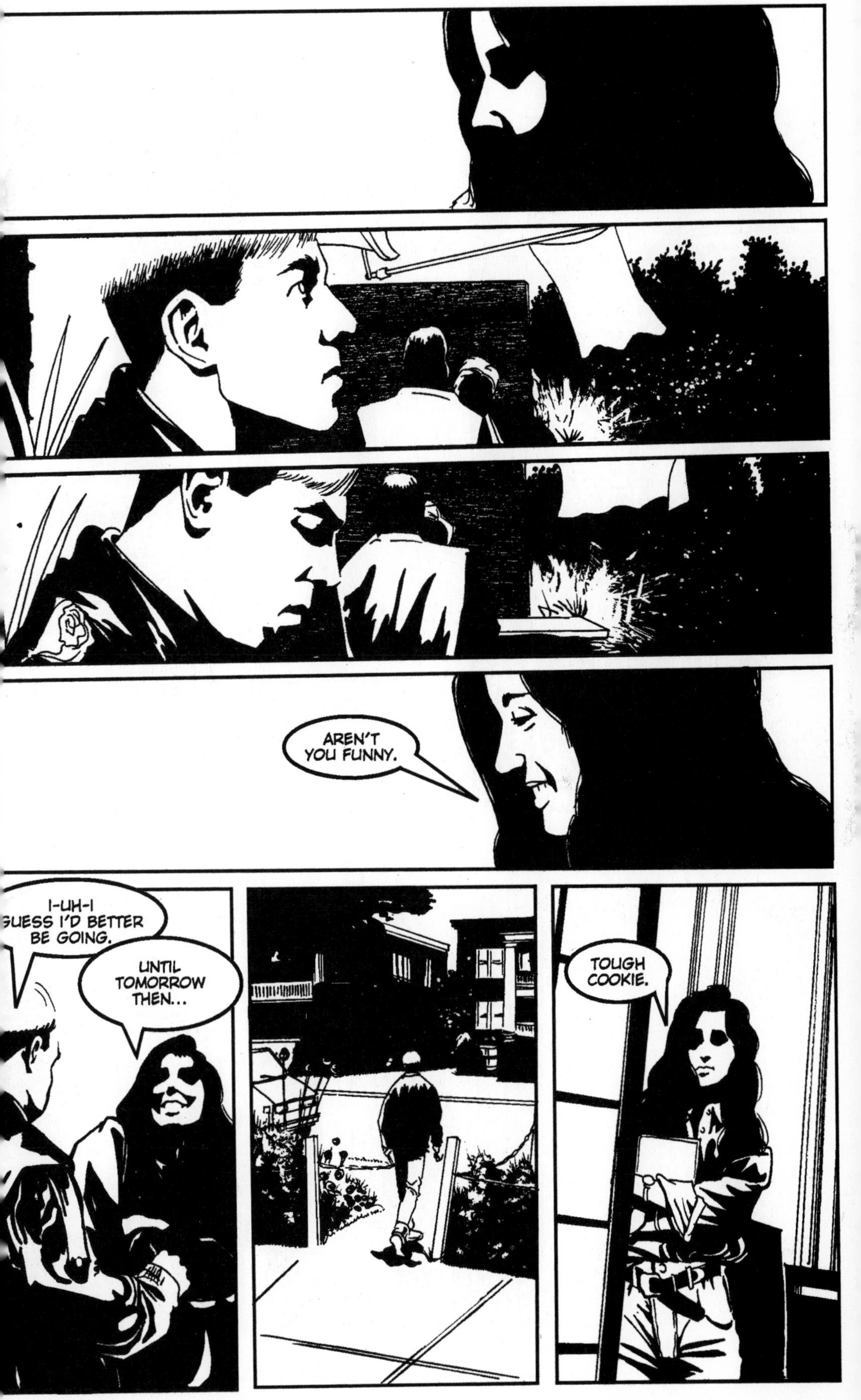
AREN'T YOU FUNNY.
I-UH-I GUESS I'D BETTER BE GOING.
UNTIL TOMORROW THEN...
TOUGH COOKIE.

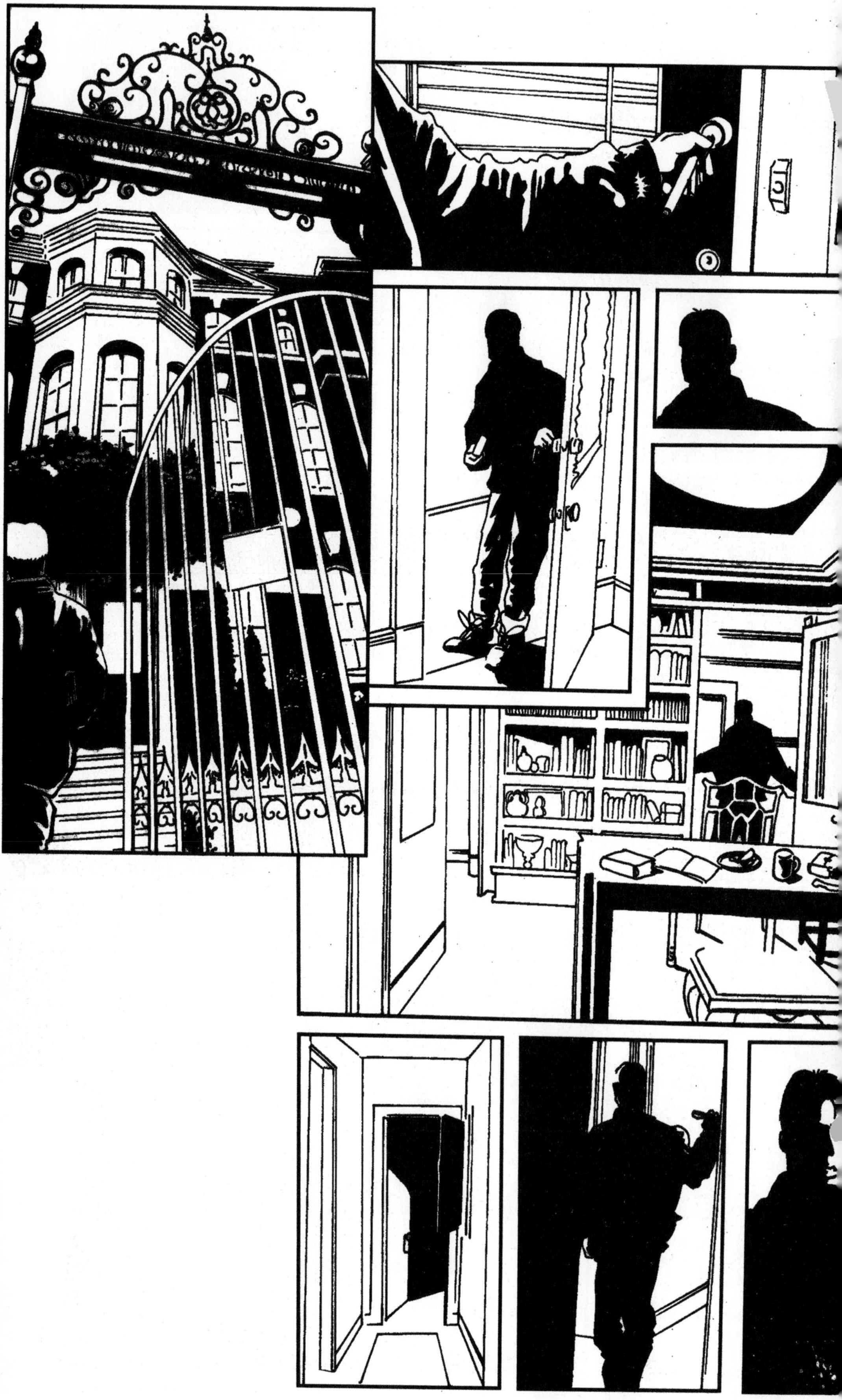

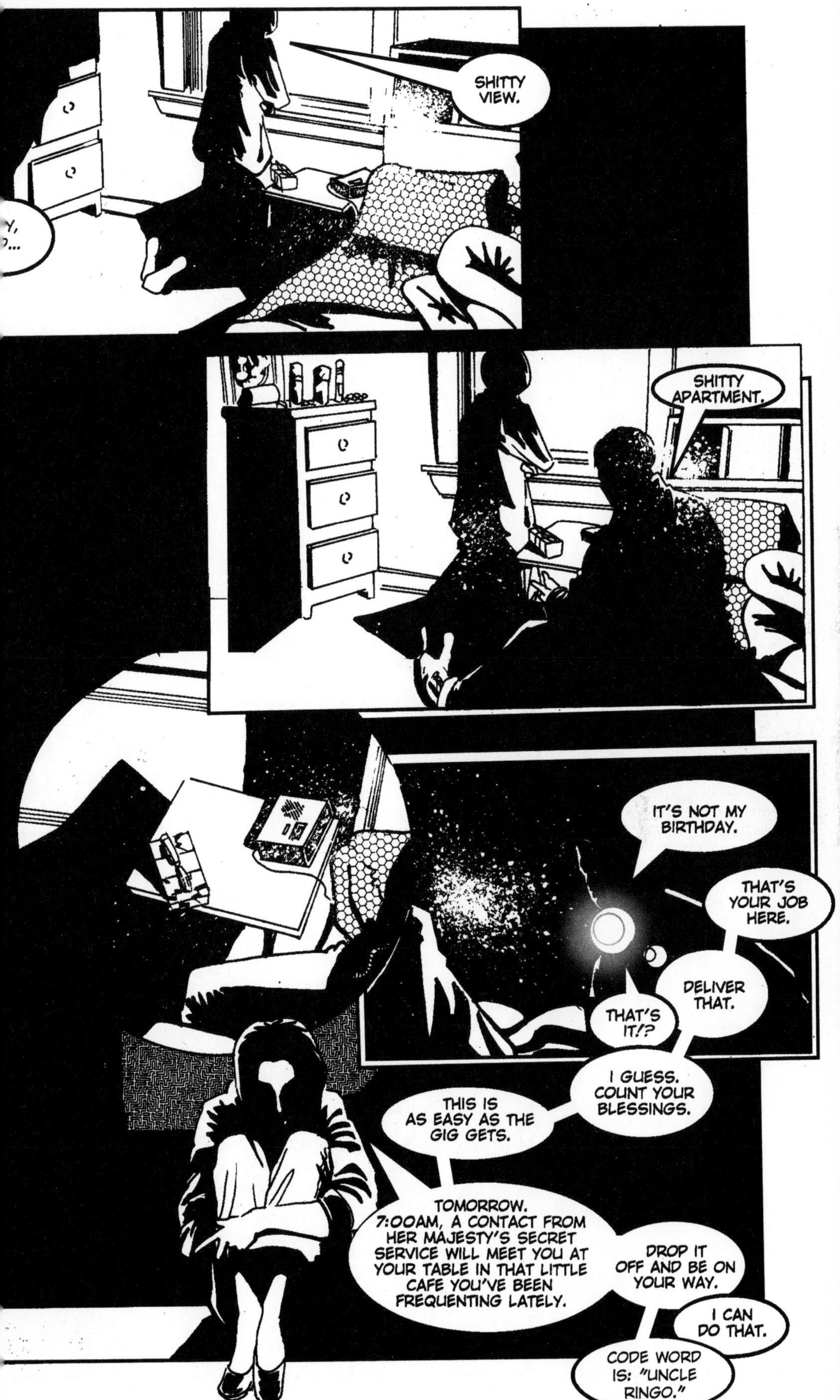
SHITTY VIEW.
SHITTY APARTMENT.
IT'S NOT MY BIRTHDAY.
THAT'S YOUR JOB HERE.
DELIVER THAT.
THAT'S IT!?
I GUESS. COUNT YOUR BLESSINGS.
THIS IS AS EASY AS THE GIG GETS.
TOMORROW. 7:00AM, A CONTACT FROM HER MAJESTY'S SECRET SERVICE WILL MEET YOU AT YOUR TABLE IN THAT LITTLE CAFE YOU'VE BEEN FREQUENTING LATELY.
DROP IT OFF AND BE ON YOUR WAY.
I CAN DO THAT.
CODE WORD IS: "UNCLE RINGO."

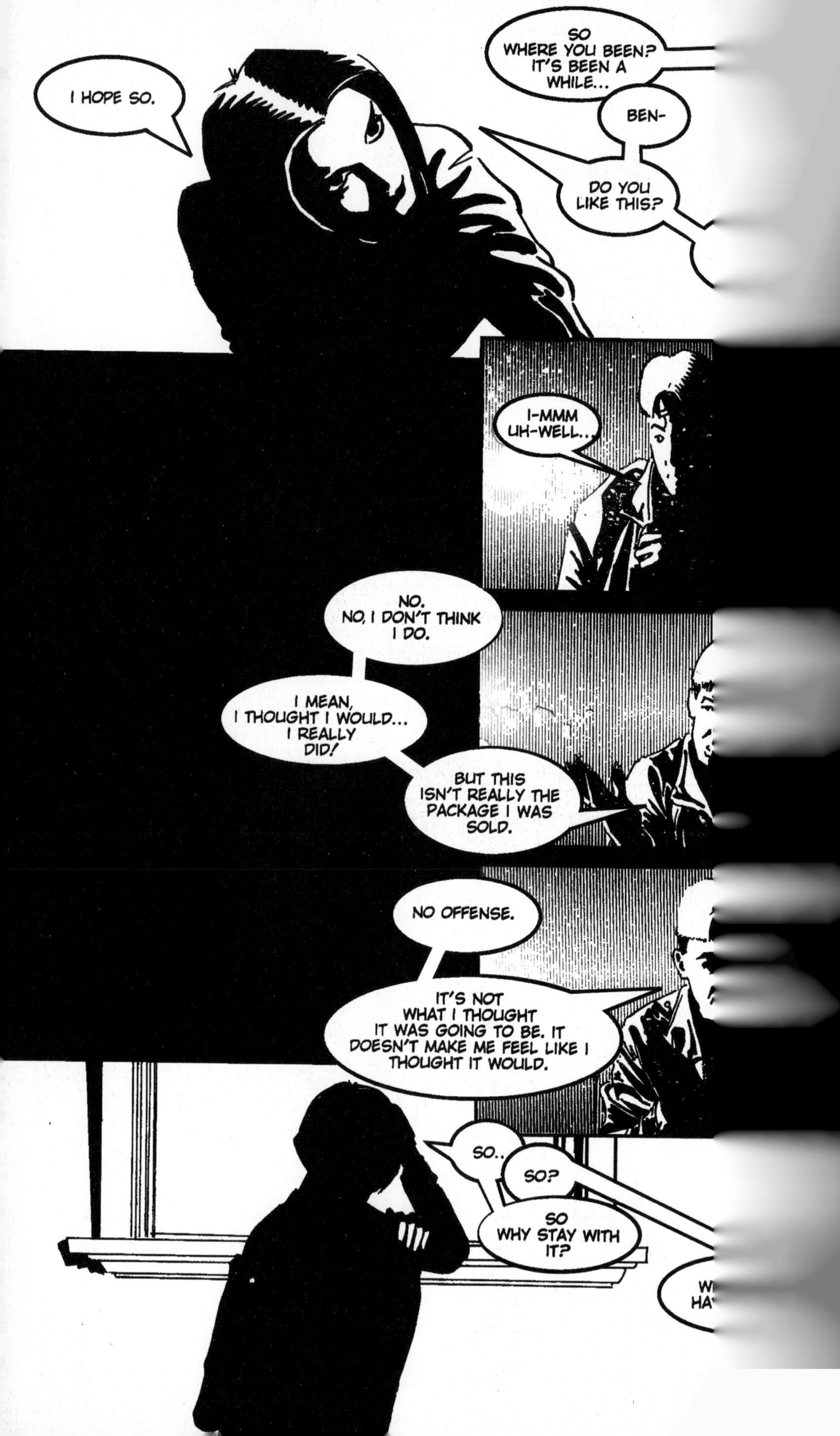
I HOPE SO.
SO WHERE YOU BEEN? IT'S BEEN A WHILE...
BEN-
DO YOU LIKE THIS?
I-MMM UH-WELL...
NO. NO, I DON'T THINK I DO.
I MEAN, I THOUGHT I WOULD... I REALLY DID!
BUT THIS ISN'T REALLY THE PACKAGE I WAS SOLD.
NO OFFENSE.
IT'S NOT WHAT I THOUGHT IT WAS GOING TO BE. IT DOESN'T MAKE ME FEEL LIKE I THOUGHT IT WOULD.
SO...
SO?
SO WHY STAY WITH IT?

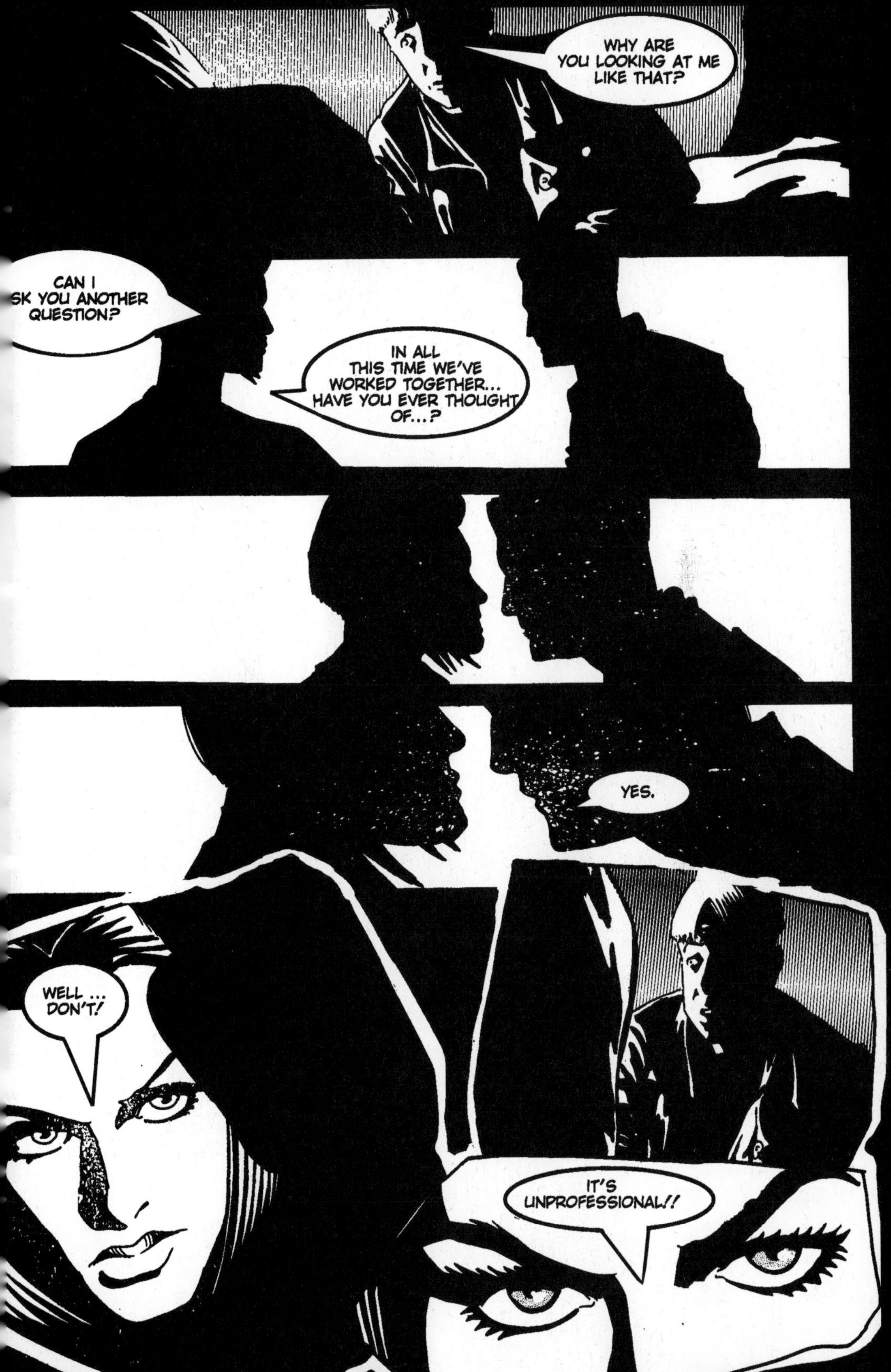
WHY ARE YOU LOOKING AT ME LIKE THAT?
CAN I SK YOU ANOTHER QUESTION?
IN ALL THIS TIME WE'VE WORKED TOGETHER... HAVE YOU EVER THOUGHT OF...?
YES.
WELL ... DON'T!
IT'S UNPROFESSIONAL!!

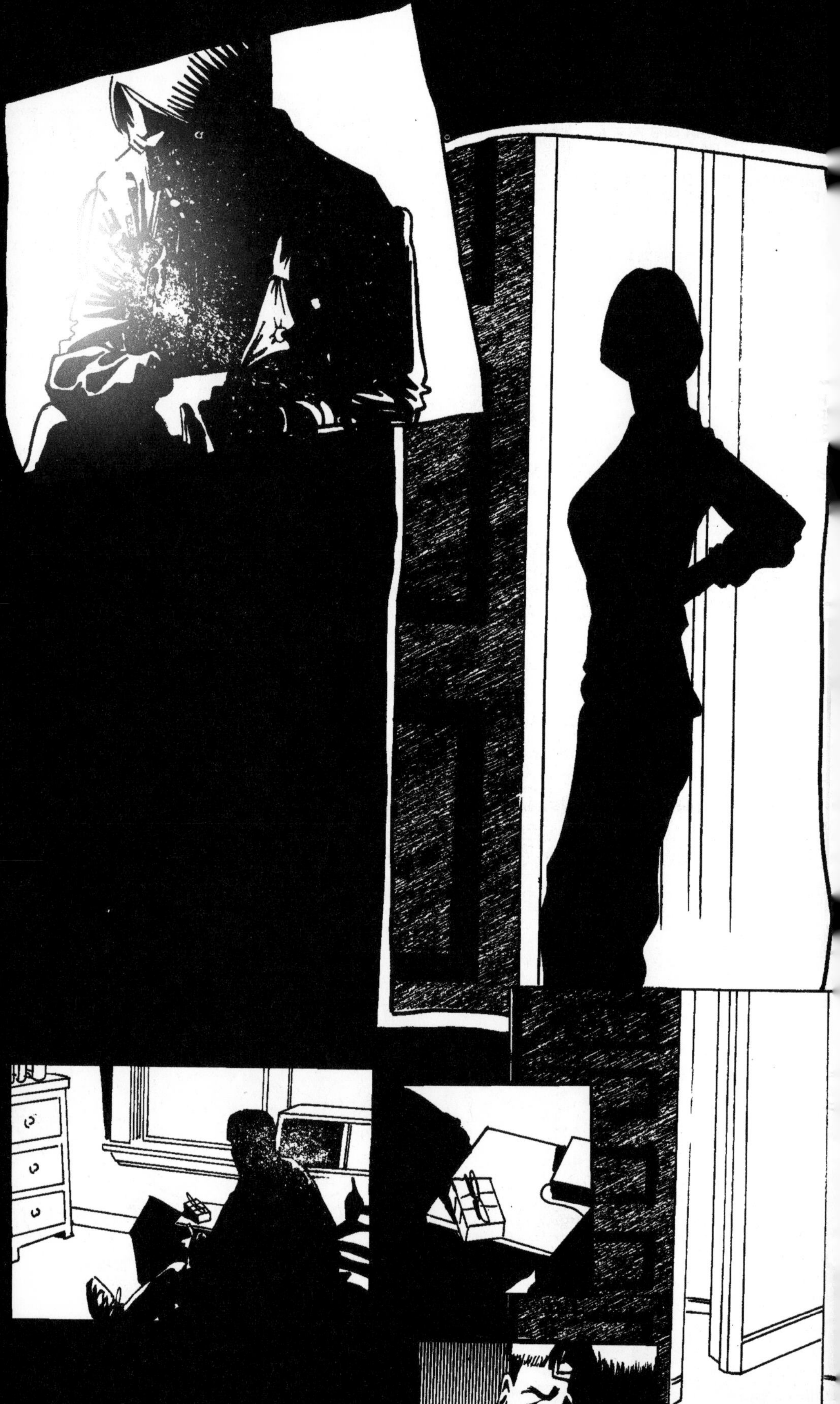

WHATEVER!

AT LEAST SHE TOOK MY MIND OFF MY HELLISH LIFE FOR A DAY.

ANYWAY, I COULDN'T WAIT TO DO THE DROP-OFF AND GET TO THE NEXT ASSIGNMENT.

BUT MAYBE I JUST NEEDED A BREAK, I THOUGHT.

TIME OFF, TIME TO LET STUFF SINK IN.

I WONDERED HOW YOU WENT ABOUT GETTING THAT TIME OFF.

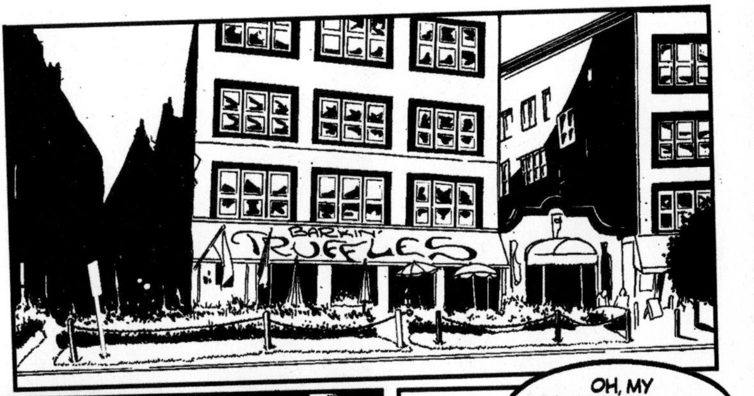
BARKIN' TRUFFLES

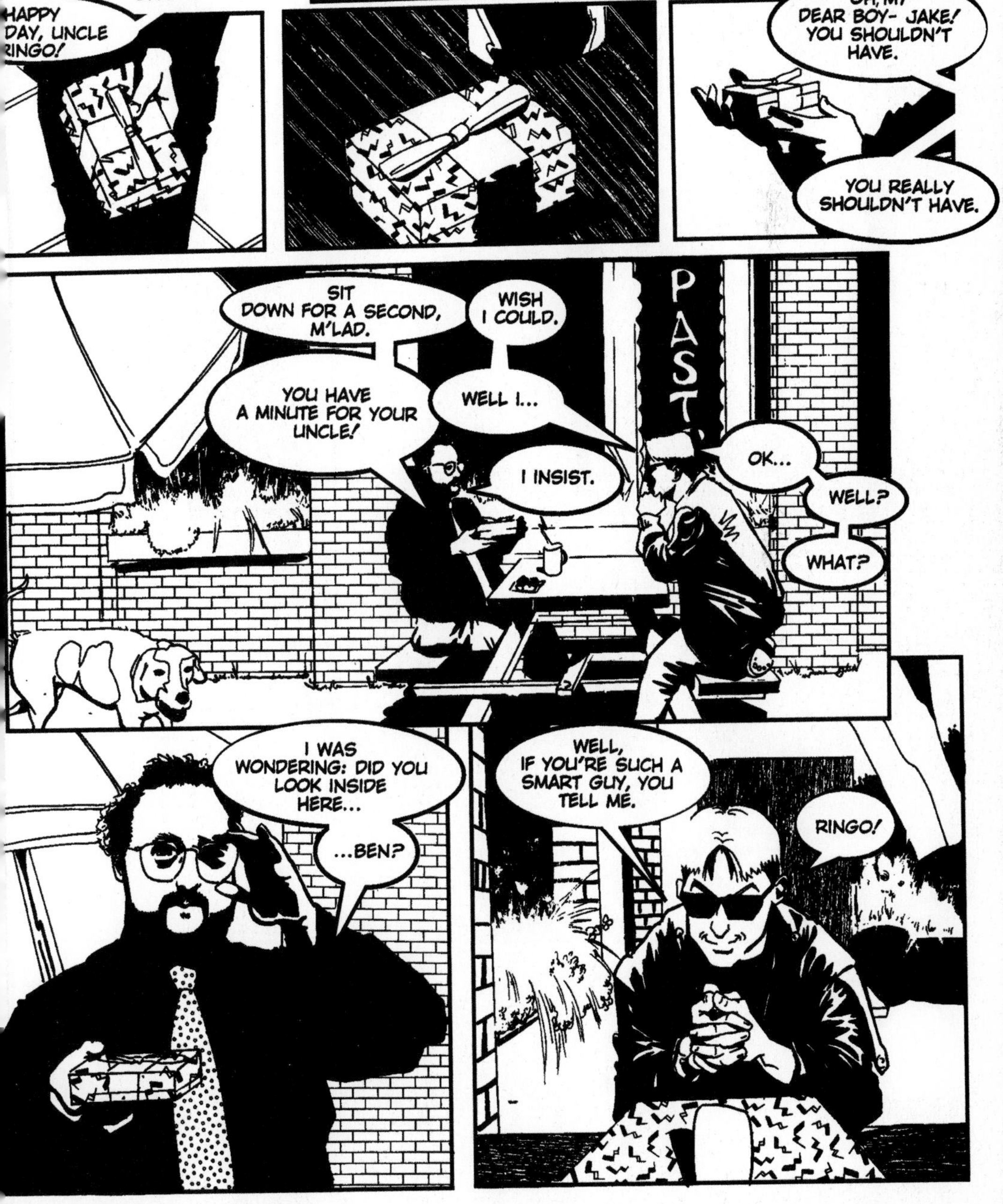
HAPPY DAY, UNCLE RINGO!
OH, MY DEAR BOY- JAKE! YOU SHOULDN'T HAVE.
YOU REALLY SHOULDN'T HAVE.
SIT DOWN FOR A SECOND, M'LAD.
WISH I COULD.
YOU HAVE A MINUTE FOR YOUR UNCLE!
WELL I...
I INSIST.
OK...
WELL?
WHAT?
PAST
I WAS WONDERING: DID YOU LOOK INSIDE HERE...
...BEN?
WELL, IF YOU'RE SUCH A SMART GUY, YOU TELL ME.
RINGO!

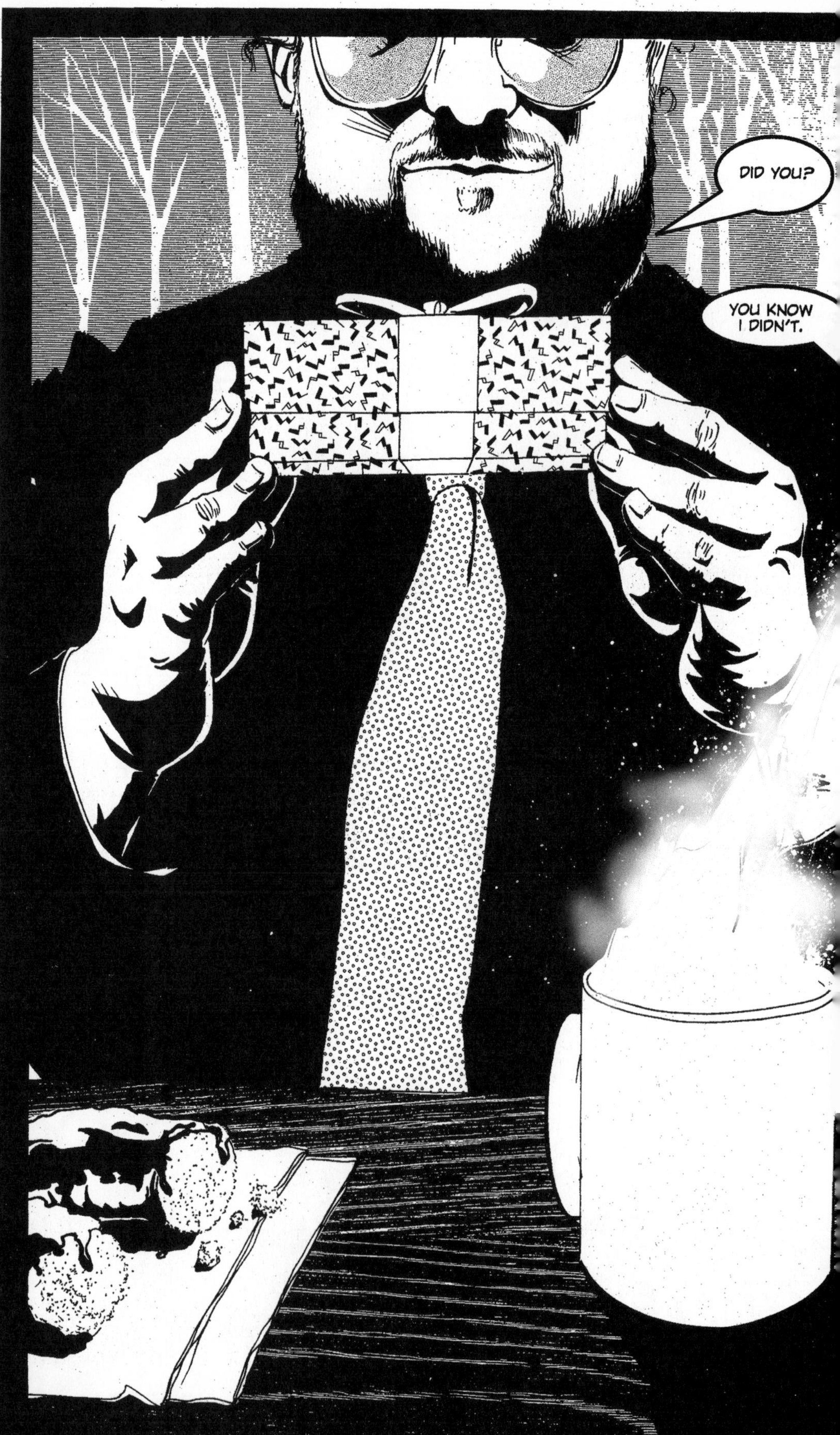
DID YOU?
YOU KNOW I DIDN'T.

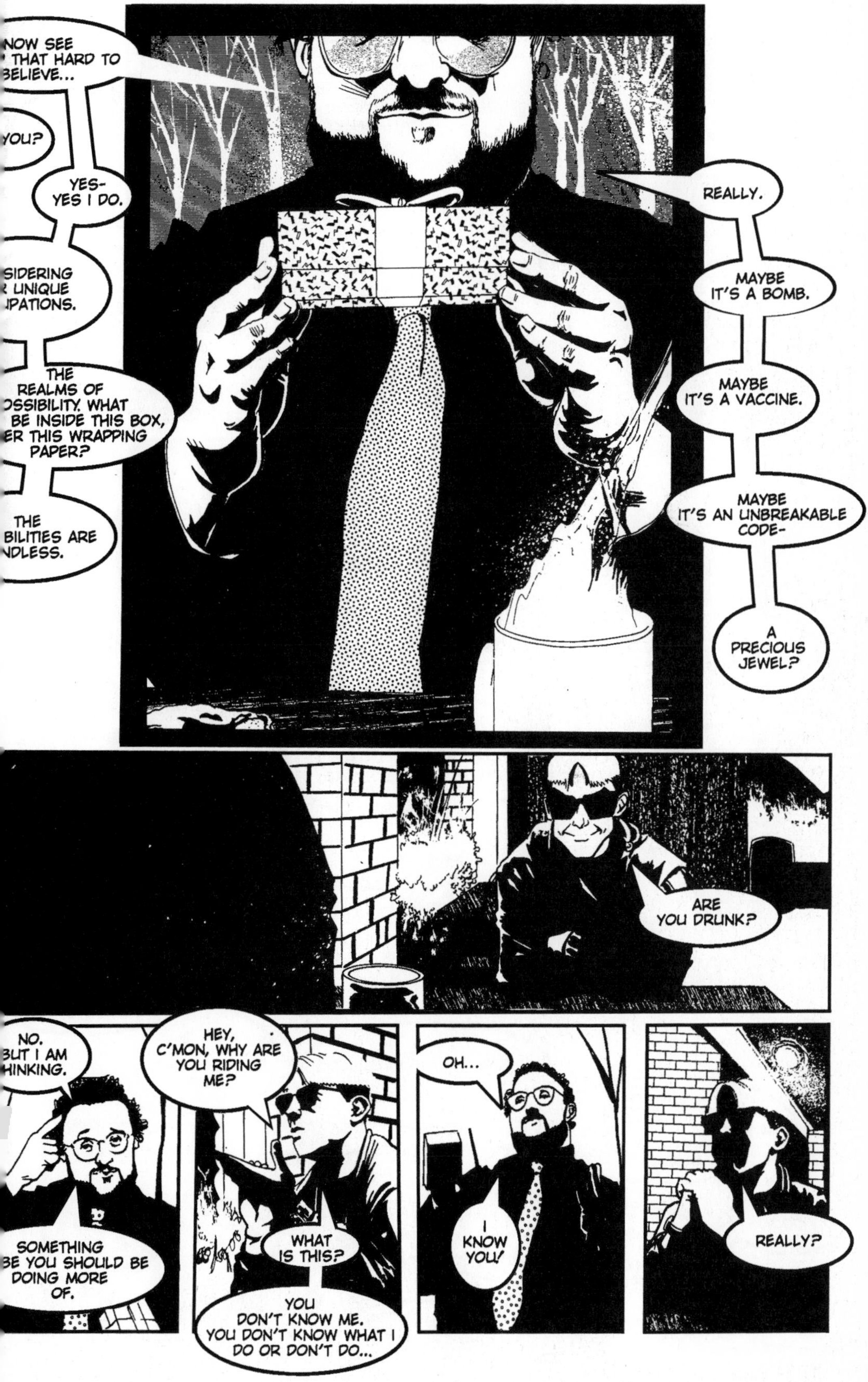

NOW SEE ' THAT HARD TO BELIEVE...
YOU?
YES- YES I DO.
SIDERING R UNIQUE UPATIONS.
THE REALMS OF OSSIBILITY. WHAT BE INSIDE THIS BOX, ER THIS WRAPPING PAPER?
THE BILITIES ARE NDLESS.
REALLY.
MAYBE IT'S A BOMB.
MAYBE IT'S A VACCINE.
MAYBE IT'S AN UNBREAKABLE CODE-
A PRECIOUS JEWEL?
ARE YOU DRUNK?
NO. BUT I AM HINKING.
SOMETHING BE YOU SHOULD BE DOING MORE OF.
HEY, C'MON, WHY ARE YOU RIDING ME?
WHAT IS THIS?
YOU DON'T KNOW ME. YOU DON'T KNOW WHAT I DO OR DON'T DO...
OH...
I KNOW YOU!
REALLY?

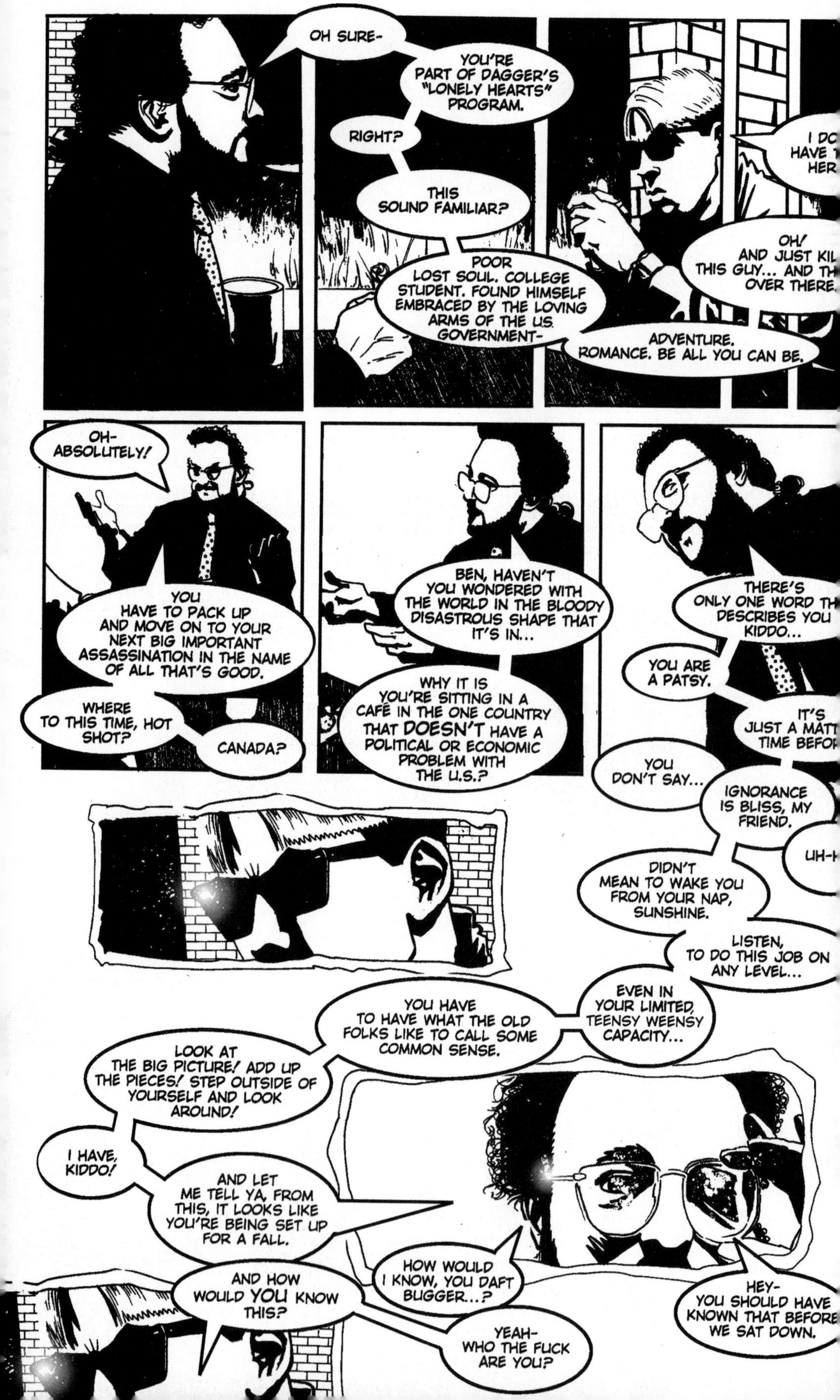
OH SURE-
YOU'RE PART OF DAGGER'S "LONELY HEARTS" PROGRAM.
RIGHT?
THIS SOUND FAMILIAR?
POOR LOST SOUL. COLLEGE STUDENT. FOUND HIMSELF EMBRACED BY THE LOVING ARMS OF THE U.S. GOVERNMENT-
ADVENTURE. ROMANCE. BE ALL YOU CAN BE.
I DO HAVE HER
OH! AND JUST KIL THIS GUY... AND TH OVER THERE.
OH- ABSOLUTELY!
YOU HAVE TO PACK UP AND MOVE ON TO YOUR NEXT BIG IMPORTANT ASSASSINATION IN THE NAME OF ALL THAT'S GOOD.
WHERE TO THIS TIME, HOT SHOT?
CANADA?
BEN, HAVEN'T YOU WONDERED WITH THE WORLD IN THE BLOODY DISASTROUS SHAPE THAT IT'S IN...
WHY IT IS YOU'RE SITTING IN A CAFÉ IN THE ONE COUNTRY THAT DOESN'T HAVE A POLITICAL OR ECONOMIC PROBLEM WITH THE U.S.?
THERE'S ONLY ONE WORD TH DESCRIBES YOU KIDDO...
YOU ARE A PATSY.
IT'S JUST A MATT TIME BEFOR
YOU DON'T SAY...
IGNORANCE IS BLISS, MY FRIEND.
UH-H
DIDN'T MEAN TO WAKE YOU FROM YOUR NAP, SUNSHINE.
LISTEN, TO DO THIS JOB ON ANY LEVEL...
EVEN IN YOUR LIMITED, TEENSY WEENSY CAPACITY...
YOU HAVE TO HAVE WHAT THE OLD FOLKS LIKE TO CALL SOME COMMON SENSE.
LOOK AT THE BIG PICTURE! ADD UP THE PIECES! STEP OUTSIDE OF YOURSELF AND LOOK AROUND!
I HAVE, KIDDO!
AND LET ME TELL YA, FROM THIS, IT LOOKS LIKE YOU'RE BEING SET UP FOR A FALL.
AND HOW WOULD YOU KNOW THIS?
HOW WOULD I KNOW, YOU DAFT BUGGER...?
YEAH- WHO THE FUCK ARE YOU?
HEY- YOU SHOULD HAVE KNOWN THAT BEFORE WE SAT DOWN.

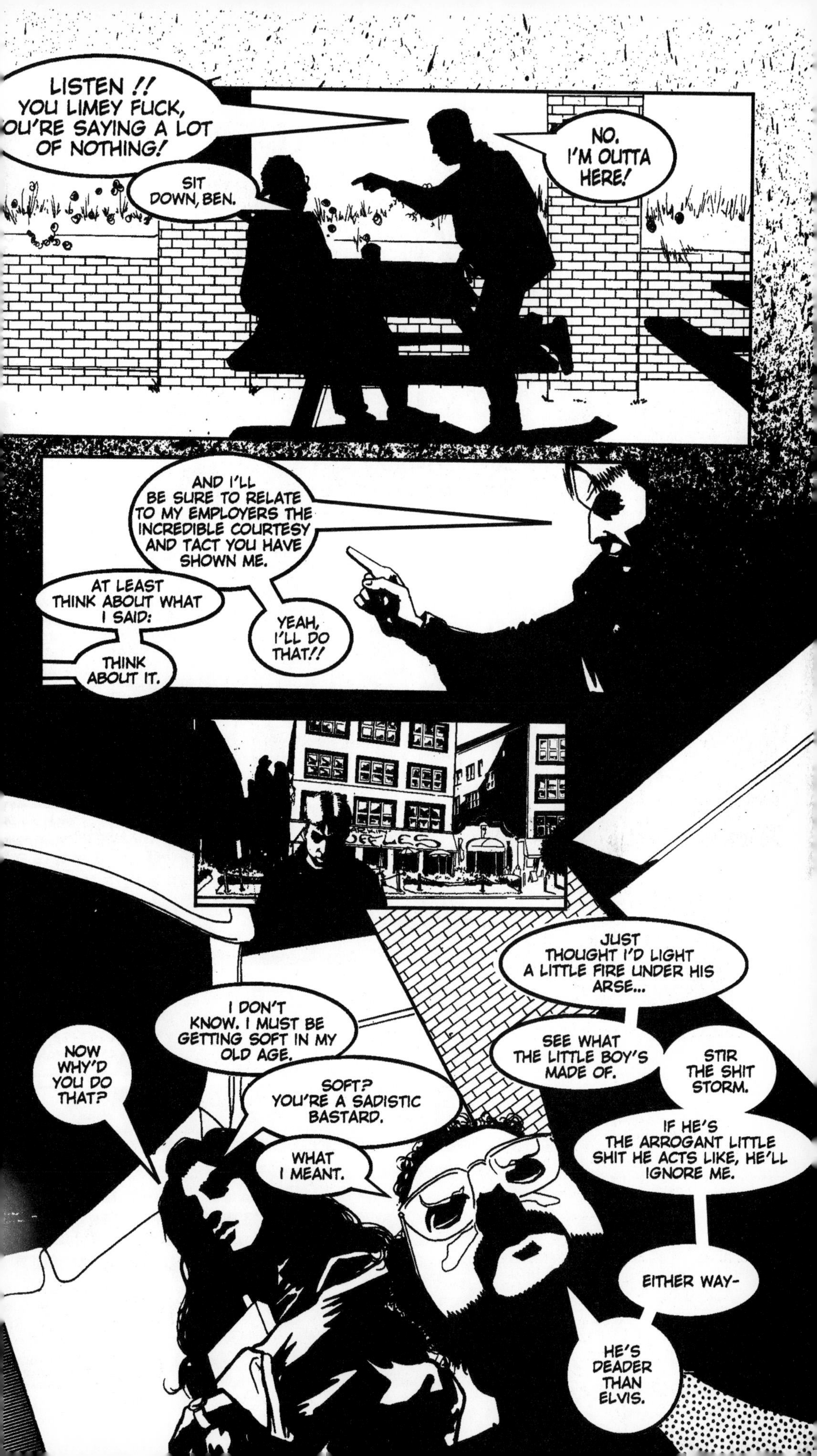
LISTEN !! YOU LIMEY FUCK, OU'RE SAYING A LOT OF NOTHING!
SIT DOWN, BEN.
NO. I'M OUTTA HERE!
AND I'LL BE SURE TO RELATE TO MY EMPLOYERS THE INCREDIBLE COURTESY AND TACT YOU HAVE SHOWN ME.
AT LEAST THINK ABOUT WHAT I SAID:
THINK ABOUT IT.
YEAH, I'LL DO THAT!!
NOW WHY'D YOU DO THAT?
I DON'T KNOW. I MUST BE GETTING SOFT IN MY OLD AGE.
SOFT? YOU'RE A SADISTIC BASTARD.
WHAT I MEANT.
JUST THOUGHT I'D LIGHT A LITTLE FIRE UNDER HIS ARSE...
SEE WHAT THE LITTLE BOY'S MADE OF.
STIR THE SHIT STORM.
IF HE'S THE ARROGANT LITTLE SHIT HE ACTS LIKE, HE'LL IGNORE ME.
EITHER WAY-
HE'S DEADER THAN ELVIS.

FUCK HIM.

"FUCK HIM!"
I THOUGHT.

FUC
FUC
AND
THIS W
SCREWE
WORLD OF SEC
LIES AND
STAB

F

HE S
W
P

I H
HEARING
I HAT
BECAUSE IT
MY WORST
REA

I WAS
OF
VAGUE
MY LIFE WA
I WAS SIC
BEING IN
DARK ALONE
MY THOUG

IT WAS WAY PAS
TIME FOR ME TO
BACK IN CON
OF MY

I REALLY D
CARE IF THAT "RIN
GUY WAS FUL
SHIT OR N

...AND I D
REALLY CARE
D.D. WAS L

THERE WERE SYMP
THAT I WAS LIVIN
A HOUSE OF CA
AND I WANTED

AND I COULD GET OUT. I COULD.
JUST DISAPPEAR. PLAY
ALONG JUST A LITTLE WHILE
LONGER- THEN I WAS GONE.
AND I MEAN GONE.

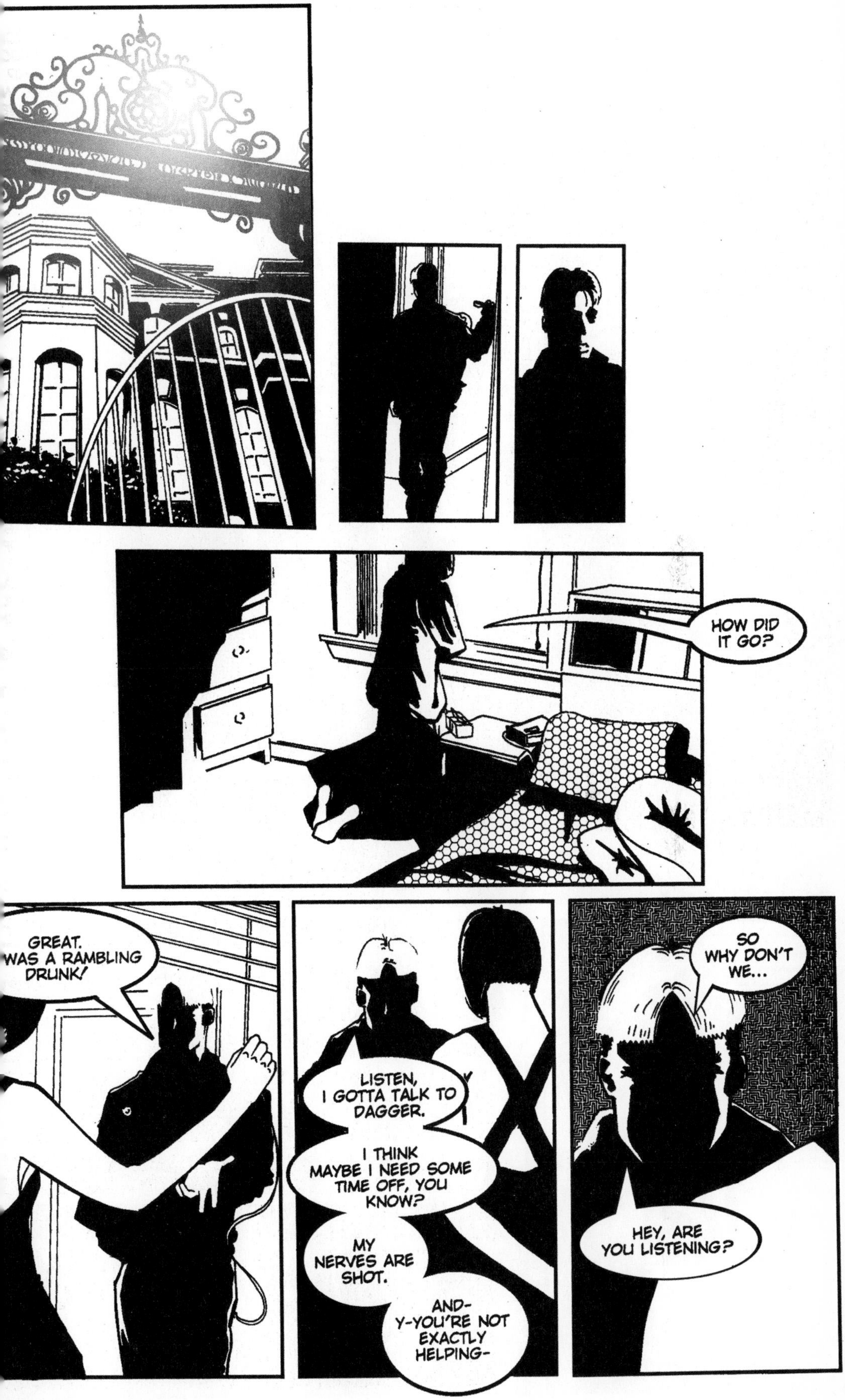
HOW DID IT GO?
GREAT. WAS A RAMBLING DRUNK!
LISTEN, I GOTTA TALK TO DAGGER.
I THINK MAYBE I NEED SOME TIME OFF, YOU KNOW?
MY NERVES ARE SHOT.
AND- Y-YOU'RE NOT EXACTLY HELPING-
SO WHY DON'T WE...
HEY, ARE YOU LISTENING?

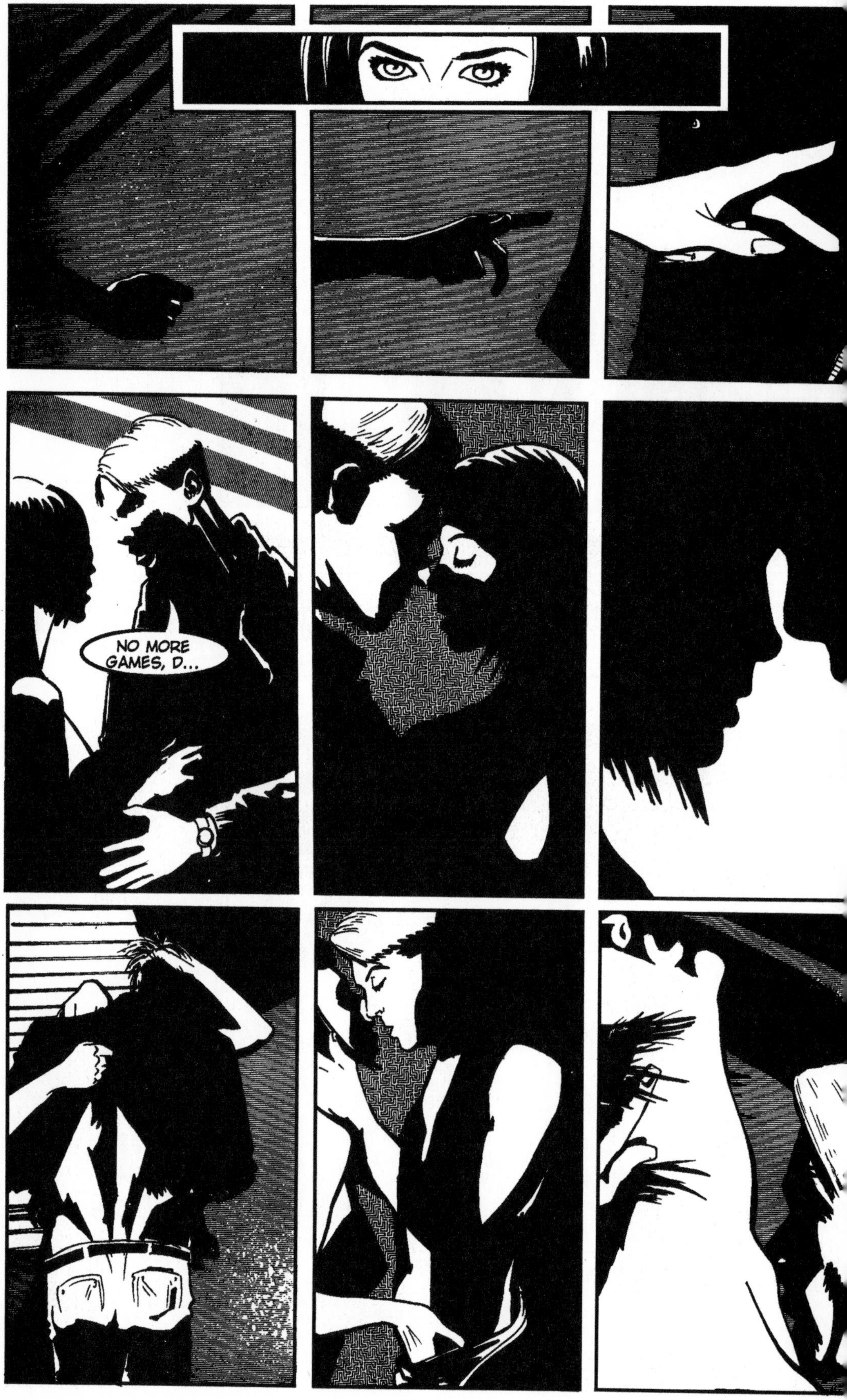
NO MORE GAMES, D...

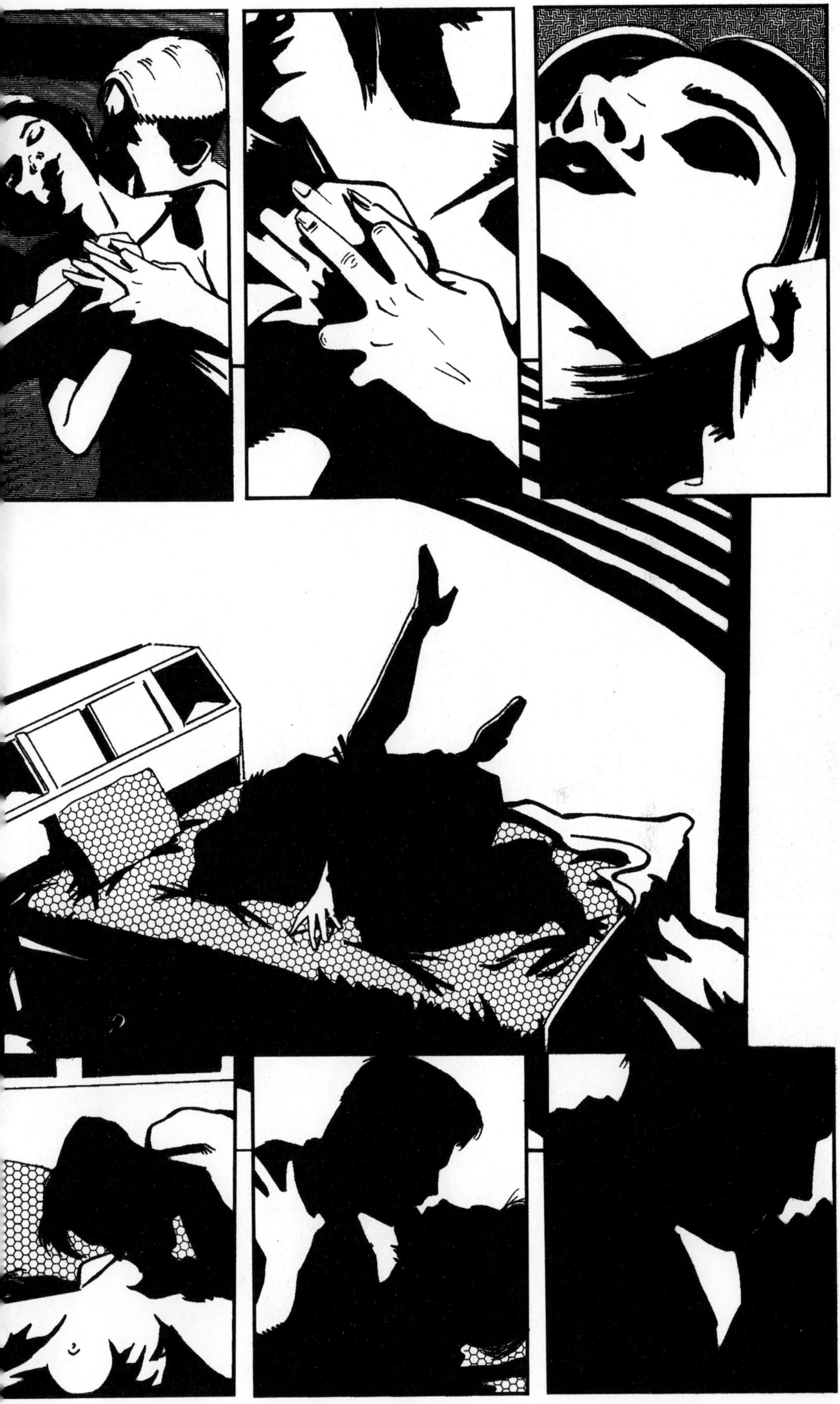

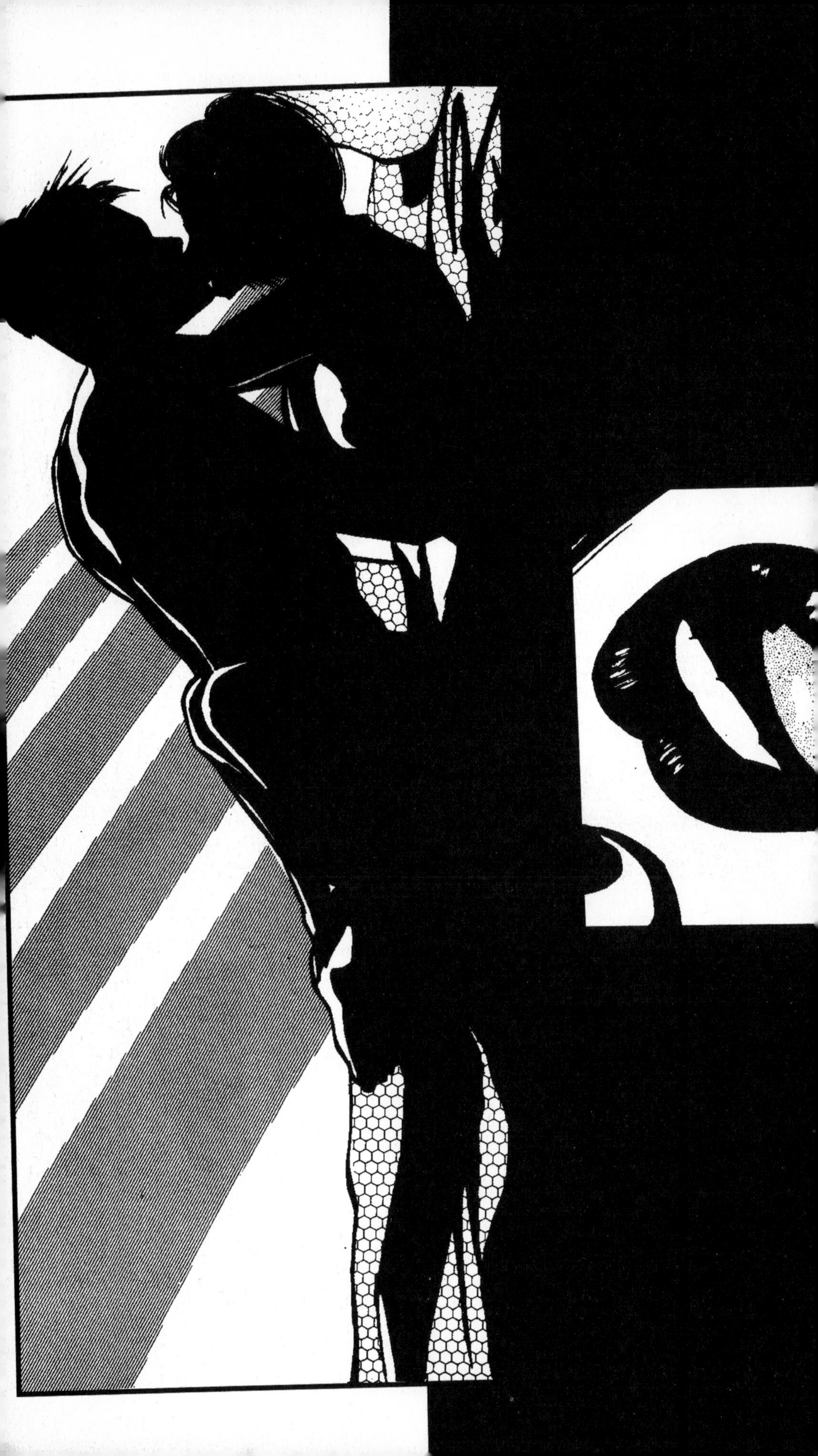

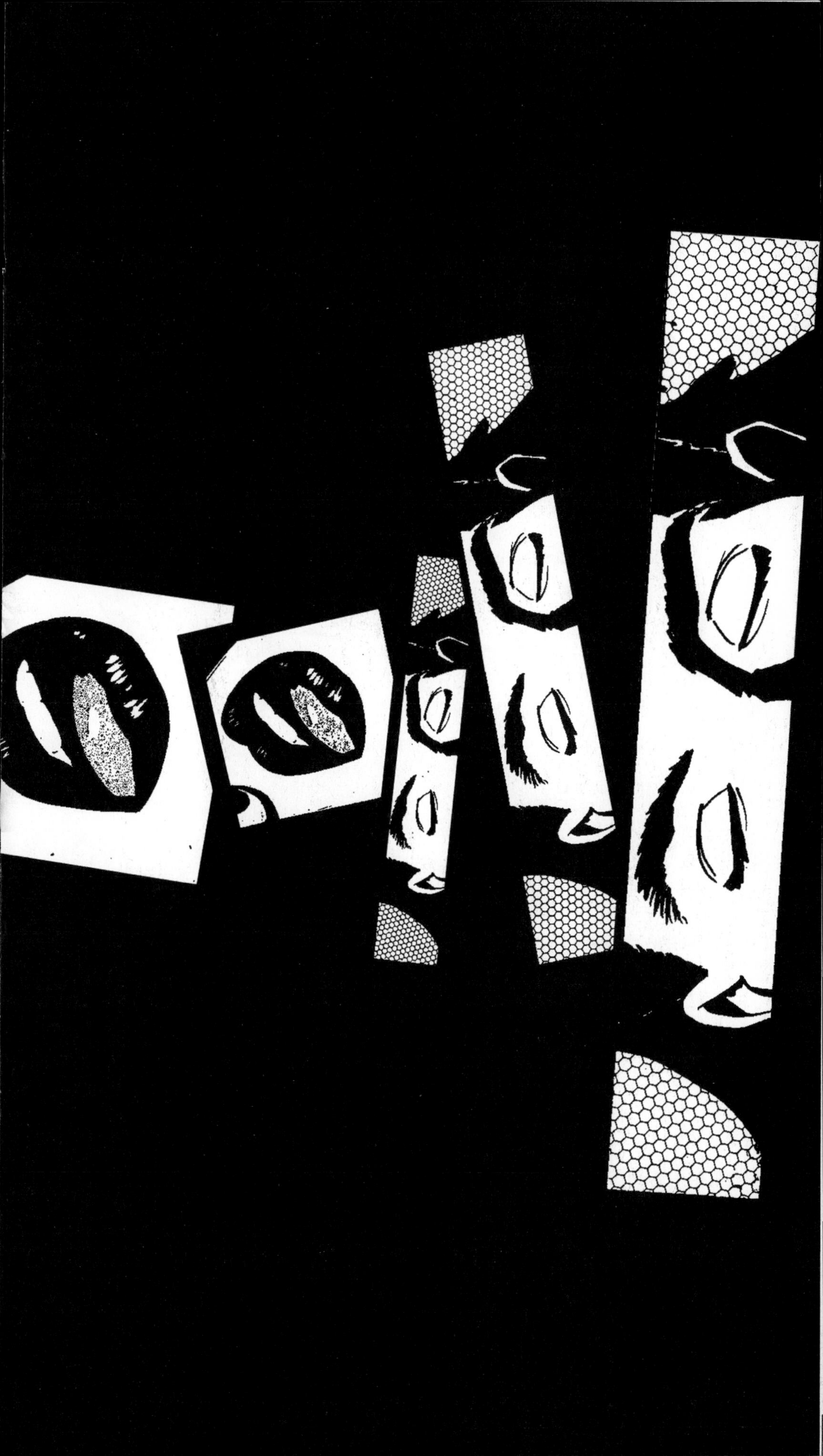

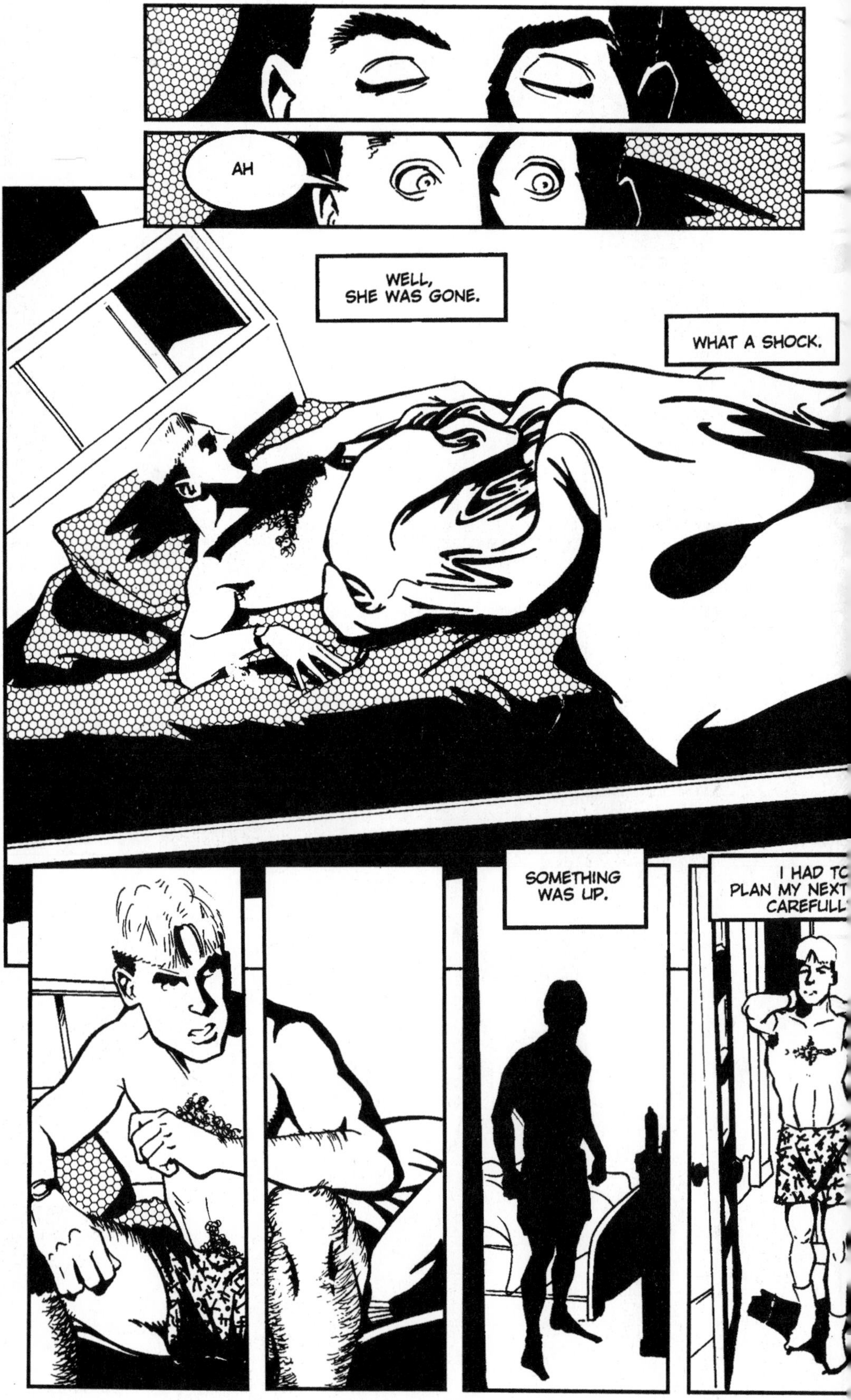
AH
WELL, SHE WAS GONE.
WHAT A SHOCK.
SOMETHING WAS UP.
I HAD T
PLAN MY NEXT
CAREFULL

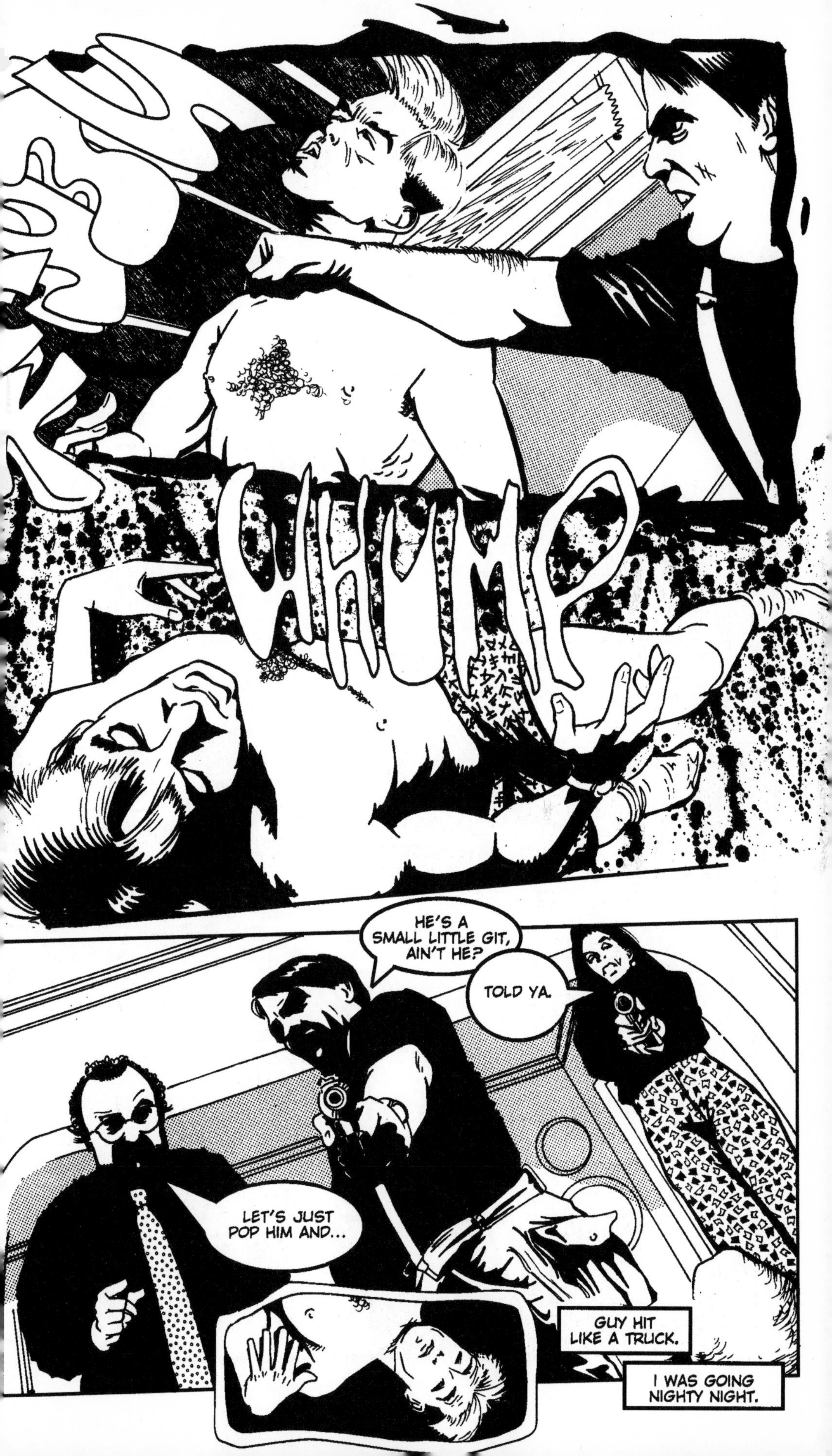
WHUMP
HE'S A SMALL LITTLE GIT, AIN'T HE?
TOLD YA.
LET'S JUST POP HIM AND...
GUY HIT LIKE A TRUCK.
I WAS GOING NIGHTY NIGHT.

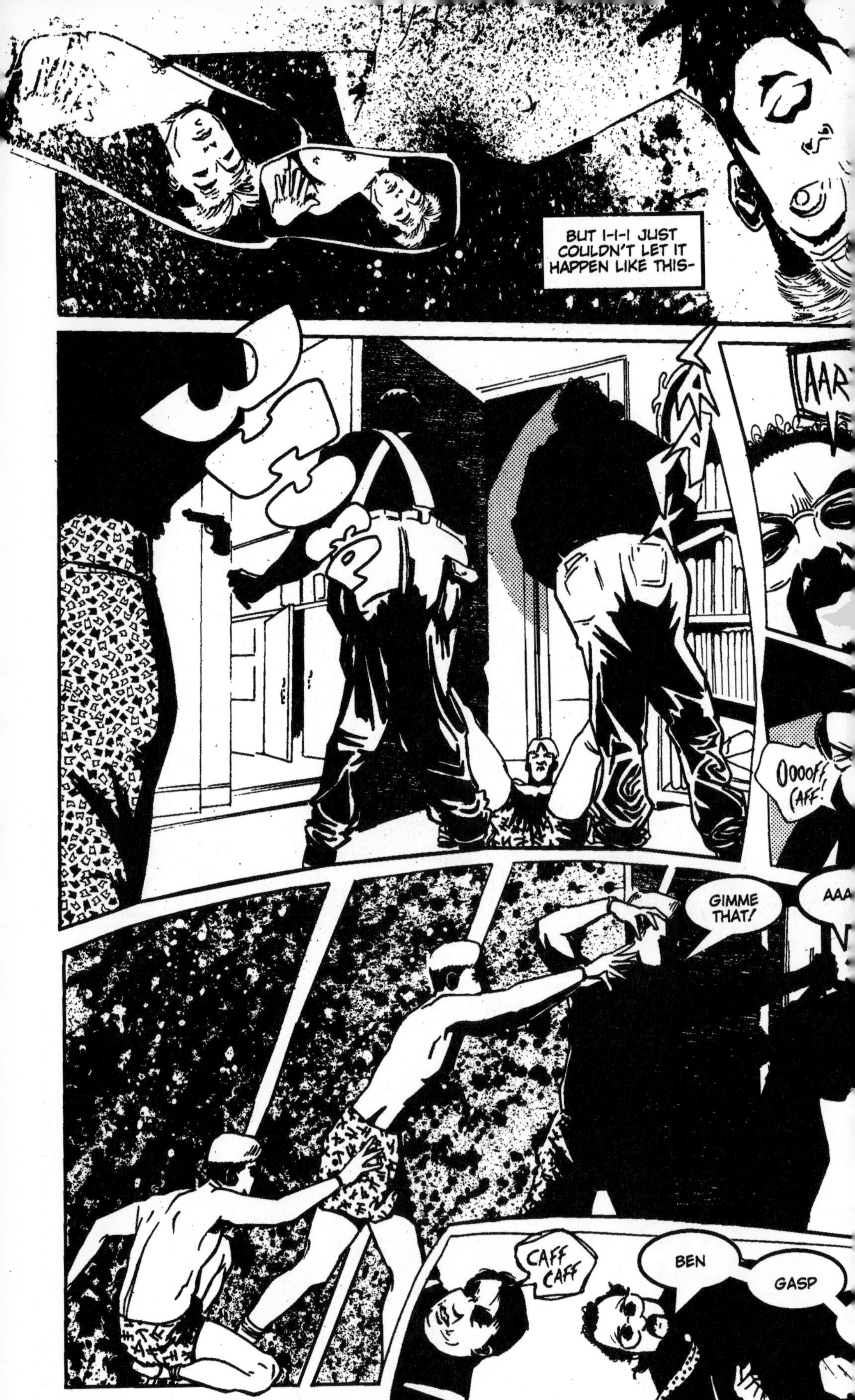

BUT I-I-I JUST COULDN'T LET IT HAPPEN LIKE THIS-
AAR
OOOOFF CAFF!
GIMME THAT!
AAA
CAFF CAFF
BEN
GASP

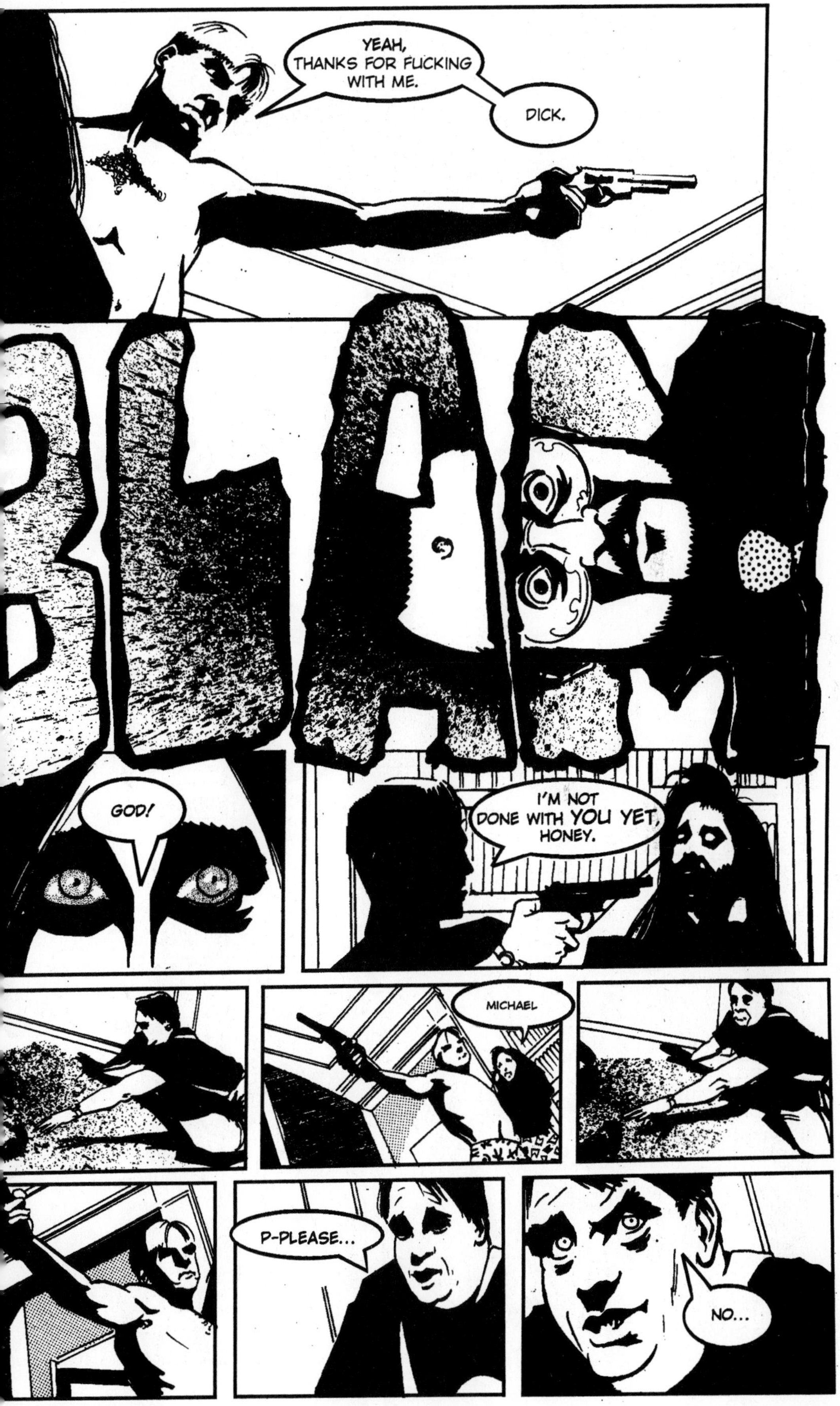
YEAH, THANKS FOR FUCKING WITH ME.
DICK.
BLAM
GOD!
I'M NOT DONE WITH YOU YET, HONEY.
MICHAEL
P-PLEASE...
NO...

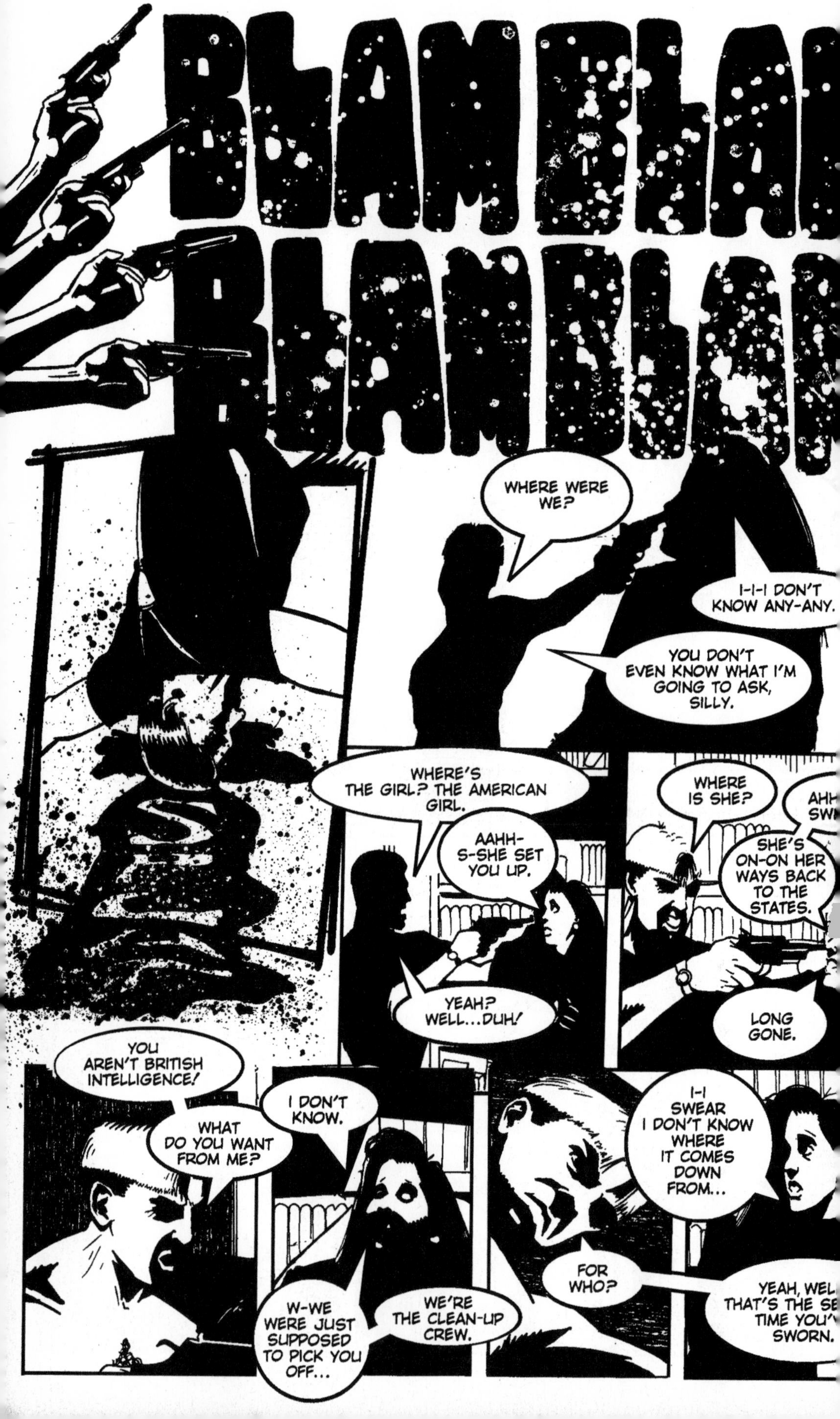
BLAM BLA
BLAM BLA
WHERE WERE WE?
I-I-I DON'T KNOW ANY-ANY.
YOU DON'T EVEN KNOW WHAT I'M GOING TO ASK, SILLY.
WHERE'S THE GIRL? THE AMERICAN GIRL.
AAHH-S-SHE SET YOU UP.
YEAH? WELL...DUH!
WHERE IS SHE?
AHH
SHE'S ON-ON HER WAYS BACK TO THE STATES.
LONG GONE.
YOU AREN'T BRITISH INTELLIGENCE!
WHAT DO YOU WANT FROM ME?
I DON'T KNOW.
W-WE WERE JUST SUPPOSED TO PICK YOU OFF...
WE'RE THE CLEAN-UP CREW.
I-I SWEAR I DON'T KNOW WHERE IT COMES DOWN FROM...
FOR WHO?
YEAH, WEL
THAT'S THE SE
TIME YOU'
SWORN.

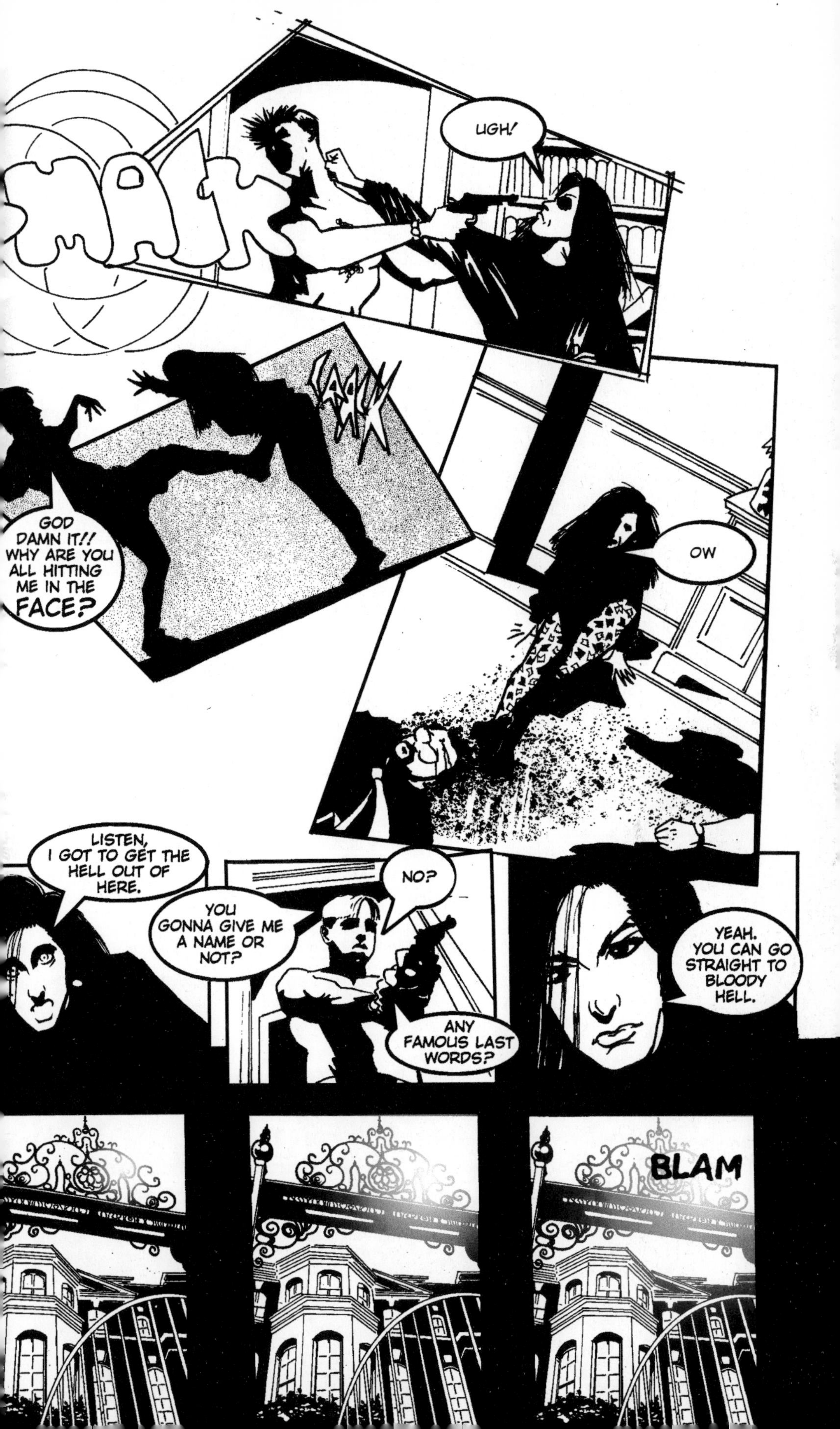

UGH!
GOD DAMN IT!! WHY ARE YOU ALL HITTING ME IN THE FACE?
OW
LISTEN, I GOT TO GET THE HELL OUT OF HERE.
YOU GONNA GIVE ME A NAME OR NOT?
NO?
ANY FAMOUS LAST WORDS?
YEAH. YOU CAN GO STRAIGHT TO BLOODY HELL.
BLAM

I WASN'T GOING TO GET ANY ANSWERS FROM HER, BUT, REALLY, I ALREADY KNEW THE ANSWERS.
I'M NOT AN IDIOT. I'M A STUBBORN PIG-HEAD FUCKER, BUT I'M NOT AN IDIOT.

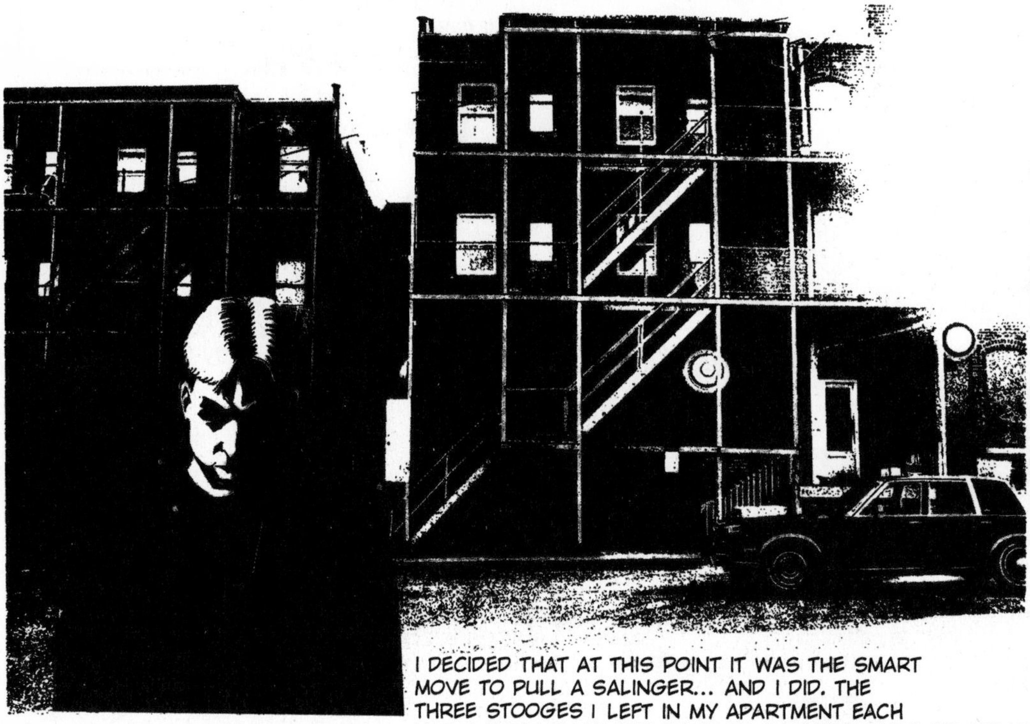

I DECIDED THAT AT THIS POINT IT WAS THE SMART MOVE TO PULL A SALINGER... AND I DID. THE THREE STOOGES I LEFT IN MY APARTMENT EACH HAD A THICK ENVELOPE OF CASH ON THEM. WHOEVER DID HIR PAID THEM UP FRONT. BETWEEN THAT AND WHAT I HAD STASHED AWAY, BECOMING A GHOST WAS EASY.

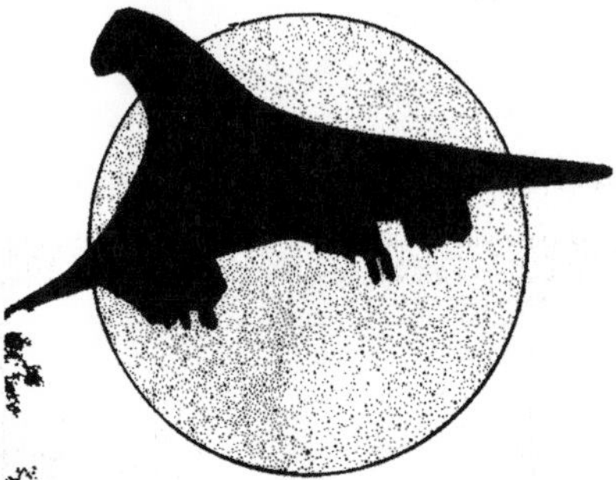

IT WAS VERY GRATIFYING TO FIND THAT I WAS AS GOOD AT THIS GAME AS I THOUGHT I WAS. I BEAT THE SYSTE

I GOT AWAY. I WON!

BUT Y'KNOW WHAT? IT WASN'T ENOUGH. NOT BY A LONG SHOT.

I LAY ON A VACATION BEACH IN MALAYSIA STARING AT THE SA
LETTING THE STING OF THIS MONUMENTAL ASS-FUCK EAT AW

FOR MONTHS I RELIVED THE HATE AND DECEIT IN MY MIND, OVER AND OVER, OVER AND OVER,

UNTIL I DRAGGED MY ASS BACK TO PROJECT FIRE.

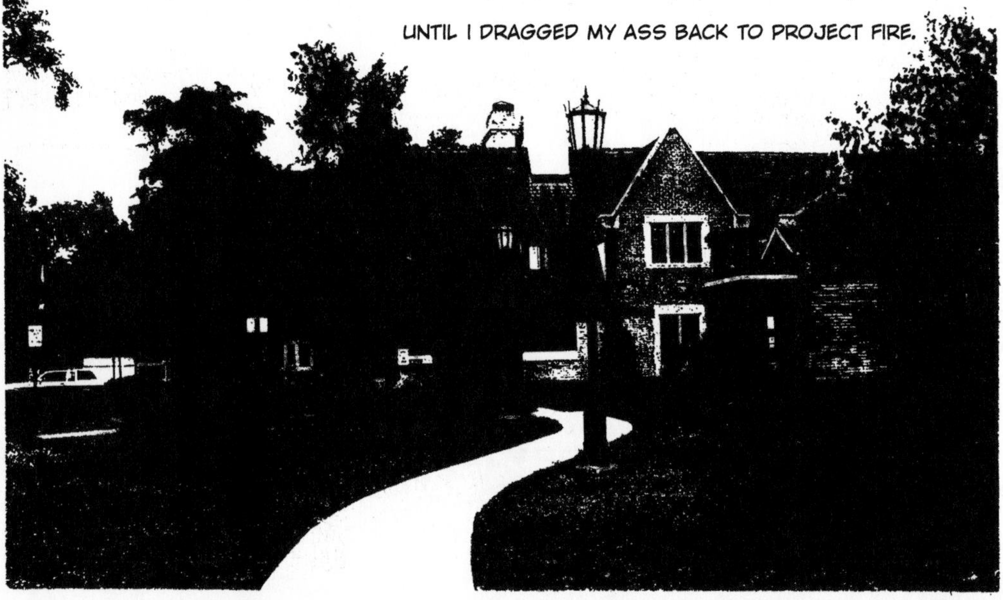

I WASN'T LOOKING FOR SOME DRAMATIC FACE-TO-FACE.

THERE WAS LITTLE TO NOTHING FOR ME TO GAIN FROM IT.

LOGICALLY SPEAKING—

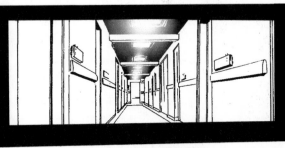

NO, I WAS DOING THIS FOR YOU.

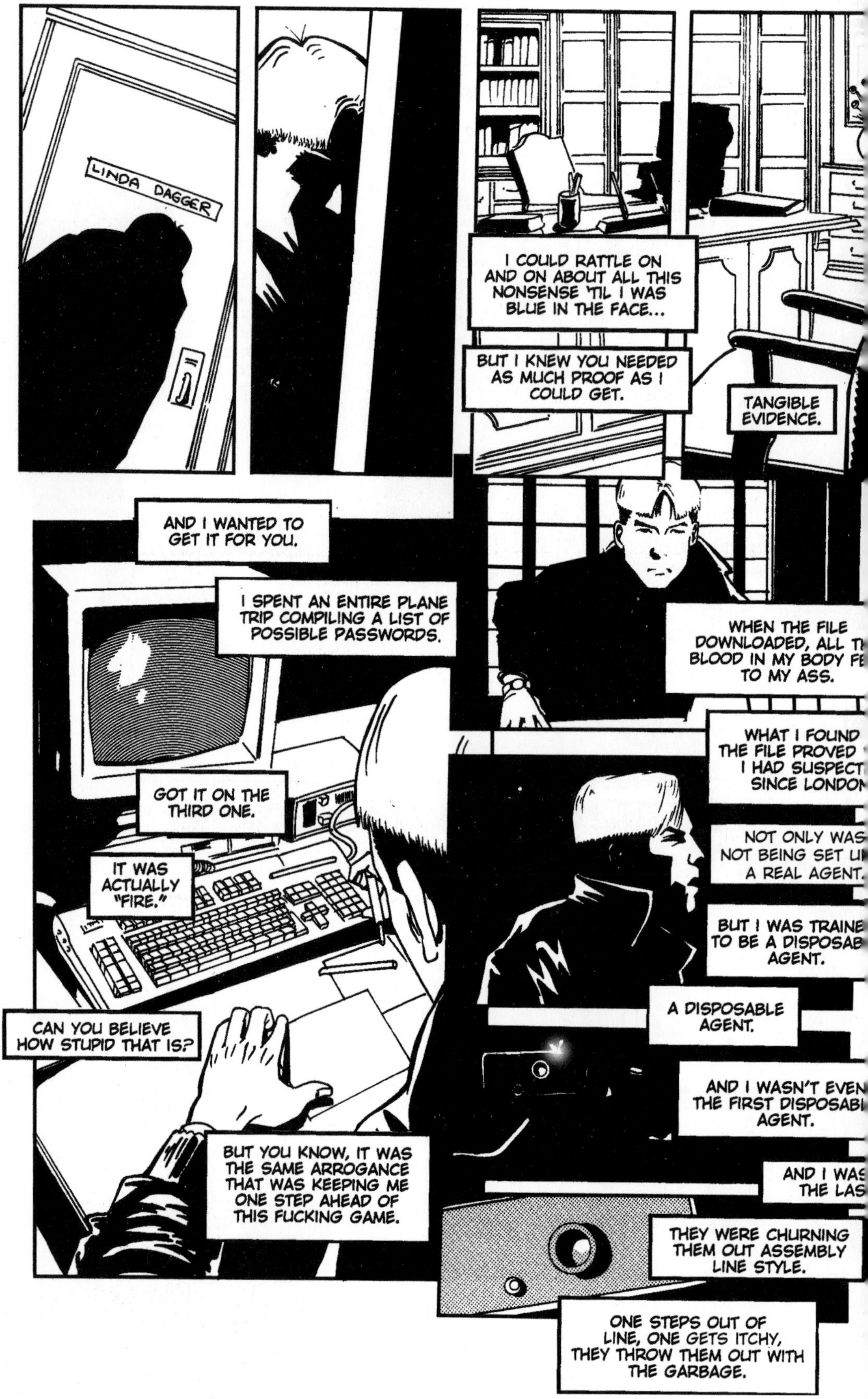

LINDA DAGGER
I COULD RATTLE ON AND ON ABOUT ALL THIS NONSENSE 'TIL I WAS BLUE IN THE FACE...
BUT I KNEW YOU NEEDED AS MUCH PROOF AS I COULD GET.
TANGIBLE EVIDENCE.
AND I WANTED TO GET IT FOR YOU.
I SPENT AN ENTIRE PLANE TRIP COMPILING A LIST OF POSSIBLE PASSWORDS.
GOT IT ON THE THIRD ONE.
IT WAS ACTUALLY "FIRE."
CAN YOU BELIEVE HOW STUPID THAT IS?
BUT YOU KNOW, IT WAS THE SAME ARROGANCE THAT WAS KEEPING ME ONE STEP AHEAD OF THIS FUCKING GAME.
WHEN THE FILE DOWNLOADED, ALL T BLOOD IN MY BODY F TO MY ASS.
WHAT I FOUND THE FILE PROVED I HAD SUSPECT SINCE LONDON
NOT ONLY WAS NOT BEING SET U A REAL AGENT.
BUT I WAS TRAINE TO BE A DISPOSAB AGENT.
A DISPOSABLE AGENT.
AND I WASN'T EVEN THE FIRST DISPOSAB AGENT.
AND I WAS THE LAS
THEY WERE CHURNING THEM OUT ASSEMBLY LINE STYLE.
ONE STEPS OUT OF LINE, ONE GETS ITCHY, THEY THROW THEM OUT WITH THE GARBAGE.

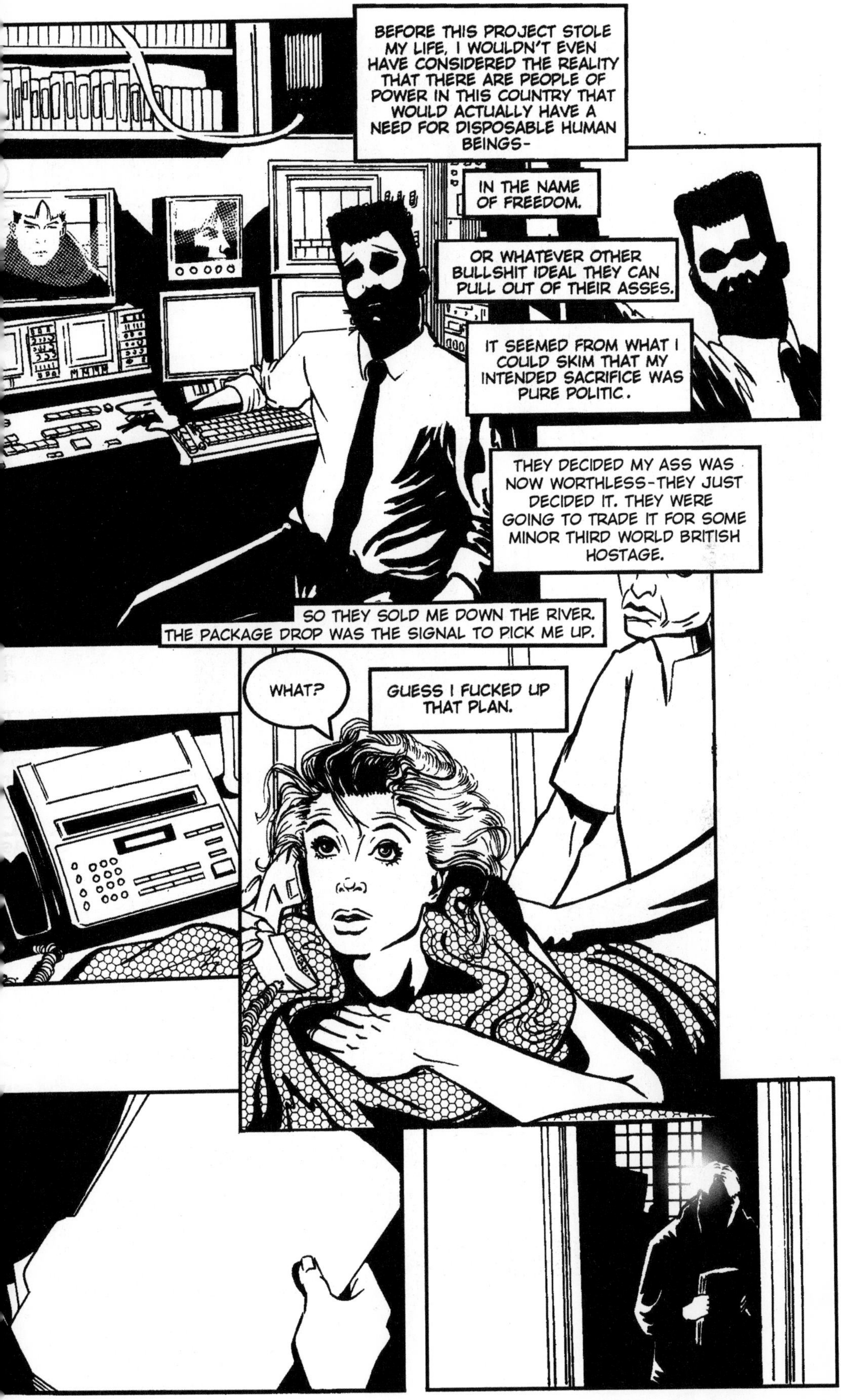
BEFORE THIS PROJECT STOLE MY LIFE, I WOULDN'T EVEN HAVE CONSIDERED THE REALITY THAT THERE ARE PEOPLE OF POWER IN THIS COUNTRY THAT WOULD ACTUALLY HAVE A NEED FOR DISPOSABLE HUMAN BEINGS-
IN THE NAME OF FREEDOM.
OR WHATEVER OTHER BULLSHIT IDEAL THEY CAN PULL OUT OF THEIR ASSES.
IT SEEMED FROM WHAT I COULD SKIM THAT MY INTENDED SACRIFICE WAS PURE POLITIC.
THEY DECIDED MY ASS WAS NOW WORTHLESS-THEY JUST DECIDED IT. THEY WERE GOING TO TRADE IT FOR SOME MINOR THIRD WORLD BRITISH HOSTAGE.
SO THEY SOLD ME DOWN THE RIVER. THE PACKAGE DROP WAS THE SIGNAL TO PICK ME UP.
WHAT?
GUESS I FUCKED UP THAT PLAN.

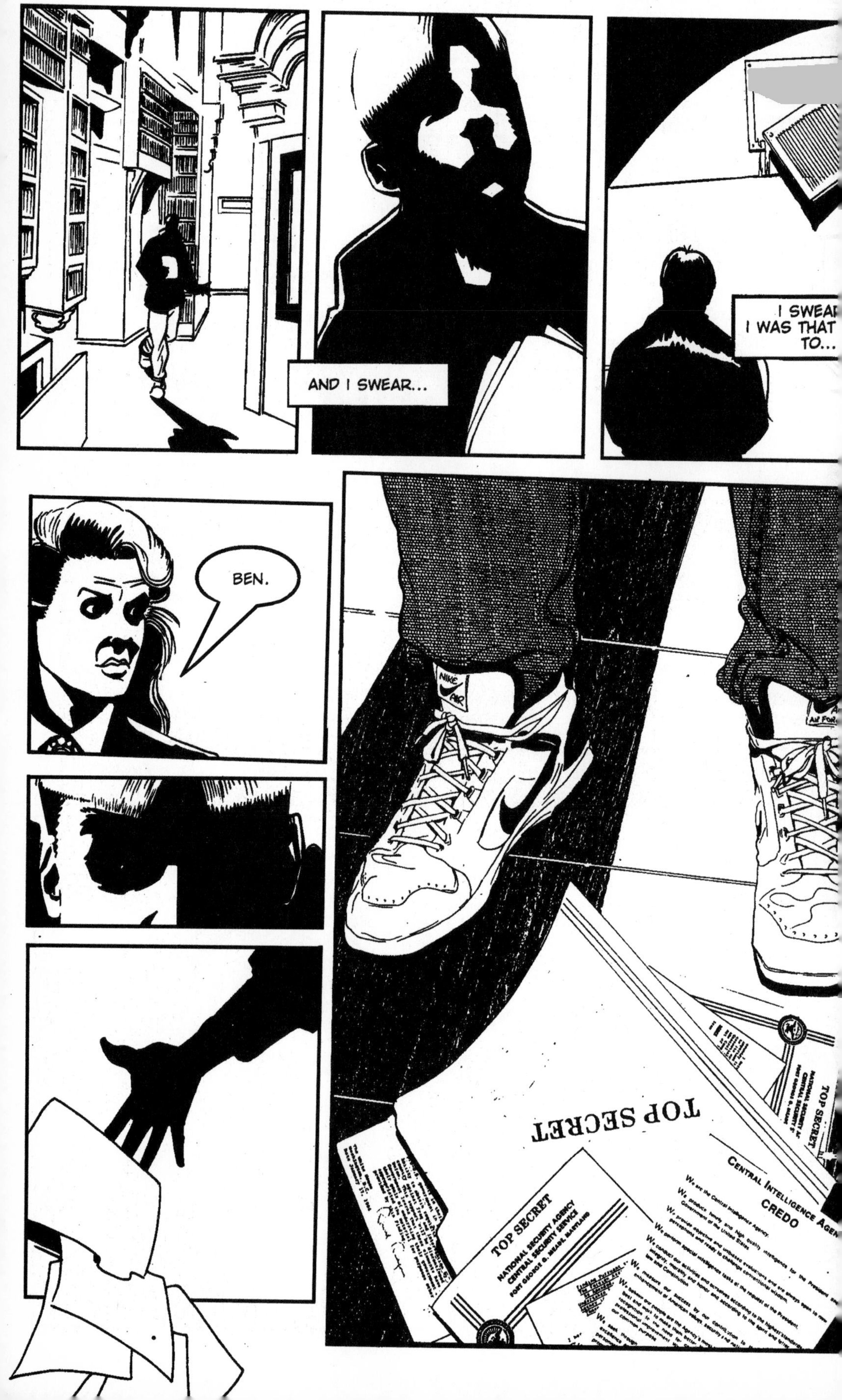
AND I SWEAR...
I SWEA
I WAS THAT
TO...
BEN.
TOP SECRET
CENTRAL INTELLIGENCE AGEN
CREDO
TOP SECRET
NATIONAL SECURITY AGENCY
CENTRAL SECURITY SERVICE

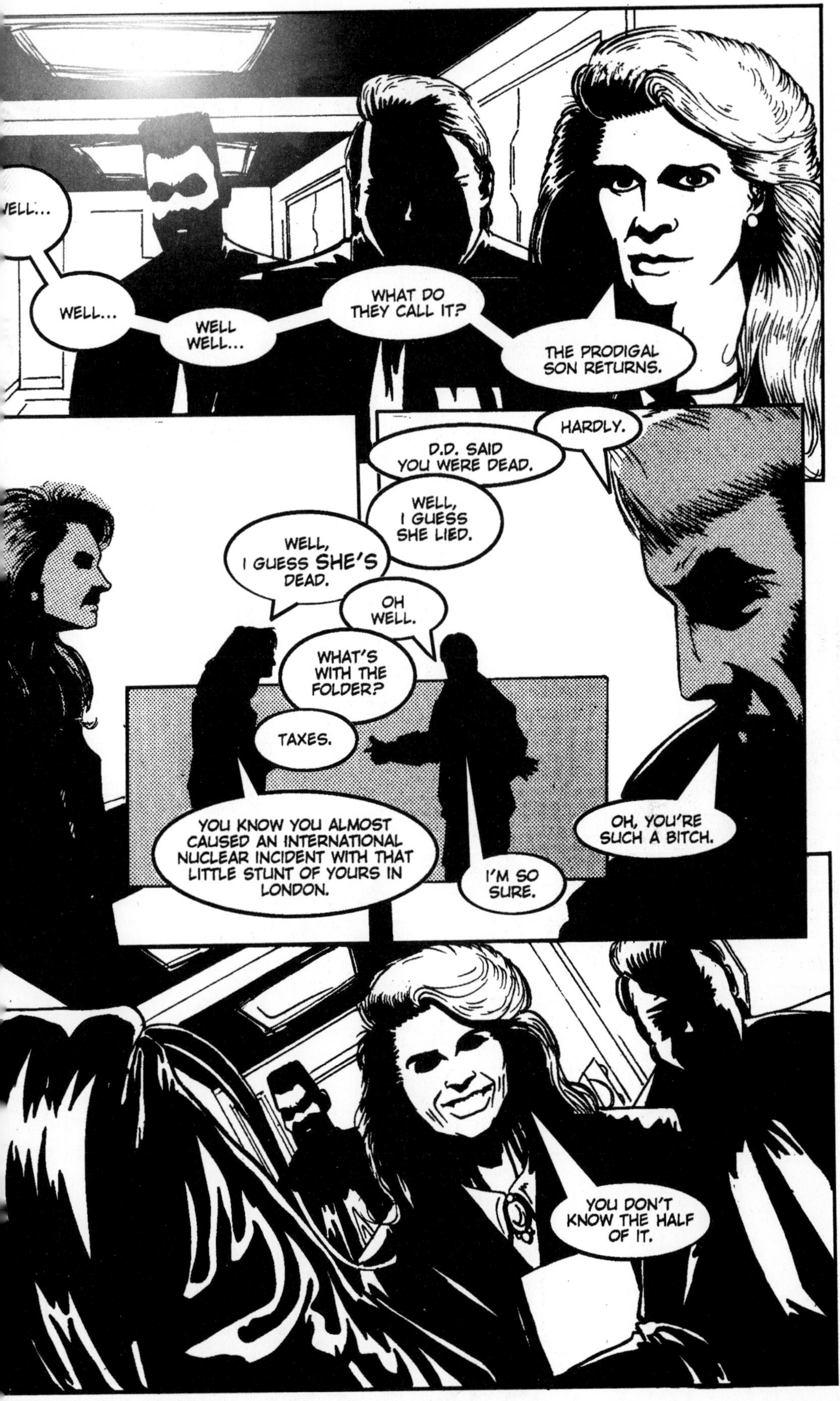
WELL...
WELL...
WELL WELL...
WHAT DO THEY CALL IT?
THE PRODIGAL SON RETURNS.
HARDLY.
D.D. SAID YOU WERE DEAD.
WELL, I GUESS SHE LIED.
WELL, I GUESS SHE'S DEAD.
OH WELL.
WHAT'S WITH THE FOLDER?
TAXES.
YOU KNOW YOU ALMOST CAUSED AN INTERNATIONAL NUCLEAR INCIDENT WITH THAT LITTLE STUNT OF YOURS IN LONDON.
I'M SO SURE.
OH, YOU'RE SUCH A BITCH.
YOU DON'T KNOW THE HALF OF IT.

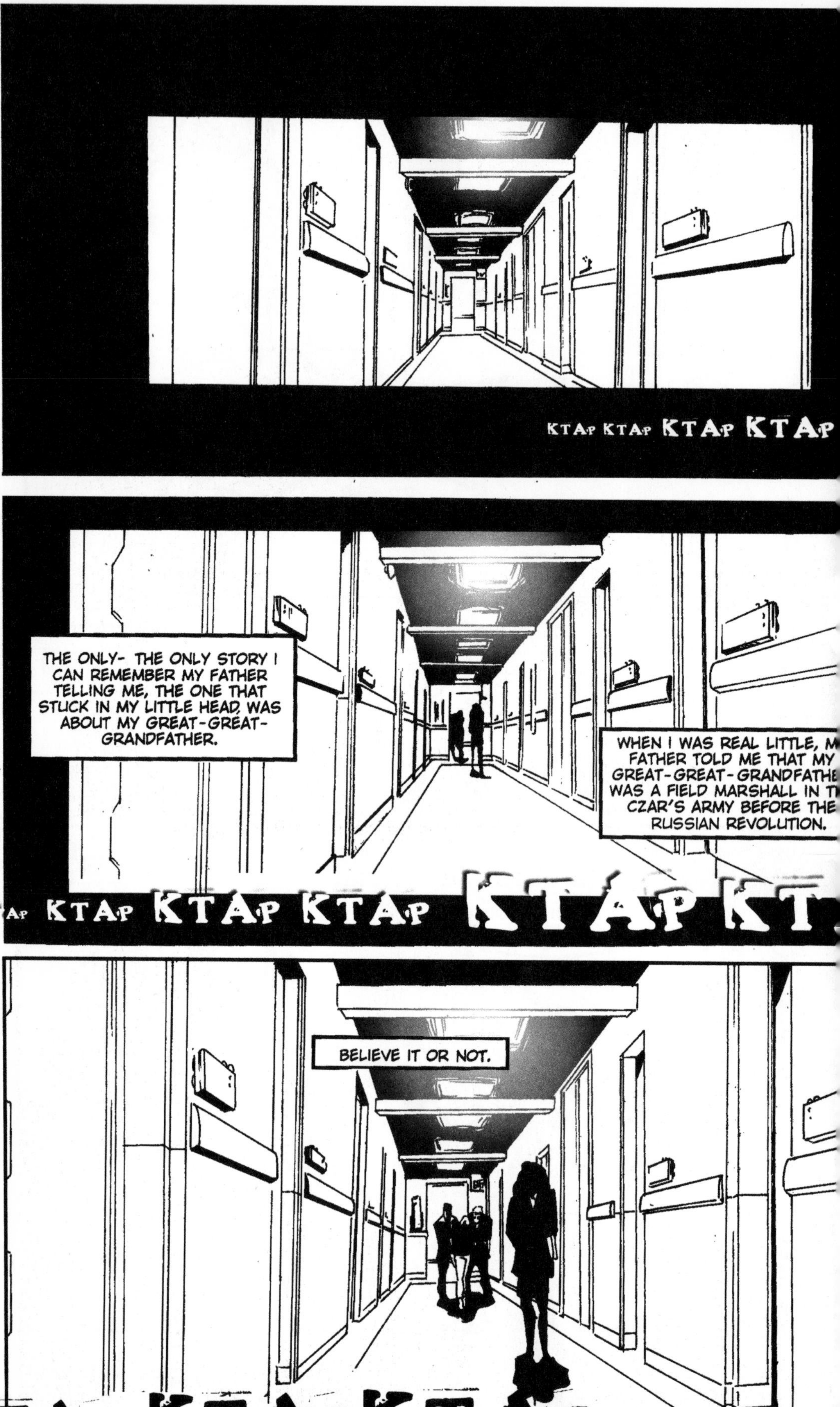
KTAP KTAP KTAP KTAP
THE ONLY- THE ONLY STORY I CAN REMEMBER MY FATHER TELLING ME, THE ONE THAT STUCK IN MY LITTLE HEAD, WAS ABOUT MY GREAT-GREAT-GRANDFATHER.
WHEN I WAS REAL LITTLE, M FATHER TOLD ME THAT MY GREAT-GREAT-GRANDFATHE WAS A FIELD MARSHALL IN T CZAR'S ARMY BEFORE THE RUSSIAN REVOLUTION.
TAP KTAP KTAP KTAP KTAP KT
BELIEVE IT OR NOT.
TAP KTAPKTAP

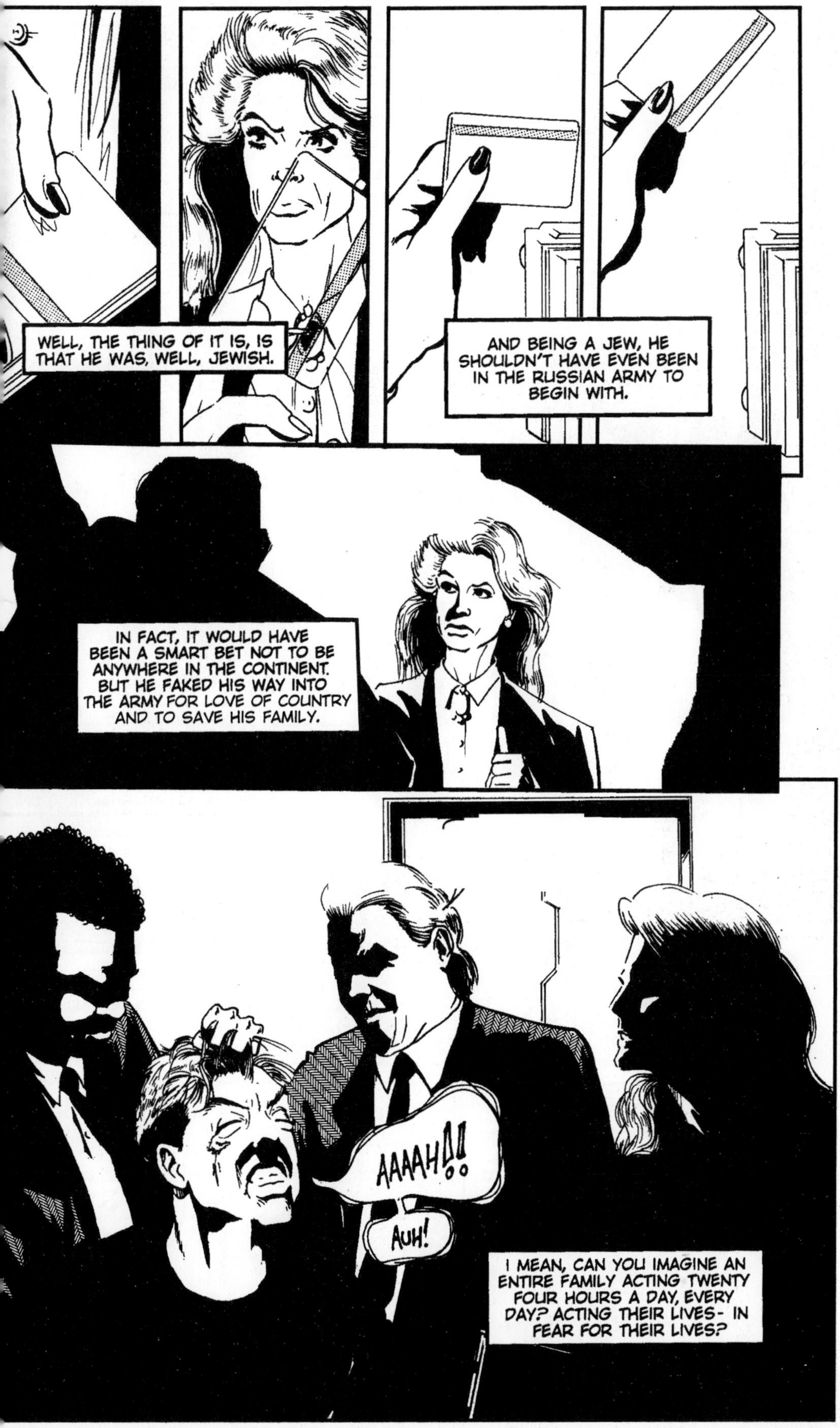

WELL, THE THING OF IT IS, IS THAT HE WAS, WELL, JEWISH.
AND BEING A JEW, HE SHOULDN'T HAVE EVEN BEEN IN THE RUSSIAN ARMY TO BEGIN WITH.
IN FACT, IT WOULD HAVE BEEN A SMART BET NOT TO BE ANYWHERE IN THE CONTINENT. BUT HE FAKED HIS WAY INTO THE ARMY FOR LOVE OF COUNTRY AND TO SAVE HIS FAMILY.
AAAAH!!
AUH!
I MEAN, CAN YOU IMAGINE AN ENTIRE FAMILY ACTING TWENTY FOUR HOURS A DAY, EVERY DAY? ACTING THEIR LIVES- IN FEAR FOR THEIR LIVES?

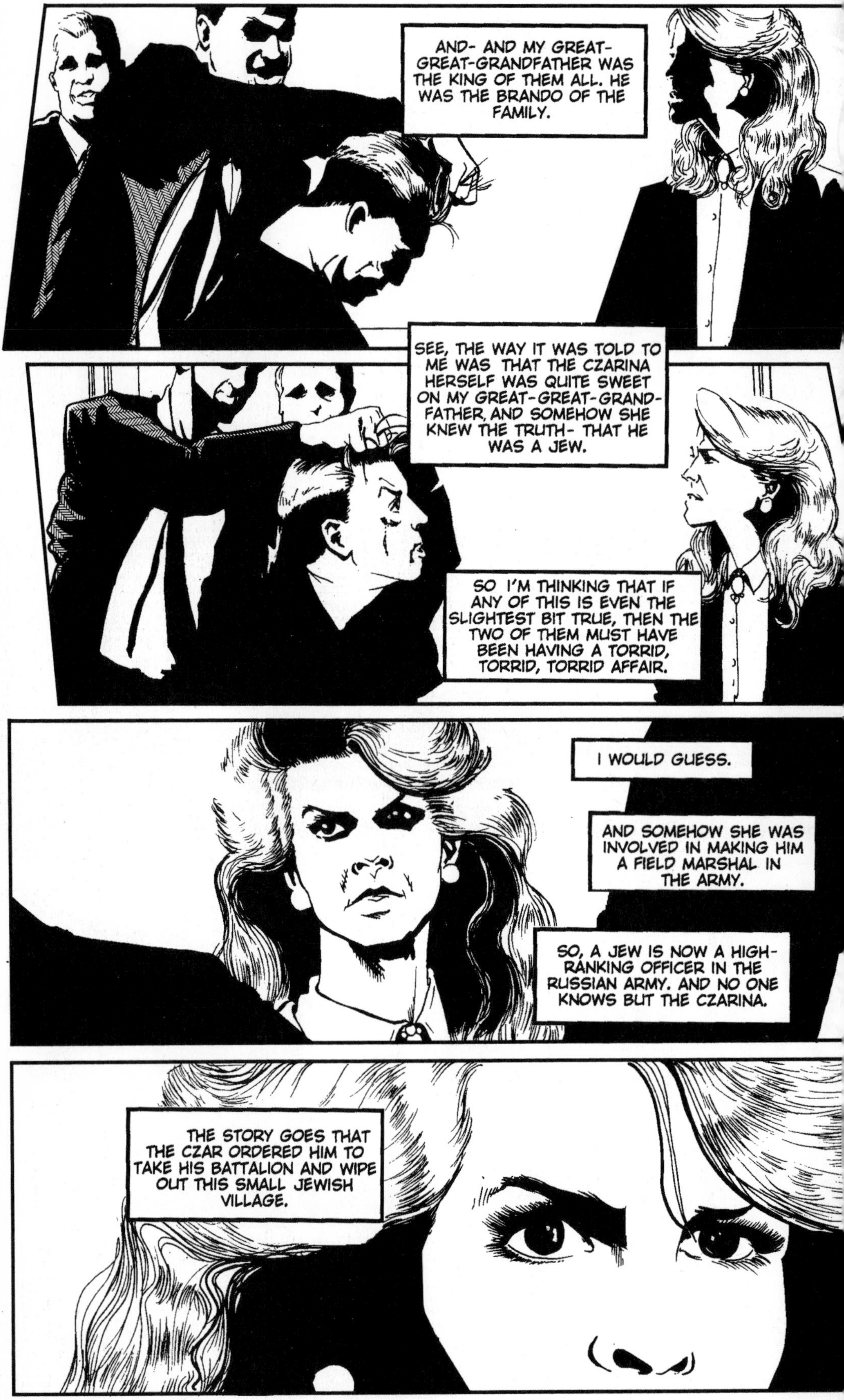
AND- AND MY GREAT-GREAT-GRANDFATHER WAS THE KING OF THEM ALL. HE WAS THE BRANDO OF THE FAMILY.
SEE, THE WAY IT WAS TOLD TO ME WAS THAT THE CZARINA HERSELF WAS QUITE SWEET ON MY GREAT-GREAT-GRANDFATHER, AND SOMEHOW SHE KNEW THE TRUTH- THAT HE WAS A JEW.
SO I'M THINKING THAT IF ANY OF THIS IS EVEN THE SLIGHTEST BIT TRUE, THEN THE TWO OF THEM MUST HAVE BEEN HAVING A TORRID, TORRID, TORRID AFFAIR.
I WOULD GUESS.
AND SOMEHOW SHE WAS INVOLVED IN MAKING HIM A FIELD MARSHAL IN THE ARMY.
SO, A JEW IS NOW A HIGH-RANKING OFFICER IN THE RUSSIAN ARMY. AND NO ONE KNOWS BUT THE CZARINA.
THE STORY GOES THAT THE CZAR ORDERED HIM TO TAKE HIS BATTALION AND WIPE OUT THIS SMALL JEWISH VILLAGE.

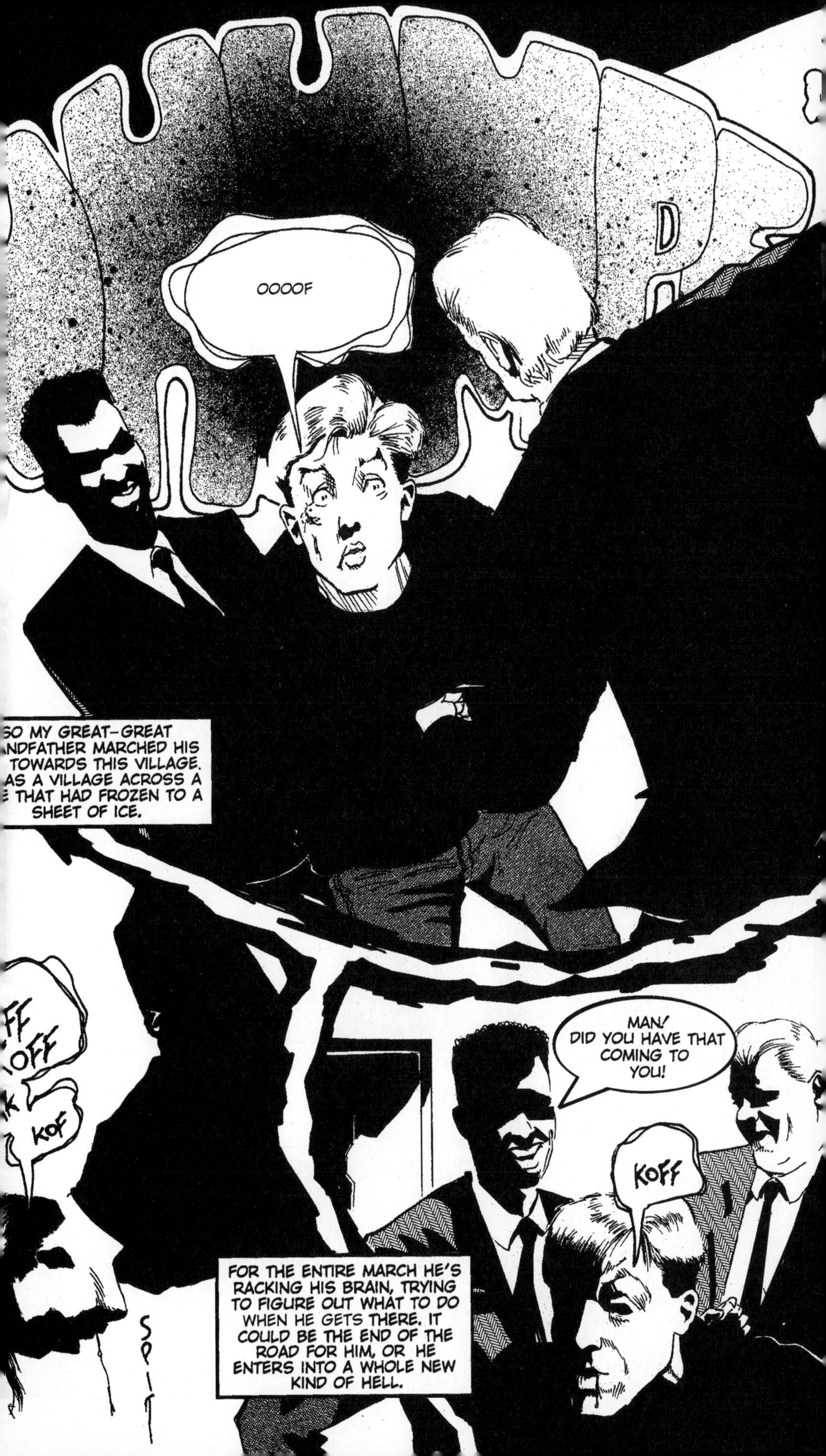
OOOOF
SO MY GREAT-GREAT
NDFATHER MARCHED HIS
TOWARDS THIS VILLAGE.
AS A VILLAGE ACROSS A
E THAT HAD FROZEN TO A
SHEET OF ICE.
KOF
SPIT
MAN! DID YOU HAVE THAT COMING TO YOU!
KOFF
FOR THE ENTIRE MARCH HE'S RACKING HIS BRAIN, TRYING TO FIGURE OUT WHAT TO DO WHEN HE GETS THERE. IT COULD BE THE END OF THE ROAD FOR HIM, OR HE ENTERS INTO A WHOLE NEW KIND OF HELL.

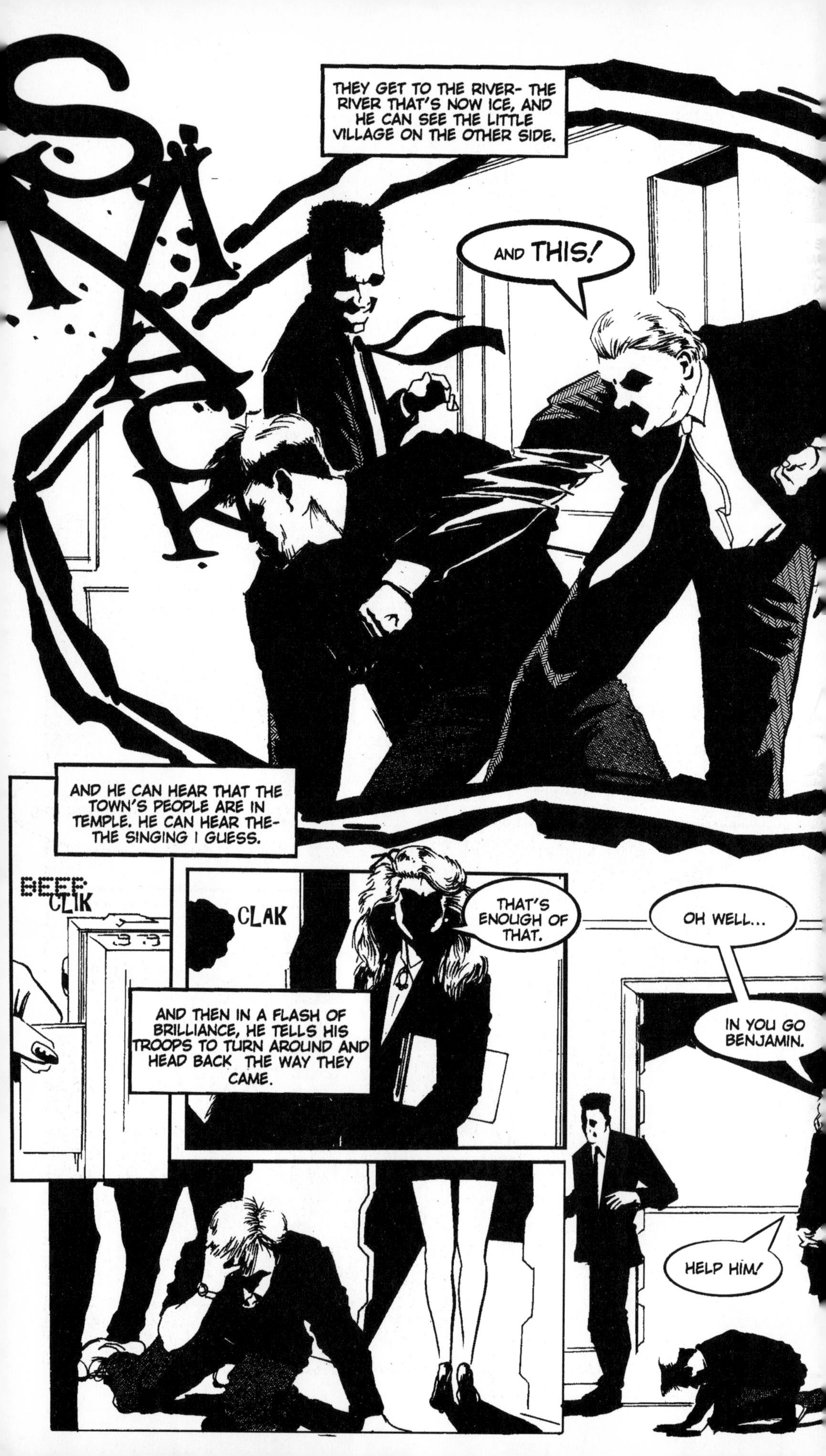
THEY GET TO THE RIVER- THE RIVER THAT'S NOW ICE, AND HE CAN SEE THE LITTLE VILLAGE ON THE OTHER SIDE.
SMACK
AND THIS!
AND HE CAN HEAR THAT THE TOWN'S PEOPLE ARE IN TEMPLE. HE CAN HEAR THE- THE SINGING I GUESS.
BEEP
CLIK
CLAK
THAT'S ENOUGH OF THAT.
AND THEN IN A FLASH OF BRILLIANCE, HE TELLS HIS TROOPS TO TURN AROUND AND HEAD BACK THE WAY THEY CAME.
OH WELL...
IN YOU GO BENJAMIN.
HELP HIM!

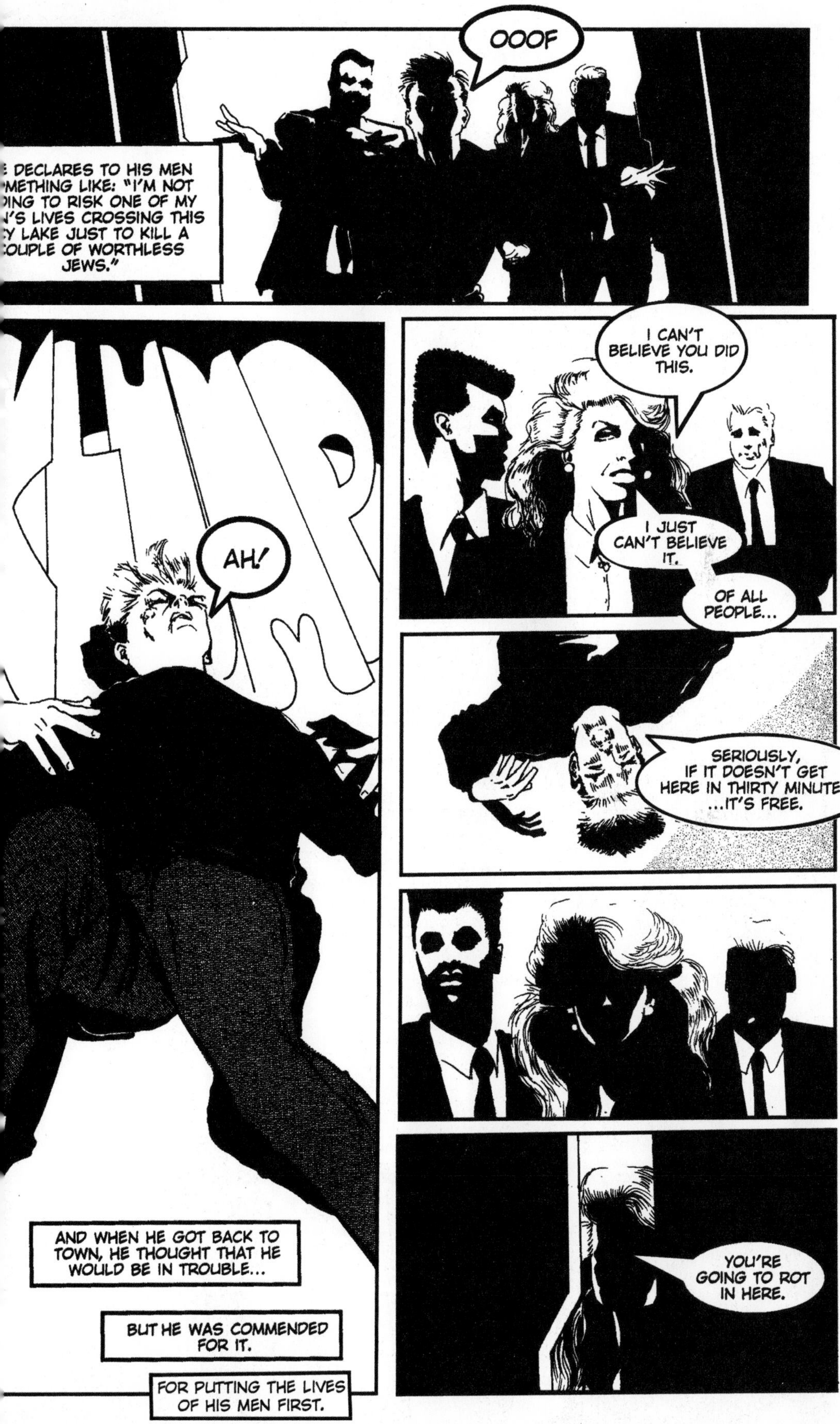
OOOF
E DECLARES TO HIS MEN METHING LIKE: "I'M NOT OING TO RISK ONE OF MY N'S LIVES CROSSING THIS Y LAKE JUST TO KILL A COUPLE OF WORTHLESS JEWS."
AH!
I CAN'T BELIEVE YOU DID THIS.
I JUST CAN'T BELIEVE IT.
OF ALL PEOPLE...
SERIOUSLY, IF IT DOESN'T GET HERE IN THIRTY MINUTES ...IT'S FREE.
YOU'RE GOING TO ROT IN HERE.
AND WHEN HE GOT BACK TO TOWN, HE THOUGHT THAT HE WOULD BE IN TROUBLE...
BUT HE WAS COMMENDED FOR IT.
FOR PUTTING THE LIVES OF HIS MEN FIRST.

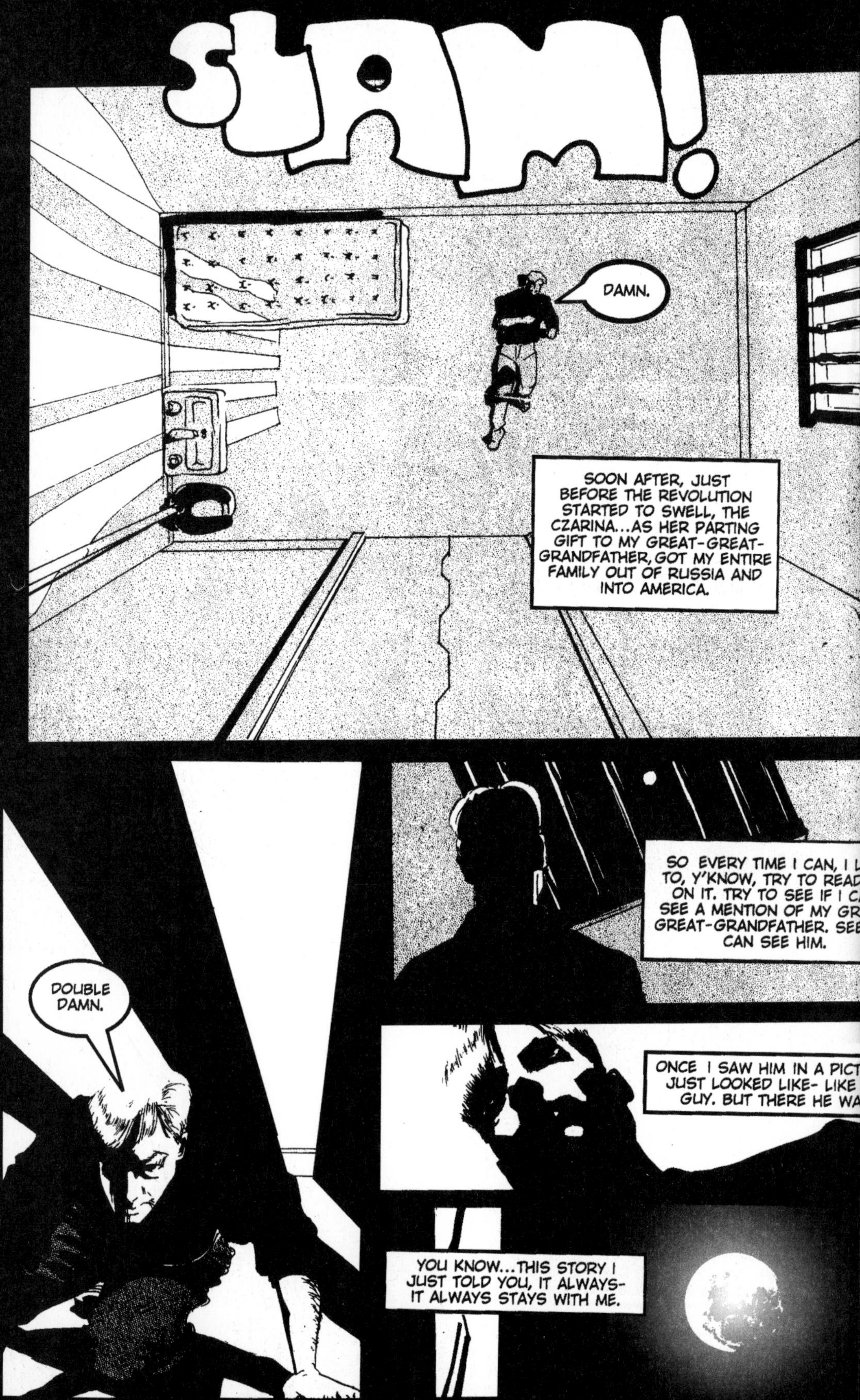
SLAM!
DAMN.
SOON AFTER, JUST BEFORE THE REVOLUTION STARTED TO SWELL, THE CZARINA...AS HER PARTING GIFT TO MY GREAT-GREAT-GRANDFATHER, GOT MY ENTIRE FAMILY OUT OF RUSSIA AND INTO AMERICA.
DOUBLE DAMN.
SO EVERY TIME I CAN, I L
TO, Y'KNOW, TRY TO READ
ON IT. TRY TO SEE IF I C
SEE A MENTION OF MY GR
GREAT-GRANDFATHER. SEE
CAN SEE HIM.
ONCE I SAW HIM IN A PICT
JUST LOOKED LIKE- LIKE
GUY. BUT THERE HE WA
YOU KNOW...THIS STORY I JUST TOLD YOU, IT ALWAYS- IT ALWAYS STAYS WITH ME.

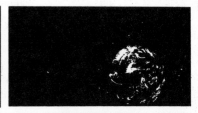

SEE, THIS WAS A MAN WHO HAD DONE SOMETHING. HE TOOK THE- THE HORRIBLE SITUATION THAT HIS LIFE FOUND ITSELF TO BE AND HE WORKED WITH IT.

HE WORKED IT FROM THE INSIDE. HE SKATED RIGHT UP TO THE VERY EDGE OF IT AND DID SOMETHING WORTHWHILE.

SO MUCH SO THAT- THAT A BILLION YEARS LATER- SOMEONE STILL KNOWS ABOUT IT.

Clik

AND HERE I AM... WITH ALL THIS- ALL THIS GOING ON AROUND ME AND TO ME, AND I CAN'T HELP BUT THINK THAT

THAT IT'S MY TURN TO DO THE SAME.

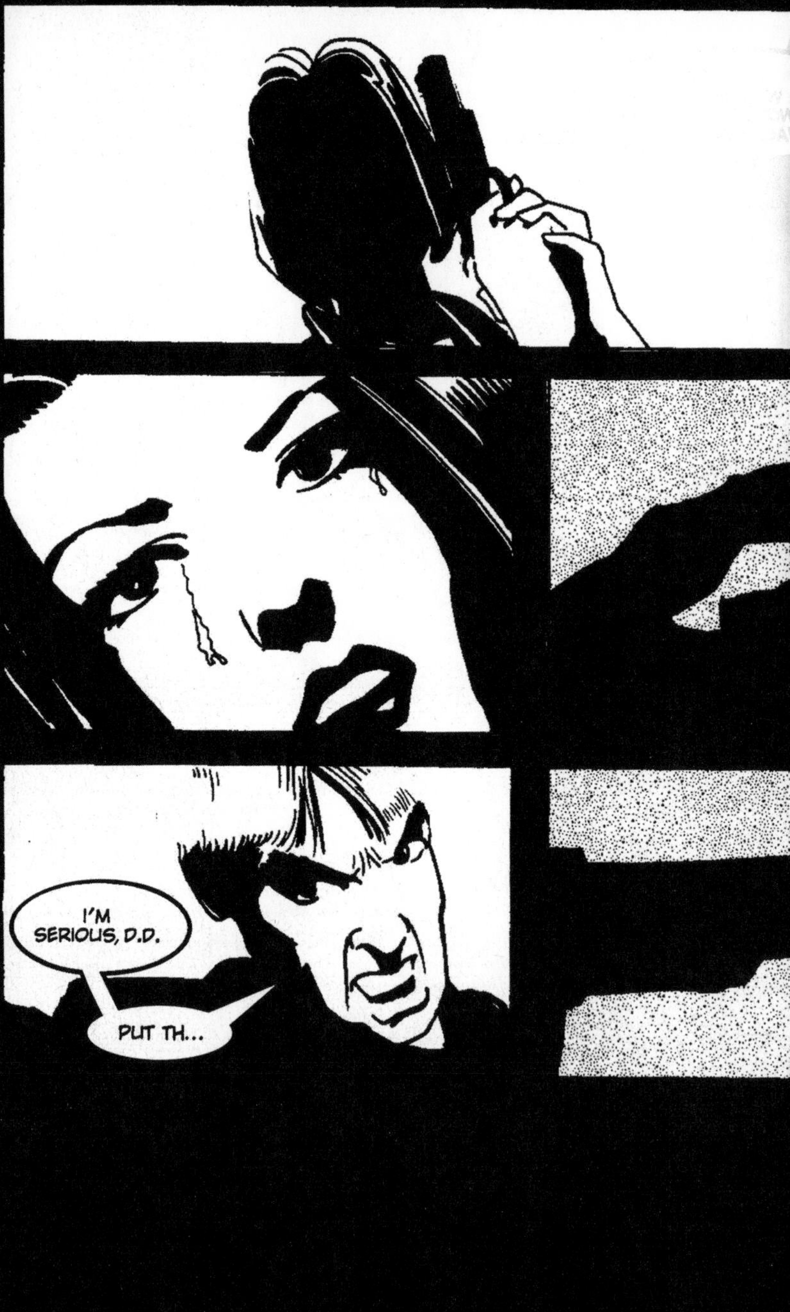
I'M SERIOUS, D.D.
PUT TH...

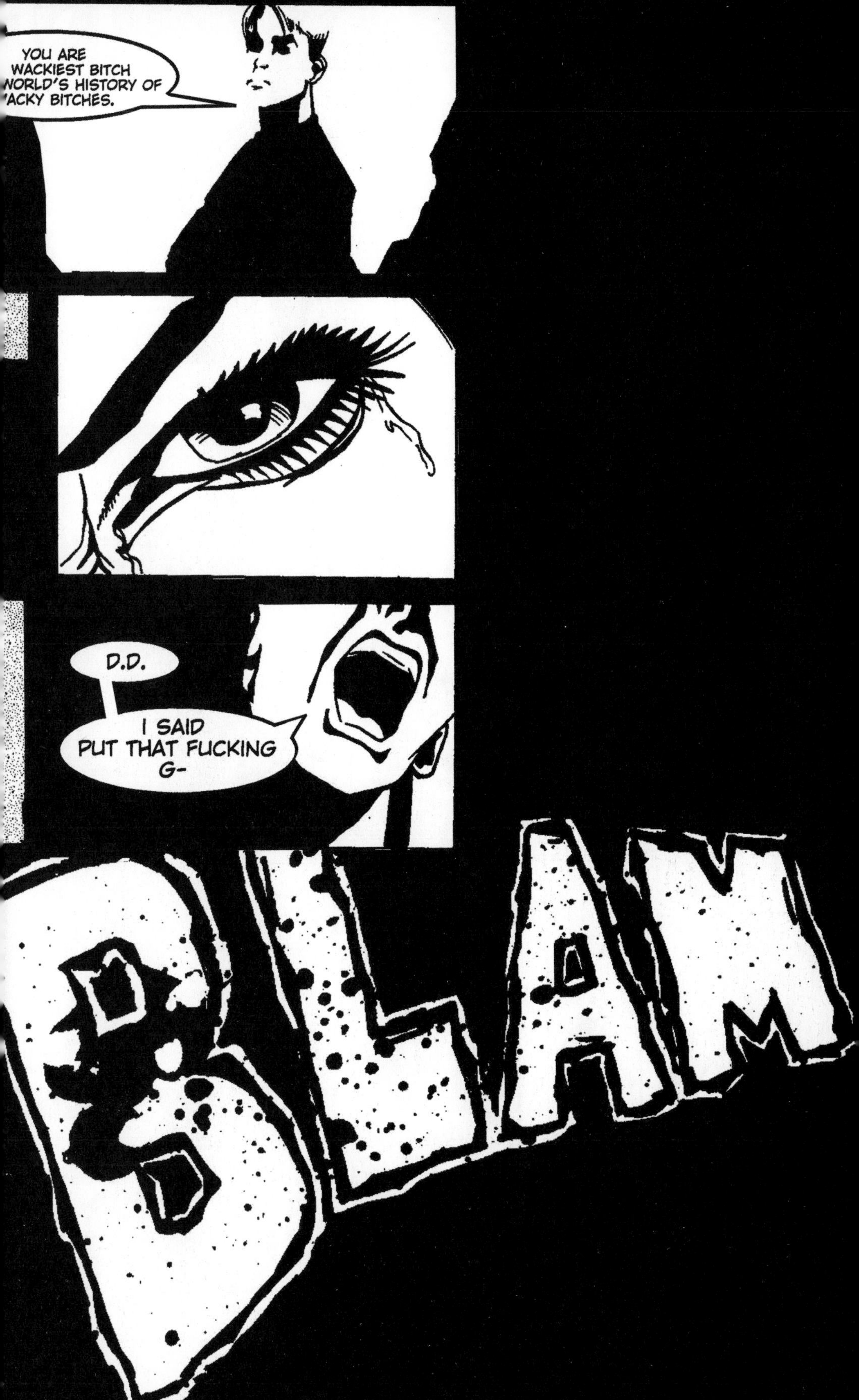
YOU ARE WACKIEST BITCH
ORLD'S HISTORY OF
ACKY BITCHES.
D.D.
I SAID PUT THAT FUCKING G-
BLAM

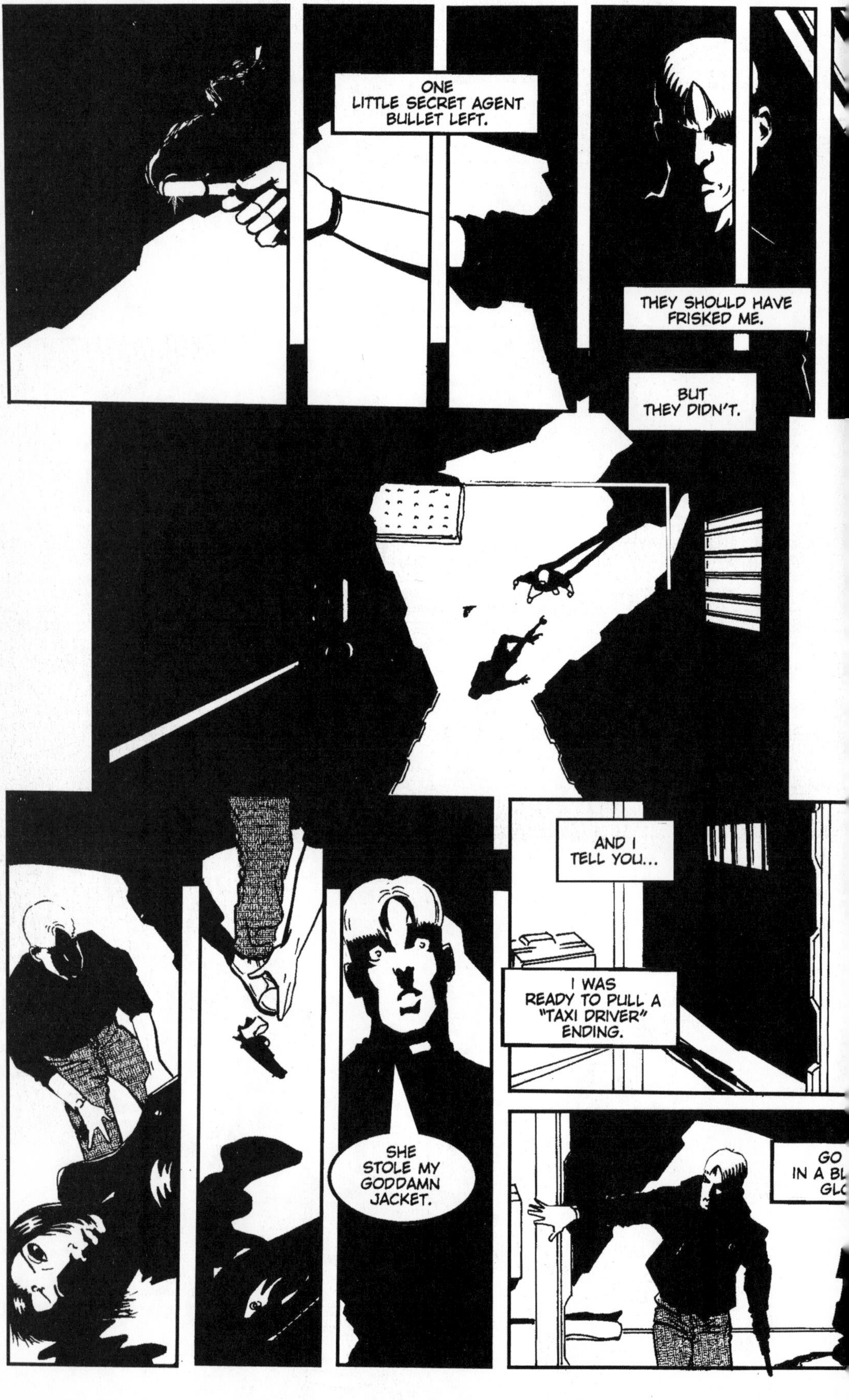
ONE LITTLE SECRET AGENT BULLET LEFT.
THEY SHOULD HAVE FRISKED ME.
BUT THEY DIDN'T.
SHE STOLE MY GODDAMN JACKET.
AND I TELL YOU...
I WAS READY TO PULL A "TAXI DRIVER" ENDING.

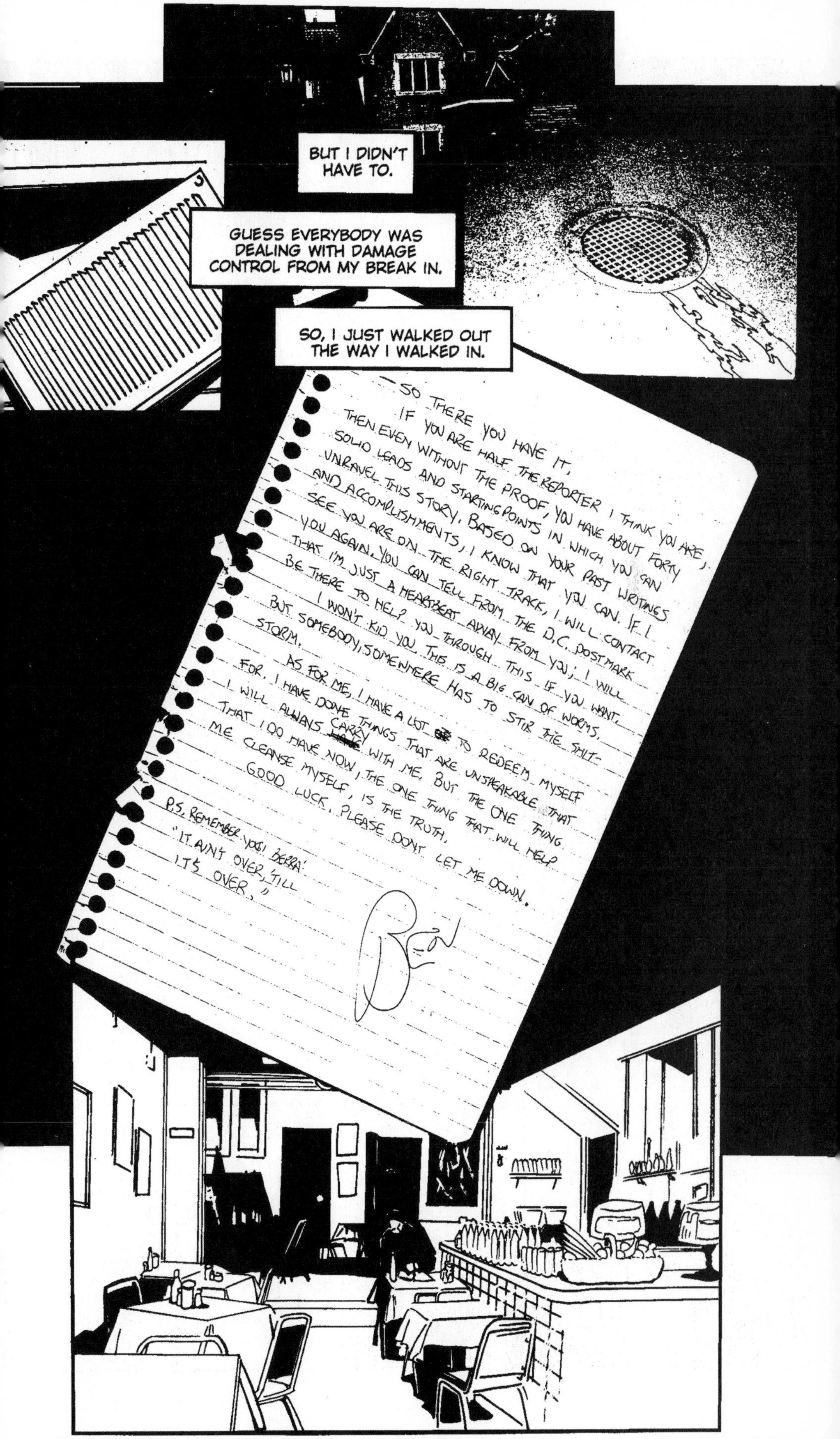
BUT I DIDN'T HAVE TO.
GUESS EVERYBODY WAS DEALING WITH DAMAGE CONTROL FROM MY BREAK IN.
SO, I JUST WALKED OUT THE WAY I WALKED IN.
— SO THERE YOU HAVE IT,
IF YOU ARE HALF THE REPORTER I THINK YOU ARE,
THEN EVEN WITHOUT THE PROOF, YOU HAVE ABOUT FORTY
SOLID LEADS AND STARTING POINTS IN WHICH YOU CAN
UNRAVEL THIS STORY, BASED ON YOUR PAST WRITINGS
AND ACCOMPLISHMENTS, I KNOW THAT YOU CAN. IF I
SEE YOU ARE ON THE RIGHT TRACK, I WILL CONTACT
YOU AGAIN. YOU CAN TELL FROM THE D.C. POSTMARK
THAT I'M JUST A HEARTBEAT AWAY FROM YOU; I WILL
BE THERE TO HELP YOU THROUGH THIS IF YOU WANT.
I WON'T KID YOU. THIS IS A BIG CAN OF WORMS,
BUT SOMEBODY, SOMEWHERE HAS TO STIR THE SHIT-
STORM.
AS FOR ME, I HAVE A LOT TO REDEEM MYSELF
FOR. I HAVE DONE THINGS THAT ARE UNSPEAKABLE THAT
I WILL ALWAYS CARRY WITH ME. BUT THE ONE THING
THAT I DO HAVE NOW, THE ONE THING THAT WILL HELP
ME CLEANSE MYSELF, IS THE TRUTH.
GOOD LUCK. PLEASE DON'T LET ME DOWN.
P.S. REMEMBER YOGI BERRA:
"IT AIN'T OVER, 'TILL
IT'S OVER."

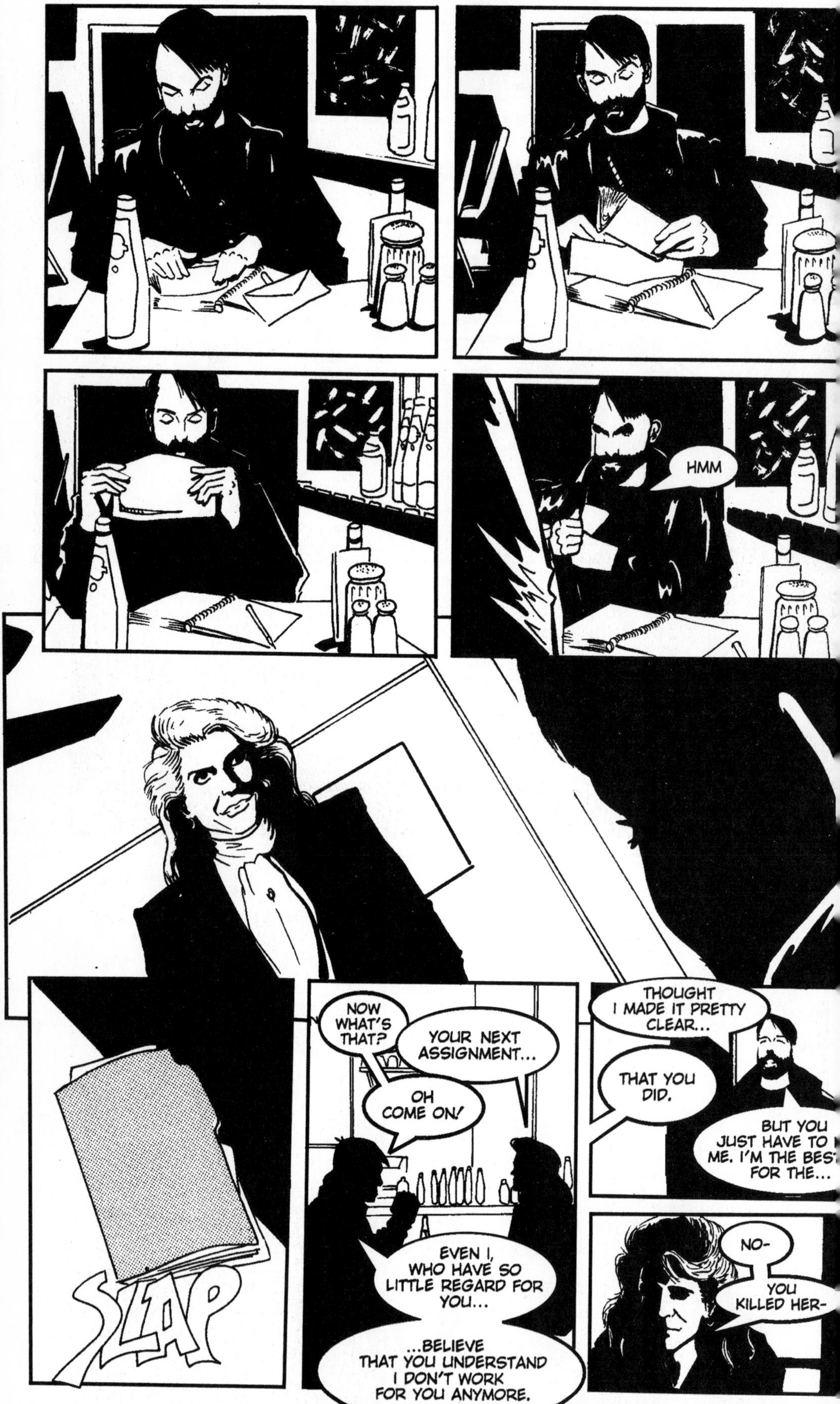
HMM
SLAP
NOW WHAT'S THAT?
YOUR NEXT ASSIGNMENT...
OH COME ON!
EVEN I, WHO HAVE SO LITTLE REGARD FOR YOU...
...BELIEVE THAT YOU UNDERSTAND I DON'T WORK FOR YOU ANYMORE.
THOUGHT I MADE IT PRETTY CLEAR...
THAT YOU DID.
BUT YOU JUST HAVE TO ME. I'M THE BES FOR THE...
NO-
YOU KILLED HER-

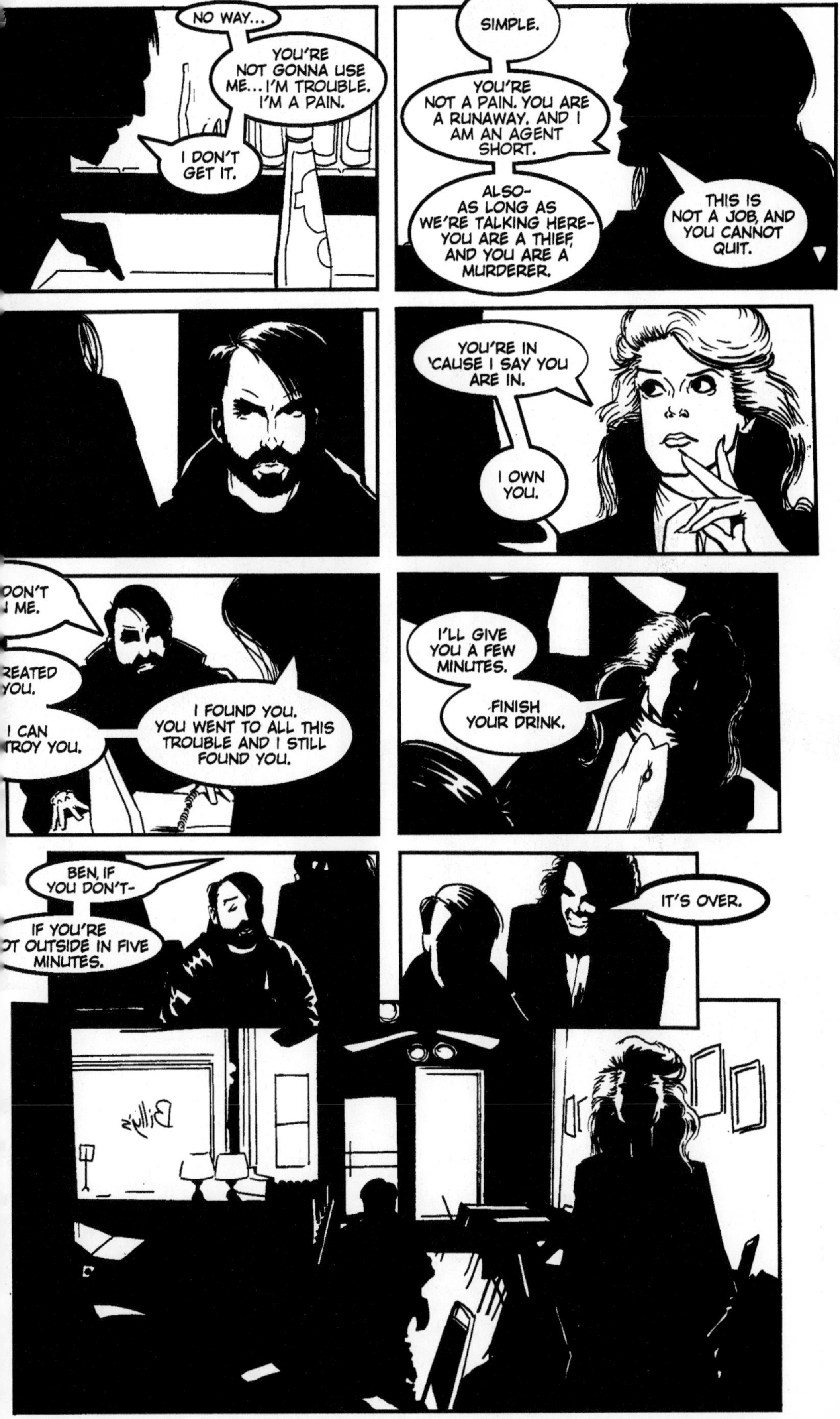
NO WAY...
YOU'RE NOT GONNA USE ME...I'M TROUBLE. I'M A PAIN.
I DON'T GET IT.
SIMPLE.
YOU'RE NOT A PAIN. YOU ARE A RUNAWAY. AND I AM AN AGENT SHORT.
ALSO- AS LONG AS WE'RE TALKING HERE- YOU ARE A THIEF, AND YOU ARE A MURDERER.
THIS IS NOT A JOB, AND YOU CANNOT QUIT.
YOU'RE IN 'CAUSE I SAY YOU ARE IN.
I OWN YOU.
DON'T ME.
REATED YOU.
I CAN TROY YOU.
I FOUND YOU. YOU WENT TO ALL THIS TROUBLE AND I STILL FOUND YOU.
I'LL GIVE YOU A FEW MINUTES.
FINISH YOUR DRINK.
BEN, IF YOU DON'T-
IF YOU'RE OT OUTSIDE IN FIVE MINUTES.
IT'S OVER.

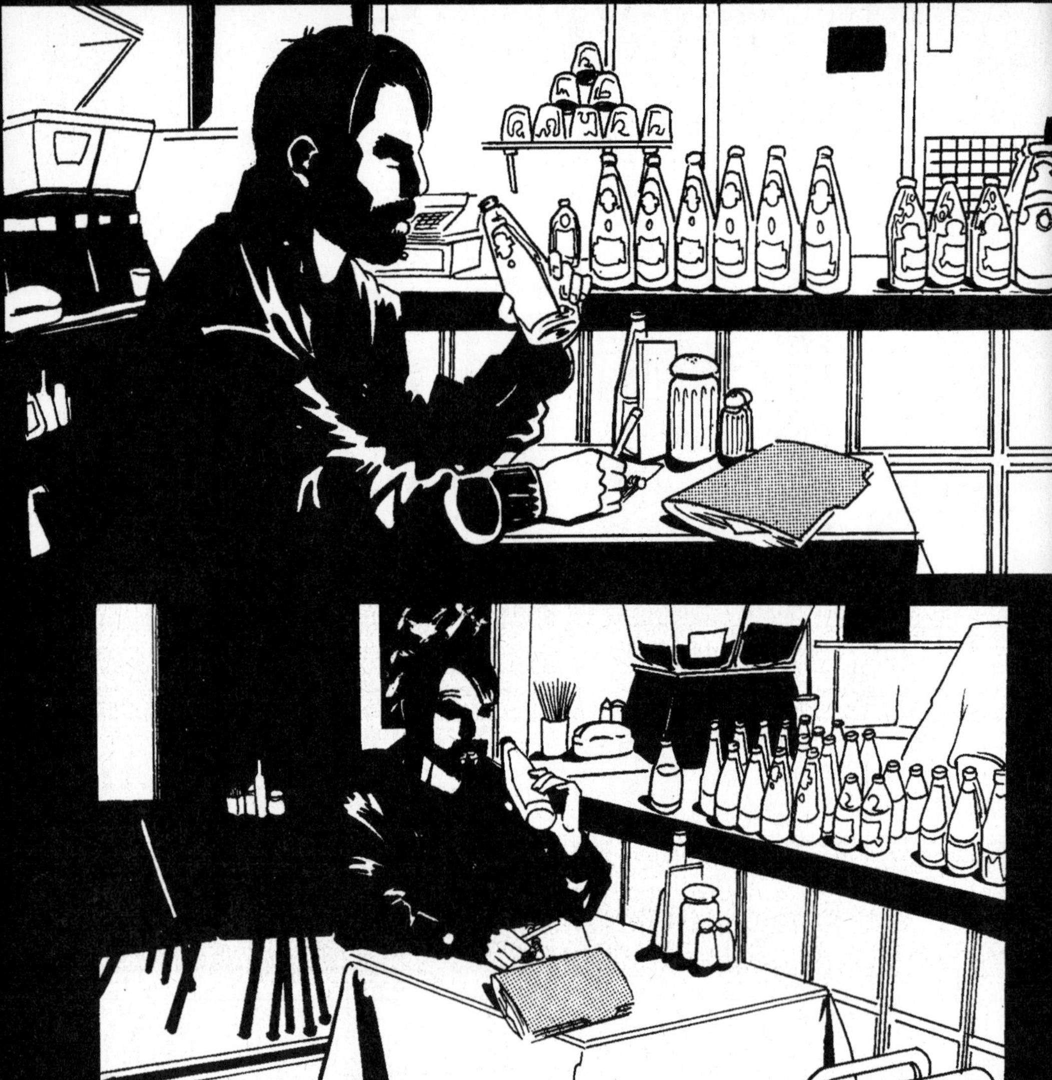

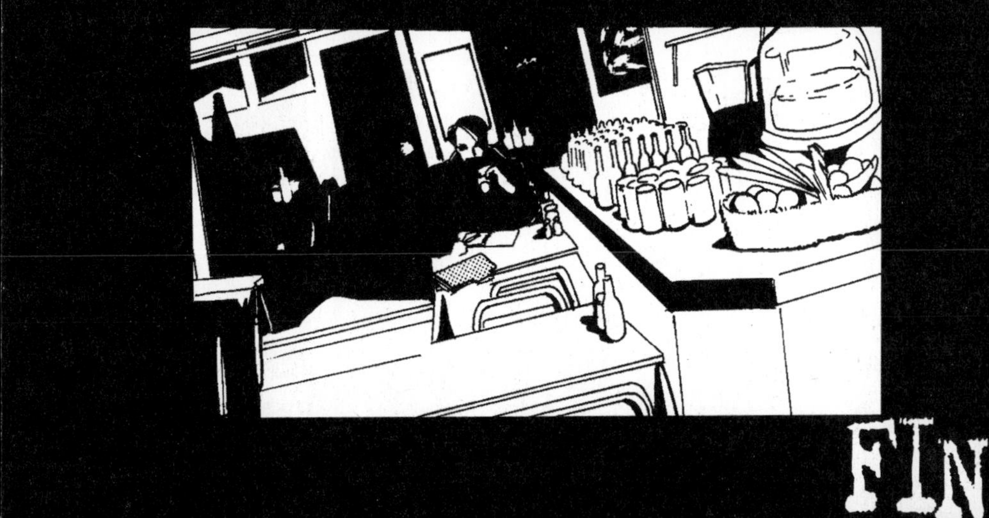

FIN

ONE MORE TIME...

Ah! Now that's better.

For five years I've been telling friends, family and strangers on public transportation that one day I was going to go back and reletter, remaster and tweak the hell out of this book and put it back on the stands.

And now I have.

When I solicited this FIRE redo, I figured no big deal—I'll just take the weekend, plow right through it and ship it off to the printer. Then I opened it up and looked inside for the first time in a few years, and...well, *fuck! Holy crap sandwich,* was I wrong!

See, this is the book that first got me some attention. And by that, I mean it was the first book I was proud o

I've always been chock-full of self-delusion. And back then, I guess my delirium included the idea that I wa a decent freehand comic-book letterer.

Now, I bet if you were generous enough to buy this book the first time, when it was solicited as a two-issue miniseries back in my fledgling Caliber Comics days, you can't even tell the difference. But let me tell you, I went through every single page of this redone novel with a sledgehammer.

There isn't *one* panel that I didn't eff with—a task that ended up taking weeks. I redid every border and ever balloon. I gave Ben a decent haircut (his hair was taking on a life of its own as mine, in real life, was going the way of the comics industry). And I tossed in some updated and snazzier dialogue.

Also, when I originally created the comic, I chickened out on a couple of turns, which I have since regretted. This includes the ending. I was afraid of what I then considered the bold risk of repeating the opening sequence at the end, and that was a decision that, in retrospect, always bothered me. Also, a version of Vaughn's Fireball story was originally written, but I took it out for some reason, and that always bothered me as well.

I did everything to this book short of redrawing it. I didn't want to actually put pen to paper, because I wanted to handle it like a remastering of an old movie—like those lunatics who went and cleaned up *Vertigo* a couple years back. I wanted to stay faithful to the source material, but not to the degree that I was going to embarrass the shit out of myself (again).

Here are a couple examples of the original and remastered versions

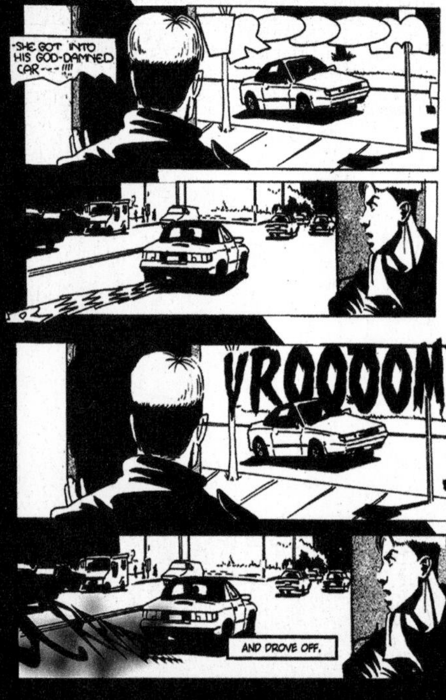
-SHE GOT INTO HIS GOD-DAMNED CAR---!!!
VROOOOM
AND DROVE OFF.

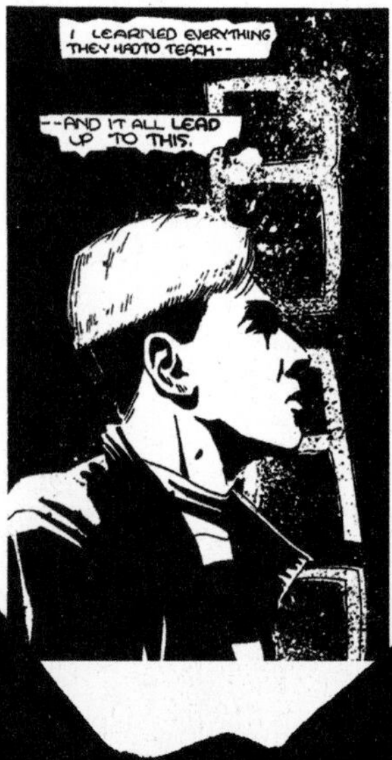
I LEARNED EVERYTHING THEY HAD TO TEACH--
--AND IT ALL LEAD UP TO THIS.

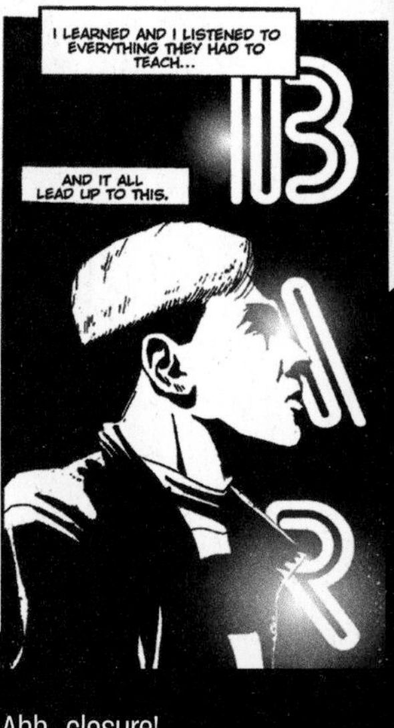
I LEARNED AND I LISTENED TO EVERYTHING THEY HAD TO TEACH...
AND IT ALL LEAD UP TO THIS.

Ahh...closure!

Bendis!
2001

THANKS

This book would not have been possible without the existence of **Izzy Schachner, Jared Bendis, David Mack, Marc Ricketts, Marc Andreyko**, the patient cast, and all of you, as well as the dazzling support and patience of my wife, **Alisa**, and my amazing children, all of whom did not exist when I originally made this graphic novel. Well, Alisa did, but she was in college somewhere and we didn't know each other. Also, the story at the end of the book is a true story from my family history. It was a story I know my Uncle Leonard had hoped to put in a book one day. So, this is for him.

SUGGESTED READING

Veil: The Secret Wars of the CIA, 1981-1987
by Bob Woodward

Crossfire: The Plot That Killed Kennedy
by Jim Marrs

All the President's Men
by Carl Bernstein and Bob Woodward

The Spy Who Came in from the Cold, The Russia House, The Night Manager and *Tinker Tailor Soldier Spy*
by John le Carré

The Once and Future King
by T.H. White

JFK: The Book of the Film
by Oliver Stone and Zachary Sklar

BIOGRAPHY

Brian Michael Bendis is a Peabody Award-winning comics creator, an Amazon and *New York Times* best-selling author and one of the most successful writers working in mainstream comics.

The announcement of Bendis' multifaceted move to DC Entertainment made international headlines and trended worldwide. He made his DC debut in the landmark ACTION COMICS #1000, and he currently writes SUPERMAN and ACTION COMICS as well as curating the new Wonder Comics line for DC, which showcases the return of YOUNG JUSTICE, DIAL H FOR HERO and WONDER TWINS and features the debut of NAOMI, an original new character for the DC Universe.

The move also brought Bendis' Jinxworld line of creator-owned comics into the DC fold. The imprint's new titles include the Yakuza epic PEARL (with art by *Jessica Jones* co-creator Michael Gaydos), the comic book industry spy thriller COVER (with art by award-winning multimedia sensation David Mack), the youth revolutionary tale SCARLET (with art by series co-creator Alex Maleev) and the alternate history mafia saga UNITED STATES OF MURDER, INC. (with art by POWERS co-creator Michael Avon Oeming).

In addition to his work in print, Bendis won a Peabody Award for his work as the co-creator of *Jessica Jones* on Netflix from Marvel TV, and he was an executive producer and consultant for the hit Sony feature film *Spider-Man: Into the Spider-Verse*, which features the character Miles Morales, the multiracial Spider-Man co-created by Bendis and artist Sara Pichelli. Morales' comics debut made international headlines and was featured on Fox News, CNN, *The Daily Show, Conan, The Howard Stern Show* and many other media channels.

Bendis' introduction of a new Iron Man character in the form of 15-year-old Riri Williams also made international headlines when the story broke in *Time* magazine. The first issue of her series, *Invincible Iron Man*, was one of the top five-selling comics nationwide the week of its launch.

In 2014 Random House published Bendis' creative guidebook *Words for Pictures*, an intricate look at the creation of comic books and graphic novels based on the graphic novel class he teaches at Portland State University. It shot to number one on its Amazon sales chart upon its release.

In his time at Marvel Entertainment, Bendis completed historic runs on *Spider-Man* (18 years), *Avengers* (9 years), *Iron Man* and *Guardians of the Galaxy*, as well as a 100-issue run on the *X-Men* franchise and the wildly successful "event" projects *Avengers vs. X-Men, House of M, Secret War, Secret Invasion, Age of Ultron, Civil War II* and *Siege*. He was also one of the main architects of Marvel's Ultimate line of comics and part of the company's creative committee which consulted on all of the Marvel movies from the first *Iron Man* through 2018's *Guardians of the Galaxy Vol. 2*.

Sony's live-action series based on his Eisner Award-winning comic series POWERS ran for two seasons on the Playstation network, with Bendis serving as executive producer and contributing writer. He is also the creator of the Jinx line of crime comics, which has spawned the graphic novels GOLDFISH, FIRE, JINX, TORSO (with co-writer Marc Andreyko) and TOTAL SELL OUT.

Bendis has received an honorary doctorate in the arts from the Cleveland Institute of Art and a certificate of excellence from the Central Intelligence Agency for his work on diversity issues, as well as an Excellence in Journalism Award from the Press Club of Cleveland. He has also won five Eisner Awards (including Best Writer two years in a row) and the prestigious Inkpot Award for comic art excellence.

Bendis lives in Portland, Oregon with his wife, Alisa; his gorgeous daughters, Olivia, Tabatha and Sabrina; his dashing son, London; and his dogs, Lucky and Max.

His TED talk and his appearance on *Late Night with Seth Meyers* are available for viewing at Jinxworld.com.